FRONTLINE
PAKISTAN

For my mother, Tahira Khatoon,
who gave me the courage to face life head-on,
and Razia Bhatti,
who taught me how to write

FRONTLINE PAKISTAN

THE STRUGGLE WITH MILITANT ISLAM

ZAHID HUSSAIN

Columbia University Press
New York

Columbia University Press
Publishers Since 1893
New York

Copyright © 2007 Zahid Hussain

Library of Congress Cataloging-in-Publication Data
A complete CIP record is available from the Library of Congress
ISBN 978-0-231-14224-3

c   10 9 8 7 6 5 4 3 2 1

CONTENTS

PREFACE

In February 2002, a mere two years after the President of the USA very publicly refused to endorse the new military government of Pakistan, Pakistan's leader, General Pervez Musharraf, stood up on a platform in Washington with US Secretary of State for Defense Donald Rumsfeld. In between the friendly badinage, Rumsfeld looked Musharraf in the eye and said warmly: 'Mr. President, we – our country – and indeed the world – [have] a big stake in your country and your part of the world, and we wish you well in your important work.'

The dramatic turn of events in the aftermath of 9/11 pushed Pakistan into a new spotlight. From being an international outcast for its long-standing support of the Taliban and militant cross-border insurgents in Kashmir, Pakistan became the key strategic partner of America's war on terror. The same military leaders who had facilitated jihadist networks to fight their proxy wars in Afghanistan and Kashmir, and who may well have turned a blind eye to the illegal sale of nuclear materials, are now being touted as the US's regional standard bearers.

General Musharraf, the man responsible for this astonishing volte-face, has had to walk a fine line between a military reluctant to break entirely with its radical clients and his status as America's key strategic partner in the region. Since he took the fateful decision to throw in his lot with the Americans, Musharraf has been a marked man. Islamic militants once trained by Pakistan's formidable spymasters, the Inter-Services Intelligence (ISI) have turned their guns onto the military leader they saw as having betrayed the jihad.

In fact, as this book explores, Musharraf's decision to forge a partnership with America meant taking Pakistan to war with itself. The outcome of this struggle will affect not only the fate of Pakistan, but the ideological climate of the Middle East, and the security of the world. It is a war which is rarely examined in any depth, as too many observers both in and outside Pakistan seem content to take the symbolic theatre of Pakistani politics at face value. The narrative which both Musharraf and his American allies are so anxious to promulgate – that the Pakistani government is 'cracking down' on 'jihadist elements' – belies the disturbing reality that jihadists have as much if not more power over Pakistani society than Musharraf himself. As the wars in Iraq and Afghanistan proceed ever more savagely, and as more and more western cities, including London, experience jihadist terror, Musharraf's idiosyncratic 'war on terror' takes on momentous significance.

Covering the fast-unravelling events have been the most testing of times for me as a journalist. Reporting is never easy in any conflict zone, but it was much harder in the politically complex climate of the region after 9/11, when strategic relationships were turned on their head, and the gap between official rhetoric and reality on the ground was so large.

On 8 November 2001, just four weeks into the US-led coalition forces air strikes in Afghanistan, I sneaked inside the Afghan border as part of a humanitarian organization, disguised as a doctor. The embattled Taliban regime had banned foreign journalists and even the slightest suspicion could have landed me in serious trouble. The risk was huge, but so was the scoop. I remember receiving frantic calls on my way to the Torkhum border, from *The Times* deputy editor Preston and foreign editor Bronwen Maddox, who were worried about my safety. Though not fully convinced by my decision, they nevertheless assured me of complete support.

The day-long stay in the war zone was, indeed, the most dangerous venture in my entire journalistic career. The trip was also the most revealing. Whilst the Pakistani government was pledging its support for the US war on the Taliban, I witnessed thousands of Pakistanis pouring into the south-eastern city of Jalalabad in response to Osama bin Laden's call to arms. In their flowing *shalwar* and *kameez*, they stood out instantly. The youngest and most fervent had already been dispatched to the front. The older men who had lived their lives in Pakistan's lawless frontier waited for their marching orders. The Taliban were routed a week later, but the war on terror was far from over. One year later, I met Taliban fighters on Pakistan's north-western borders

waiting for the call from their leaders to join the resistance against the
occupying troops.

After 9/11, I closely followed the hunt for al-Qaeda leaders and
travelled many times to Pakistan's lawless Waziristan tribal region to
report on the military operation against the militants. One of the world's
most difficult terrains, it has become the new base for international
terrorism and a possible lair for bin Laden and Zawahiri. Thousands
of Pakistani troops have been locked in an impossible war in this
high mountainous region against the fiercely independent tribesmen
refusing to hand over their foreign 'guests'.

Direct interaction with the jihadist groups has provided me with a
unique insight into their operations and their links with the Pakistani
military. I have encountered hundreds of Islamic fighters over the
years, many of them in their teens, eager to achieve martyrdom. I met
the radical Islamic leaders, who believe that jihad was the only way
to end the oppression of Muslims across the world and establish the
dominance of Islam. They were the product of Islamic madrassas as
well as secular educational institutions.

As luck had it, on several occasions I happened to be in the right
place at the right time, which gave me a rare insight into some of
the most important events. I was present at Kandahar airport on 31
December 2000 when Masood Azhar, one of Pakistan's most feared
militant leaders, and Ahmed Omar Saeed Sheikh, the British-born
militant, were exchanged to secure the release of passengers of an
Indian Airlines plane hijacked by Kashmiri militants. A week later, I
happened to see Azhar resurfacing in Karachi and delivering a vitriolic
speech from the pulpit of a mosque. The nexus between the militants
and Pakistan's Inter-Services Intelligence was only too obvious.

Interviews with General Musharraf (who I have interviewed several
times since he took over power, including an exhaustive session in
January 2002 for a *Newsweek* cover story) and other senior Pakistani
military and civilian leaders have provided me with a valuable insight
into the new face of the Pakistan-US alliance.

It was because of all these experiences that I wanted to write a
book which showed the reality of Pakistan's 'war on terror'. *Frontline
Pakistan* is the result. I hope that it fills in some of the gaps left by the
official version of events.

The book is divided into three parts. The first part looks at how
Musharraf came to throw in his lot with the Americans after 9/11, and
why this was such a momentous decision. The second part uncovers

the forces ranged against him: the jihadists and their allies. The third part looks at the battle between them – how it is being fought and who is winning.

ACKNOWLEDGEMENTS

I owe a huge debt of gratitude to my colleagues at *Newsline*, especially editor Rehana Hakim and Samina Ibrahim for their support and editorial advice. They have always been a source of strength for me. I am extremely proud of being part of the courageous team who bring out this fiercely independent magazine. *Newsline* has also been the main venue for most of my investigative reports over the last 17 years.

I am extremely grateful to Kathy Gannon and Françoise Chipaux, who convinced me to write this book. They encouraged me at every stage. Special gratitude to Steve Levine of the *Wall Street Journal*, a great friend who painstakingly went through the first draft and gave valuable suggestions.

It is now over 20 years since I started writing for *The Times*, and I owe my editors, especially foreign editor Bronwen Maddox, thanks for enormous support and encouragement. It is largely thanks to *The Times* that I have been able to travel through the region, including Afghanistan.

My thanks as well to *Newsweek* and the *Wall Street Journal* for providing space for my stories on Pakistan and Afghanistan. Ron Moreau, *Newsweek*'s South Asia Bureau chief, has always been a source of support.

I have greatly benefited from the intellectual input from Maleeha Lodhi and Ahmed Rashid, two of my best friends in and out of journalism. Samina Ahmed too has been source of intellectual inspiration.

There are many others who helped me accomplish this book in different ways. Zaman Kazmi as usual has been available for all kinds of help.

Many thanks to Abigail Fielding Smith, my editor at I.B.Tauris, who from the outset believed in this project.

Finally, thanks to my friend Zaba Satthar, without whose support this project would not have been possible. She was the first one to see the initial draft and her comments have helped to shape this book.

PROLOGUE

PAKISTAN
AGAINST ITSELF

From the tinted glass window of his speeding Mercedes Benz, President Musharraf could see a van racing towards his motorcade from the opposite side of the road, crushing to death a policeman who tried to block its way. It was a national holiday on 25 December 2003, and the road was deserted. Within seconds the van blew up with a huge explosion after hitting a security car at the tail end of the convoy. It was dark all around. The driver involuntarily pressed the brakes. 'Accelerate. Don't stop,' the President shouted at him. The car had moved just 150 yards when another vehicle rammed into the car just behind him detonating 60 pounds of high explosives. The President's car was trapped between the two explosions. Three of the tyres on the armour-plated presidential Mercedes were burst by the impact. Blood and body parts covered the vehicle. The driver pressed the accelerator and drove home on a single tyre.[1] The assailant almost got him. 'It was very close,' the President later recalled. He was saved, perhaps, because a third bomber could not reach the assigned place in time.

It was the second attempt on Musharraf's life in less than two weeks. Both attempts had taken place in Rawalpindi, the seat of the Pakistani military headquarters. The fact that explosives were placed under a bridge along the route of Musharraf's motorcade, and that the terrorists' vehicles were able to access his convoy in a zone where, supposedly, not the slightest movement could escape detection, was baffling. The assailants chose the same spot for both attacks. The route was used nearly every day by General Musharraf as he travelled from his residence to his presidential offices in Islamabad. Security was always tight when he travelled, with roads closed to allow his long motorcade to pass rapidly. It was even more vigilant on that day as Pakistan's tiny Christian community celebrated Christmas. In both the attempts it was clear that the perpetrators had the assistance of experts and were given tracking and other devices not usually available to local terrorists. Having travelled to Islamabad hours before for a dinner he had hosted, Musharraf attributed his survival to 'Allah's blessings, his mother's prayers and the nation's goodwill'.[2]

There was little doubt, however, about who was behind the attack. Professionally planned, it bore all the hallmarks of international terrorists, for whom General Musharraf had been a marked man. By official admission, it was the fourth attempt on General Musharraf's life since 13 September 2001, when he decided to throw Pakistan's lot in with the US war on terror. By unofficial accounts this might even have been the fifth or sixth such attempt. The General had been the *bête noire* of many people and groups out there, but especially the Islamist extremists.

Musharraf had put his own survival at stake by deciding to curb Islamic militancy after 9/11. Security around him had been tightened. His movements were kept secret and his travel route often changed because of growing fears of his meeting the fate of Anwar Sadat, the Egyptian President who was assassinated by an Islamic militant after he made peace with Israel. The President became one of the most stringently protected men in the world. All traffic was stopped on his travel routes at least half an hour before he passed. The entire route was cleared by bomb disposal squads. But when it came to suicide bombing coordinated by insiders, one could not do much.

The assassination attempts right in the centre of Army Headquarters could not have been possible without inside contacts. The country's intelligence agencies could not possibly be unaware of the identity of the groups and their ringleaders. Musharraf had tried to rein in his intelligence organizations, but with mixed results. Some of the 'ideologized' operatives were sidelined, but many more remained in important places from where they could continue to help the militants. It eventually emerged that it was soon after the US attack on Afghanistan in October 2001 that some 20 Islamic militants, many of them Afghan and Kashmir war veterans, had gathered at a house in Islamabad to discuss a plan to assassinate Musharraf for allying with the United States. The meeting was apparently organized by Ahmed Omar Saeed Sheikh and Amjad Hussain Farooqi, the two protaganists of the December 1999 hijacking of an Indian Airlines plane. Among the participants were two Pakistani army soldiers belonging to the elite special force.[3]

It was hard to believe that the man they sought to kill had once been the doyenne of the jihadists and their allies in the military intelligence service. I first met General Musharraf at his official residence: a sprawling white colonial mansion in the middle of Rawalpindi cantonment, ten days after the coup which brought him to power in October 1999. His piquant sense of humour, frankness and affable personality came as a marked contrast to General Mohammad Zia ul-Haq, the last military strongman who ruled the crisis-ridden country from 1977 to 1988. Unlike the austere General Zia, Musharraf was known for a certain flamboyance in dress and a penchant for music and dancing. He was an officer of the old school with a secular bent. General Musharraf provoked strong reactions from radical Islamists when he appeared in public holding his two poodles. He came across as a moderate and pragmatic man as he talked about the problems and challenges faced by his new government. Known as a consummate soldier's soldier, he clearly enjoyed being at the helm of political power of the world's most ungovernable nation. 'It is a tough job, but the feeling of being in charge when having the confidence makes it enjoyable,' he asserted.[4]

His confidence had certainly been boosted by the public euphoria that greeted his coup and the milder than expected international reaction. General Musharraf, who described himself as a 'reluctant coup maker', made it very clear that there was no question of the country soon returning to democracy.

Musharraf's background bears all the hallmarks of the maverick yet intensely driven politician he was to become. The second of three sons, Musharraf was born into a middle-class family of Delhi that migrated to Pakistan after the partition in August 1947. The family was settled in Karachi where his father was a foreign ministry employee. His mother was a rarity for her era, an educated Muslim working woman, who had a long career with the International Labour Organization. Musharraf received his army commission in 1964.[5] He almost got thrown out for indiscipline a few months later. He subsequently faced court martial as a second lieutenant for another disciplinary infringement. The proceedings were stopped because of the war with India in 1965. A gallantry award saved him from the court martial. He received another gallantry award in 1971. Despite his performance, his indiscipline almost brought his career to an end again as a lieutenant colonel. 'My rise to the post of army chief is a miracle,' Musharraf admitted.[6]

General Musharraf was serving as a corps commander at Mangla[7] when he was invited by the then Prime Minister, Nawaz Sharif, to take over the army command. Sharif had already been ousted from power by his army chief once, and was determined not to let it happen again. The obvious candidate for the head of the army would have been Lt.-General Ali Quli Khan, a powerful Pashtun who belonged to one of Pakistan's most influential political families. But precisely because of this strong power base Sharif was reluctant to choose him. The Sand-hurst-trained General had also won Sharif's disfavour because of his closeness to General Waheed Kakar, the army chief who had forced Sharif to quit during his first term in office in 1993. Musharraf, a relative outsider and Mohajir (a minority ethnic group) rather than Pashtun, suited Sharif's purposes much better. Or so he thought. It did not take much time for Musharraf to show that he was nobody's man.

As Chief of Army Staff, Musharraf presided over an undercover military operation with far-reaching consequences, which was kept secret from the Prime Minister. When Indian troops took their annual winter season retreat from the icy Kargil peaks of Indian-occupied Kashmir in May 1999, the Pakistani military took up their abandoned positions. This caused a terrifying escalation in India-Pakistan tensions, and Sharif, taken by surprise, had to make humiliating concessions insisted upon by President Clinton to avoid a full-scale war. This left him very weak domestically.

In a desperate attempt to reduce the tension between the civil leadership in Islamabad and the military leadership in Rawalpindi, Sharif gave General Musharraf the additional charge of Chairman of the Joint Chiefs of Staff Committee and assured the General that he did not have any intention to fire him. It was almost certainly a ploy to put Musharraf off guard. Musharraf did not take the bait and instead provocatively sacked a senior corps commander for meeting the Prime Minister without his permission.

Despite the rising tensions, it seemed to General Musharraf that the situation was under control when he accepted a long-standing invitation from the chief of the Sri Lankan army in October 1999. The month before, the army top brass had decided on a contingency plan to move in if the Prime Minister decided to fire their chief. Musharraf appointed his loyalist Brigadier Salahuddin Satti as the commander of the pivotal 111 Brigade, which was responsible for the security of Islamabad. In the event of a military takeover, the brigade was the first to move. Military Intelligence kept a close watch on Sharif's movements. Musharraf had complete faith in his commanders. 'You don't have to worry. Everything is under control,' he was reassured by General Aziz, Chief of General Staff as he left for Sri Lanka.[8]

On the return flight, Musharraf busied himself jotting down notes on how the army could contribute to the country's governance. As the plane entered Pakistani airspace, the link with the control tower at Karachi airport crackled to life with an inexplicable message that the flight be diverted to some other airport outside Pakistan. At 6.50 pm, Brigadier Taj told Musharraf that the pilot wanted to talk to him. In the cockpit, Captain Sarwat informed him of the radio message. 'That is when I knew that something had gone wrong and presumed it was concerning me,' Musharraf later recalled.[9] It was perhaps the most testing time for the war-hardened soldier during his thirty-five-year army career.

The Prime Minister himself was flying back to Islamabad from Punjab at around 2 pm, about the time that General Musharraf was boarding his flight in Colombo. He was said to be visibly preoccupied during the flight. Retired Lt.-General Iftikhar Ali Khan, Defense Secretary, was at the airport to receive the Prime Minister. On the way to PM House, Sharif informed him that he had decided to fire Musharraf. A dumbfounded Ali asked if he should not wait for Musharraf to return. 'No, I have decided to appoint General Ziauddin as the new chief,' the Prime Minister replied.[10] Being a former senior army officer, General Iftikhar Ali Khan could foresee the repercussions. But Sharif had decided to take a calculated gamble. Only a year earlier, he had forced another army chief, General Jehangir Karamat, to resign, and he felt confident enough to do it a second time. He wanted the new army chief to take over while Musharraf was still airborne. At 5 pm he issued the orders for the appointment of General Ziauddin. The fateful decision set the army's contingency plan rolling.

Lt.-General Mahmood Ahmed, the corps commander at Rawalpindi, and Lt.-General Mohammed Aziz, Chief of General Staff, were playing tennis when they heard about Sharif's decision. The two generals rushed to the General Headquarters to mobilize their forces for the counter coup. The situation was delicately balanced. Loyalties were not clearly defined. Entrenched in the PM House, General Ziauddin was issuing orders and making new appointments. He was desperately trying to garner the support of the commanders He sacked both General Aziz and General Mahmood. But it was too late. Brigadier Satti's 111 Brigade had already moved to seal the PM House. There was utter confusion in the country as the state-controlled Pakistan Television went off the air. Within an hour it became increasingly apparent that Sharif was losing the battle. But he was not prepared to give up. He was constantly in touch with civil aviation officials in Karachi, urging them not to let the PK 805 land. The endgame depended on the fate of General Musharraf. If he was kept out of the country, most of the commanders might accept the change, he believed.

At Karachi airport there was confusion among the army officers, who were there to receive the chief. Several times the flags from the staff car were removed and then replaced. The civil aviation authorities switched off the landing lights and blocked the runway with fire trucks. It was only at about 7.20 pm that the army from the nearby Malir cantonment moved in and seized control of the airport and the air control tower. Musharraf was totally clueless as to what was going on below, as the plane, with just thirty minutes of fuel left, was diverted to Nawabshah, a small airport some 200 miles from Karachi. It was then that Major-General Malik Iftikhar; the commanding officer, came on the line and requested Musharraf to turn back to Karachi. 'Sir, the situation is all right. We have taken over,' the officer said.[11] Musharraf was still not sure about the situation as the plane landed. He insisted on speaking to General Usmani, the local commander, before disembarking from the plane. The endgame came smoothly. The military takeover was complete as night fell.

By March 2000, Sharif was in jail. Sharif's jail term was, however, cut short when Musharraf, under pressure from the Saudi government commuted his sentence and sent him in exile to Jeddah. It was still pitch dark on 10 December 2000 when the former Prime Minister was taken from his prison cell in the sixteenth-century military fort of Attock, some 40 miles from the capital, and whisked away in a Saudi embassy black Mercedes.[12] A government announcement at midnight said that, under the terms agreed with General Musharraf, Sharif's life sentence stood commuted, but he would have to forfeit $8.3 million in property and stay out of politics for the next 21 years. In a nationwide TV address a few days later, General Musharraf justified his decision, saying that he wanted to end the politics of hatred. But in the same breath he warned that the exiled family would not be allowed to return to the country for ten years.

Although Sharif's release from jail came about as a result of the efforts of the Saudi royal family, the move had strong American backing. The Clinton administration had been hugely indebted to Sharif for his cooperation, particularly in the efforts to capture Osama bin Laden. A few months before the coup, he had promised to deliver the Saudi fugitive to the USA and crack down on Islamic militants. The USA had paid $25 million to the Sharif government to help the ISI to raise a commando force to capture bin Laden. The Pakistani leader had earlier won American support for his move to normalize relations with India and pull out Pakistani troops from Kargil. It did not come as surprise when Washington quickly hailed the amnesty.[13]

Ironically, the man who usurped America's most pliant ally in the region on a wave of nationalist feeling, would within a few years of taking command, stake his power – and his life – on support for the USA's foreign policy.

The 12 October coup was yet another episode of the Pakistani soap opera of alternation between authoritarian rule by an elected government and authoritarian rule by a self-appointed leader from the army. Most Pakistanis were disillusioned with the ineptitude of successive civilian leaders, and welcomed the military takeover, though warily. General Musharraf had stepped into a situation that had not been faced by past military rulers: a nation armed with nuclear weapons falling apart as a result of worsening ethnic and sectarian violence. Years of financial mismanagement and rampant corruption had pushed the country to the brink of bankruptcy.

It was, however, a military takeover with a difference. Musharraf appeared like a 'benevolent dictator', allowing both a free press and political freedom. He did not impose martial law or use coercive means to silence the political opposition. He called himself Chief Executive. An admirer of the father of the modern secular state of Turkey, Mustafa Kemal Ataturk, he presented himself as a reformist, promising to take Pakistan on a liberal course. The General appeared more in the mould of the first Pakistani military ruler, Field Marshal Ayub Khan, [14] than the most recent, General Zia.

He received widespread approbation when, in his first major policy speech, he announced his seven-point agenda, which included the eradication of Islamic extremism and sectarianism. He pledged to undo General Zia's radical legacy by transforming Pakistan into a moderate Muslim state. The liberal profile of his cabinet, comprising western educated professionals, had raised hopes for better governance and a clean administration. The liberal image was also necessary to win the support of the international community, wary of the spread of Islamic extremism in the region. But his policies were full of paradoxes.

The inconsistencies of Musharraf's position were revealed in his first major policy battle with the Islamists. Musharraf found himself pitted against the hardline Islamic groups when in April 2000 he moved to change the notorious Blasphemy Law, enforced as part of the Islamization process in 1981 by General Zia's military rule. Under the law anyone could be imprisoned merely on the basis of an accusation of defiling the image of the Prophet Mohammed or desecrating the Qur'an. The law that carried the death sentence had long become the handiest instrument for mullahs to persecute rivals, particularly members of the Christian community and the liberals.[15]

Musharraf had promised to bring about some procedural changes in the filing of blasphemy cases. Under the proposed amendment, cases could be registered only after an investigation by the local administrations. Just the prospect of minor procedural change inflamed religious activists who used the proposed amendment to launch an attack on the Musharraf government. Thousands of Islamic activists poured onto the streets of Karachi and other cities, vowing to defend Islamic laws. Pakistan's financial and commercial capital looked like a city under siege with the Islamists on the rampage, bringing normal life to a halt for several days in the second week of May 2000.

It was the first major test for Musharraf as he tried to move the country away from General Zia's orthodox Islamic legacy. But he beat a hasty retreat under the pressure and withdrew the amendment. The backtracking on the blasphemy issue was a serious blow to his cred-ibility. 'One step forward and one step back' was to become a charac-teristic of Musharraf's approach while dealing with the issue of Islamic extremism. The military government's defensive attitude further em-boldened the religious extremists who upped the ante by demanding enforcement of what they described as a complete Islamic system.

The most alarming aspect of the situation in the first years of Musharraf's rule was the growing assertiveness of jihadist organizations in Pakistan's domestic politics. Their increasing influence was quite evident during the violence on the blasphemy issue. Hundreds of their gun-wielding activists joined the protesters. These groups, which had been fighting in Kashmir and Afghanistan, were deeply entwined with the Pakistani intelligence service, the ISI, and for that reason the military was not willing to take them on. The military government's dividedness on domestic issues and its support for Islamic militancy in Kashmir contributed to a state of confusion and inertia.

The blasphemy issue also exposed divisions within the military leadership. Some members of the junta, who were often described as 'jihadist generals', were openly sympathetic to hardline Islamic groups. They were opposed to any move to change Islamic laws. The two decades of war in Afghanistan and conflict in Kashmir had produced men at arms who considered themselves soldiers of Islam. The confused and conflicting policies indicated that there existed multiple power centres in the country.

The uncertain political situation was conducive to the rise of extremist and conservative Islamic elements. The jihadist groups that the military government supported and the sectarian outfits that it claimed it wanted to wipe out overlapped. The jihadists behaved like paramilitaries, swaggering about with automatic weapons in public. Religious schools – madrasas – proliferated by the thousands.

The military coup had brought to power the military officers who had authored the ill-fated Kargil operation in May 1999. Once in power, Musharraf himself pursued a more aggressive policy on Kashmir and stepped up support for the Kashmiri militants. Despite his professed secularist agenda, General Musharraf equated support for their cause with support for the mujahidin (holy warriors) against the Soviet occupation of Afghanistan. The resultant tension between India and Pakistan was further heightened at the end of 1999, with the hijacking of an Indian Airlines jet en route from Kathmandu, Nepal, to New Delhi. The suspected involvement of the ISI in the hijacking had almost led to Washington declaring Pakistan a terrorist state.

There was a perceptible toughening in the tenor of senior American officials who visited Islamabad in January 2000, as they asked Pakistani military leaders to curb Islamic militant organizations perpetrating terrorism. The message was starkly clear: that Pakistan faced the imminent threat of being put on the list of nations sponsoring terrorism unless it heeded the American demand of banning the Harkat-ul-Mujahideen (HuM), [16] which Washington believed was responsible for the Indian Airlines hijacking.[17]

It was not the first time that the USA had conveyed its serious concern over Pakistan and Afghanistan becoming a hub for Islamic extremist groups involved in terrorist activities worldwide. The pressure had intensified, particularly after the hijacking and the arrest of several Islamic militants in the USA, Jordan and other countries with alleged links in Afghanistan and Pakistan. In early 2000, Karl Inderfurth, the US Assistant Secretary of State, told Pakistani leaders that the US administration was particularly concerned about the links between the ISI and HuM, the militant Kashmir liberation group. Although US officials stopped short of reading the riot act, the warning was clear. The military government was told that Pakistan's failure to curb Islamic militants might lead to stern action by the USA, including stoppage of all financial lending from the World Bank and the IMF.[18]

Musharraf rejected US allegations that the Islamic organizations fighting in Kashmir were terrorists, or working under the patronage of the ISI. He insisted that a differentiation should be made between terrorists and freedom fighters. The differences between Islamabad and Washington further increased, after Karl Inderfurth repeated the US demand for the banning of HuM at a press conference in Islamabad.

Musharraf managed to deflect these demands without overtly rejecting them. He was at this stage concerned above all else with consolidating his power base domestically. This was made abundantly clear in July 2001 when he shed his ambiguous title of Chief Executive and assumed the Presidency. Casting off his military uniform, he donned a black sherwani as he took the oath of his new office amidst much pomp and show at Islamabad's grand, white marble presidential palace. The atmosphere in the Darbar hall was visibly sullen. The cabinet ministers and senior government officials present at the ceremony had only learned of Musharraf's imminent oath-taking through the morning newspapers. Ambassadors from the USA and European countries were conspicuous by their absence.[19] It was almost a second coup. Musharraf had appointed himself the country's President replacing Rafiq Tarrar, the last vestige of the ousted elected government. The fate of the Parliament, which had remained under suspension for almost two years, was also sealed through an administrative order dissolving it.

The decision to assume the role of President was kept secret even from the corps commanders and the cabinet until the day before his swearing-in. Only three generals, the ISI chief, Lt.-General Mahmood

Ahmed, Chief of General Staff, Lt.-General Mohammed Yousuf and his Chief of Army Staff, Lt.-General Ghulam Ahmed, were in the loop. Pakistan's Foreign Minister, Abdul Sattar, was visibly embarrassed when he heard about the development back home as he came out of a meeting with US Secretary of State, Colin Powell, in Washington.[20]

Musharraf's assumption of the presidency provoked strong condemnation from the United States and other western countries, who believed the move would lead Pakistan further away from democracy. The development came just as the Bush administration was sending signals indicating its desire to improve relations with Pakistan and lift some of the sanctions placed on it following the nuclear tests. 'That process may be stalled at least for the time being,' commented a senior official. The Commonwealth, which had suspended Pakistan's membership after the coup, also warned of a tougher stance.

But as things turned out, the crisis unleashed by the events of 11 September provided Musharraf with an opportunity to end Pakistan's and his own isolation. The 'you're either with us or you're against us' mentality of the Bush administration gave him little choice but to take it. He did so with gusto. By joining the US 'war on terror', Pakistan once again took centre-stage in the international limelight, much as it had after the Soviet invasion of Afghanistan. Formerly ostracized as a military dictator, Musharraf became a valued friend to the West. He promised to steer Pakistan away from its long and troubled drift towards Islamic fundamentalism and extremism.

Policy was one thing, reality quite another. The forces ranged against Musharraf were not only non-state actors, but also their allies in the powerful military establishment. Musharraf, the ultimate operator, had, as he discovered on that day in December 2003, very limited space in which to manoeuvre.

1

PAKISTAN'S UNHOLY ALLIANCE

THE MILITANTS AND THE MILITARY

The heavily guarded, high-walled concrete structure right in the heart of Islamabad has no signboard. But everyone in the capital knows that the sprawling compound surrounded by barbed wire houses the Directorate for Inter-Services Intelligence (ISI). The spy agency has been the country's big brother. It is powerful, ubiquitous and has functioned with so much autonomy from the central government that it has almost become a state within a state. It is not only responsible for intelligence gathering, but also acts as a determinant of Pakistan's foreign policy and a vehicle for its implementation. For every civilian and military government, control of the ISI was seen as crucial to maintaining a firm grip on power. The agency had been so powerful for so long that it played by its own rules. Its various heads had contrasting profiles, but emerged among the most powerful figures in the country's establishment. For years they ran semi-independent operations in Afghanistan and Kashmir and helped to form and topple civilian governments.

For more than two decades the ISI had sponsored Islamic militancy to carry out its secret wars. It was a crucial partner in the CIA's biggest covert operation ever, one that forced the Soviet Union to pull out of Afghanistan and served as a catalyst to the disintegration of the communist superpower. In Afghanistan, as well as Kashmir, the agency discovered the effectiveness of covert warfare as a method of bleeding a stronger adversary, while maintaining the element of plausible deniability. The ISI falls directly within Pakistan's military chain of command and had also served as an instrument for promoting the military's domestic political agenda and the guardian of its self-professed 'ideological frontiers' of the country. Almost all ISI officers are regular military personnel, who are rotated in and out for a fixed tenure. However, there have been some exceptions.

The export of jihad sponsored by the ISI had its blowback. It had allowed the Islamists a huge space for their activities. State patronage, in the form of an 'unholy alliance' between the military and the mullahs, resulted in an unprecedented rise of radical Islam. The ISI had helped to create much of the Islamic militancy and religious extremism that Musharraf was confronted with. That unholy alliance had been a major factor in the country's drift to Islamic fundamentalism.

Founded in 1948 by a British army officer, Major-General R. Cawthome, then Deputy Chief of Army Staff in Pakistan, the agency was initially charged with performing all intelligence tasks at home and abroad. Its scope of operation extended to all areas related to national security. Until the 1960s, the ISI largely remained an obscure organization that confined itself to playing its specified role. But in the mid 1970s its scope was expanded to domestic politics. Ironically, it was a civilian leader, Zulfikar Ali Bhutto[1] who created the ISI's internal wing which played a critical role in the ousting of his government a few years later. It was to cast its heavy shadow over the country's politics in later years.

A charismatic and populist leader, Bhutto took over a humiliated military and a brutally truncated Pakistan in search of a new identity, following the Indian-supported secession of East Pakistan (now Bangladesh), in 1971. The country had been dismembered by civil war and Indian military action. It was no longer the country created by Mohammed Ali Jinnah.[2] The Pakistan that emerged from the ashes of defeat required a different geopolitical orientation. A revolt by young Turks in the army in the aftermath of a humiliating defeat in the war had forced the military ruler, General Yahya Khan,[3] to hand over power to Bhutto. His legitimacy was rooted in the country's first democratically held elections in 1970. Bhutto's socialist Pakistan People's Party had swept the fateful polls in the western wing of then-united Pakistan, trouncing the right-wing Islamic parties.

The scion of a feudal family of Sindh and a former foreign minister, Bhutto was seen as the savior of the new Pakistan. He successfully negotiated with India the release of 90,000 troops taken prisoner by Indian forces. He had come to power with the largest support base of any Pakistani leader since the inception of the country in 1947. But he failed to sustain the confidence of the nation. Bhutto was ideally placed to put into practice the objective of social democracy and develop secular ideas and institutions. But it did not happen. Bhutto's strategy was to bring the disparate elements of this divided society together through a kind of Islamic nationalism, which was then supposed to create the cohesion and stability necessary for socialist economic reforms, but unfortunately all Bhutto succeeded in doing was to rehabilitate religious extremism. Under pressure from the religious parties whose cooperation they were courting, Bhutto's government increased the religious content in school syllabuses and, succumbing to pressure from Saudi Arabia as well as to the demands of religious parties, declared the Ahmedis, an Islamic sect, to be non-Muslim.[4] This apparently minor action had long-term implications for the country as it fuelled Islamic zealotry and sharpened the sectarian divide. Bhutto's attempt to co-opt religious elements merely emboldened them, and eventually the clergy joined hands with their traditional ally, the military, to plot the overthrow of his government.

Bhutto's attempt to establish an authoritarian rule led him to rely more and more on the coercive apparatus of the state and the intelligence agencies. Bhutto did little to strengthen democratic institutions and to make the process of democratic reform irreversible. Instead, his entire effort was aimed at promoting a personalized rule. He did not trust anyone. Given his overwhelming paranoia and insecurity, Bhutto geared up the ISI to keep surveillance not only on his opponents, but also on his own party men and cabinet ministers. The agency kept dossiers on politicians, bureaucrats, judges and anyone else considered important.

The collapse of democratic institutions and the Constitution's loss of sanctity created a vacuum of authority that provided a favourable condition for the Bonapartist generals. Bhutto's use of the army to crush the uprising in Pakistan's western province of Balochistan provided an opportunity to the military to reassert itself in the country's politics. Bhutto's politics of expediency and attempts to appease the country's religious lobby allowed the Islamists, who were routed in the 1971 elections, to revive themselves. A nationwide agitation, led by right-wing Islamic parties in the aftermath of the controversial elections in 1977, shook his government. In a desperate attempt to appease the Islamists, Bhutto prohibited the sale and use of alcoholic beverages, banned gambling and closed down nightclubs. But the die had already been cast.

Bhutto had handpicked General Zia ul-Haq, a lesser-known officer, for the post of army chief in 1976 over the heads of half a dozen senior officers, believing he did not have any personal ambitions. General Zia was a devout Muslim and Bhutto thought he would never betray his trust. Once elevated to the top position, the General did not take much time to develop secret contacts with hardline religious groups and conspired with them to overthrow his benefactor.

On 5 July 1977, a bloodless military coup brought an end to Bhutto's six-and-a-half-year civilian rule. There was a complete convergence of interests between the Islamists and the military leadership which had ousted the Bhutto government. Several accounts of Bhutto's last days in power revealed that Major-General Ghulam Jilani, Bhutto's handpicked chief of the ISI, played a key role in the coup plan. Two years later, in April 1979, Bhutto was hanged after a dubious trial on charges of murdering a political rival. A secularist, elected with an overwhelming mandate in 1970, Bhutto probably had the best chance of any leader of taking on the Islamists and winning. His inglorious demise can only fill Pakistan's current leader, attempting a similar task, with foreboding.

Bhutto's usurper, General Zia, came from a humble lower-middle-class background. His father, a religious man, held a clerical government post during British rule in India. Despite his poverty, he provided his son with a decent education. Zia was educated at Delhi's most prestigious St Stephen's College before getting a commission in the Royal Indian Army in 1942.[5] He was a captain at the time of the creation of Pakistan in 1947. He was a hard-working officer, but lacked brilliance. Many of his colleagues believed he was lucky to be promoted beyond Colonel. From a young age, Zia was actively involved with the popular religious movement, Tablighi Jamaat, [6] one of the most influential grassroots Islamic movements in the South Asian subcontinent, which had hardline traditionalist views on the role of Islam in modern society.

A short man with a thick moustache, Zia bore a strong resemblance to the British comedian, Terry-Thomas. But he was by no means a fool. He was shrewd enough to know how to make his way up. He convinced Bhutto of his absolute loyalty and more importantly of his incapacity to be otherwise.[7]

Zia was not only an authoritarian; he also aspired to turn Pakistan into an ideological state ruled by strict Islamic sharia laws. He was an unpopular and controversial leader, whose survival in power largely owed to the external factors that emerged after the invasion by Soviet forces of Pakistan's northern neighbour, Afghanistan, in 1979. Pakistan became a frontline state and a bulwark in the West's war against communism.

General Zia brought in his close confidant, Lt.-General Akhter Abdur Rehman, to head the ISI in 1979, as the spy agency became a crucial cog in the resistance against the Soviet forces. Its tentacles started to spread far and wide. An artillery officer, General Rehman 'had a cold, reserved personality, almost inscrutable, always secretive, with no intimates except his family.' His officers remembered him as a hard man to serve due to his brusque manner and reputation as a strict disciplinarian.[8] 'That made him an ideal man for the job,' said Brigadier Mohammed Yousuf, a former ISI officer who served under him. General Rehman ran the organization until 1987. He was not a radical Islamist, but a staunch Muslim nationalist.

Under General Rehman, the ISI, in partnership with the CIA, conducted the biggest covert operation in modern history. The two organizations had secretly collaborated for years, yet General Zia was not prepared to give a free hand to the CIA. He laid down strict rules to ensure that the ISI would maintain control over contacts with Afghan mujahidin groups. No CIA operatives would be allowed to cross the border into Afghanistan. Distribution of weapons to the Afghan commanders would be handled only by the ISI. All training of mujahidin would be the sole responsibility of the ISI. While the CIA supplied money and weapons, it was the ISI that moved them into Afghanistan.[9] The Americans relied almost entirely on the Pakistani service to allocate weapons to the mujahidin groups. The framework provided the Pakistani spy agency with almost total control over the covert operation inside Afghanistan. The decade-long secret war raised the organization's profile and gave it huge clout. With the active help of the CIA and Saudi Arabia, the ISI turned the Afghan resistance into Islam's holy war.

The decade-long conflict in Afghanistan gave the Islamic extremists a rallying point and a training field. Young Muslims around the world flocked to Afghanistan to fight against a foreign invader. Some 35,000 holy warriors joined the Afghan war from 1979 to 1989.[10] The largest number came from the Middle East. Some were Saudis, among whom was a young man called Osama bin Laden. The 23-year-old son of a wealthy construction magnate said he arrived in Peshawar for the first time in 1980. He was a very shy person who had no experience of war and, as a fresh graduate from the King Abdul Aziz University, bin Laden had left the luxury of his home to help the mujahidin fighting jihad in Afghanistan. It was the beginning of his long association with Afghan and Pakistani Islamic radicals. By 1984 he was spending most of his time in Peshawar, sometimes with Abdullah Azzam, a Palestinian Islamic scholar and an ideologue who inspired the rush of foreign Muslims to fight in Afghanistan.[11] It was also during this period that he developed links with the ISI, which had become the main conduit for arms and training for the Islamic warriors.

The Afghan war placed enormous resources at the agency's disposal. Weapons provided by the CIA were channelled to Afghan fighters through the ISI. By the mid 1980s, every dollar given by the CIA was matched by another from Saudi Arabia. The funds, running into several million dollars a year, were transferred by the CIA to the ISI's special accounts in Pakistan.[12] The backing of the CIA and the funnelling of massive amounts of US military aid helped the ISI develop into 'a parallel structure wielding enormous power over all aspects of government.' It became all-pervasive and there was an unprecedented expansion in the surveillance of political opponents.

Even those in the army were not spared. According to a former senior intelligence officer, part of the ISI's function was to keep a careful watch on the generals and ensure their loyalty to the regime. In the words of Brigadier Yousaf, 'So powerful had the ISI become that apprehension, even fear, of what the ISI could do, was real.'[13] The Afghan war provided the agency with the public profile that it did not have before. Former ISI officials point out that the general expansion the agency underwent as a consequence of its Afghan role had a bearing on its overall functioning. While its role in supervising a successful covert operation in Afghanistan won the ISI international acclaim, at home it was a dreaded name.

The Afghan resistance was projected as part of the global jihad against communism. The ISI's training of guerrillas was integrated with the teaching of Islam. The prominent theme was that Islam was a complete socio-political ideology under threat from atheistic communists. The Afghan war produced a new radical Islamic movement. Besides the holy warriors from Islamic countries, thousands more joined madrasas set up with funding from Saudi Arabia and some other Muslim countries. More than 100,000 foreign Muslim radicals were directly influenced by the Afghan jihad.

The military's involvement in the politics of religion, however, had started long before the Afghan jihad. General Zia not only ushered Pakistan into its longest period of military rule, but also tried to turn the country into an ideological state. He extended the army's role in domestic politics much further than defined by earlier military rulers. Previously, the military was seen as the ultimate guarantor of the country's territorial integrity and internal security. But Zia expanded its role as the defender of Pakistan's ideological frontiers as well.[14] Addressing army officers, Zia argued that, as Pakistan was created on the basis of the two-nation theory and Islamic ideology, it was the duty of the 'soldiers of Islam to safeguard its security, integrity and sovereignty at all costs, both from internal turmoil and external aggression'. He claimed the state was created exclusively to provide its people with the opportunity to follow 'the Islamic way of life.' Preservation of the country's Islamic character was seen to be as important as the security of the country's geographical frontiers.[15] Zia's military rule differed by its very serious attempt to create an ideological basis for all areas of activities of the state and society.

General Zia cleverly used Islam to consolidate his power and legitimize his military rule. The Islamization process became the most important feature of his eleven- year rule and its *raison d'être*. For General Zia, Pakistan was an Islamic ideological state and therefore politics could not be separated from religion. He believed that he had a divine obligation to establish an Islamic society ruled in accordance with the Qur'an and sharia. Afraid to face a free electorate and having no mandate to govern, the General turned to Allah.

He introduced a rigid interpretation of Islamic sharia, thus empowering the clergy. The move to Islamize the state found ready allies among the religious parties, many of which already had close ties with the military. The Jamaat-i-Islami and other Islamic groups were co-opted by the government. For the first time in Pakistan's history, the Islamists occupied important government positions. Being in power helped Jamaat-i-Islami, the most influential and organized mainstream religious party, penetrate state institutions. Thousands of party activists and sympathizers were given jobs in the judiciary, the civil service and educational institutions. These appointments strengthened the hold of the Islamists on crucial state apparatuses for many years to come.

The process of the Islamization of the state and society took place on two levels. Firstly, changes were instituted in the legal system. Sharia courts were established to try cases under Islamic laws. For the first time, the government assumed the role of the collector of religious taxes. Secondly, Islamization was promoted through the print media, radio, television and mosques. Through a series of religious decrees, the government moved to Islamize the civil service, the armed forces and the education system. School textbooks were overhauled to ensure their ideological purity. Books deemed un-Islamic were removed from syllabuses and university libraries. It was made compulsory for civil servants to pray five times a day. Confidential reports of government officials included a section in which the staff were given marks for regularly attending prayers and for having a good knowledge of Islam.

General Zia's move to Islamize the army carried the most critical implications. Pakistan's army, carved out of the British Indian army, inherited British traditions and remained a secular organization until General Zia tried to give it a new Islamic orientation. Islam was incorporated into the army's organizational fabric. For the first time Islamic teachings were introduced into the Pakistan Military Academy.[16]

Islamic training and philosophy were made a part of the curriculum at the Command and Staff College.[17] A Directorate of Religious Instruction was instituted to educate the officer corps on Islam. Islamic education also became a part of the promotion exams. The officers were required to read *The Quranic Concept of War*, a book written by a serving officer, Brigadier S. K. Malik. The officers were taught to be not just professional soldiers, but also soldiers of Islam. In his foreword to the book, General Zia wrote: 'The professional soldier in a Muslim army, pursuing the goals of a Muslim State, cannot become "professional" if in all his activities he does not take on "the colour of Allah".'[18] To gain promotion an officer was required to be a devout Muslim. Scores of highly professional and secular officers were sidelined for not meeting the criterion of a 'good Muslim'.

As a consequence of this policy, many conservative officers reached the senior command level. Radical Islamist ideology permeated the army with the free flow of religious political literature in the armed forces training institutions. Friday prayers at regimental mosques, a matter of individual choice in the past, became obligatory. Mullahs belonging to the Deobandi sect were appointed to work among the troops. They were supposed to be the bridge for officers between the westernized profession and the faith. Units were required to take non-combatant mullahs with them to the front line. Soldiers were encouraged to attend 'Tablighi' gatherings. The purpose was to indoctrinate cadets and young officers with an obscurantist interpretation of Islam. Many of those cadets later rose to positions of power and took control of sensitive institutions, including the ISI.

The change in the social composition of the officer corps also led to the ideological reorientation of Pakistan's army in the 1980s. The army officer corps, till the 1970s, was elitist in character and composition. But the trend changed. In the past, members of the upper class or the rural aristocracy had largely dominated the army ranks; now the new officers mostly came from the lower and middle social strata. The rank and file of junior officers since the 1970s had come, not from prosperous central Punjab, but from the impoverished and relatively backward northern districts where a fundamentalist religious ethos prevailed.[19] Unlike their predecessors, the new officers did not come from elite English-language schools, but were the product of modest state-run educational institutions. The spirit of liberalism, common in the 'old' army, was practically unknown to them.[20] They were products of a social class that, by its very nature, was conservative and easily influenced by Islamic fundamentalism. They were distinctively less westernized.

Their narrow nationalist orientation and education, professional training and culture made them very receptive to the influence of Islamic groups, particularly to the Jamaat-i-Islami (JI), which freely carried out propaganda work among the officers and circulated Islamic literature. Most importantly, the JI's propaganda among vast numbers of troops was officially sanctioned by commanding officers on the battalion level and above. That led to the evolution of a long lasting alliance between the military and the mosque. The main objective of the JI was to penetrate the army and use it to seize state power. The practice introduced by General Zia of sending combat officers to universities in Pakistan, in which the JI often had pervasive influence, facilitated the party's objective.

The influence of the JI was particularly visible among officers from rural and semi-urban backgrounds. They had a high level of religious intolerance and held extremist views regarding 'external enemies' and the threat to Islam. The number of officers sporting beards for religious reasons had visibly risen. These young officers constituted the main base for General Zia's regime. According to a retired general, 25 to 30 per cent of the officers had Islamic fundamentalist leanings.

Many of them regularly attended 'Tablighi' groups that propagated the faith. They would take time off to join missionary bands preaching a return to purist Islamic values and recruiting other Muslim men to join them. Thousands of soldiers and army officers would join the annual gathering of the TJ at Raiwind on the outskirts of Lahore. More than one million faithful from across the country and abroad attend this Muslim congregation, the largest after the Haj in Mecca. Even the liberals adopted the philosophy on issues like jihad and support for militancy in Kashmir. The humiliating military defeat by the Indian army in the 1971 war, coupled with the disintegration of the country, also had a very deep impact on the psyche of army officers. Many young officers turned to religion for solace and became born-again Muslims.

Given this situation, it was not surprising that radical Islamic officers made unsuccessful coup attempts in the mid 1980s. They wanted to bring about an Islamic revolution and establish a theocratic state. The fact that the attempts were crushed and the rebel officers were charged with treason indicated that, notwithstanding its Islamization, the state was not prepared to tolerate a theocratic rule.

The situation in Afghanistan provided inspiration to a whole generation of Pakistani Islamic radicals who considered it their religious duty to fight the oppression of Muslims anywhere in the world. It gave a new dimension to the idea of jihad, which till then had only been employed by the Pakistani state in the context of mobilizing the population against the arch rival – India. The Afghan war saw the privatization of the concept of jihad. Militant groups emerged from the ranks of traditional religious movements, who took the path of an armed struggle for the cause of Islam. The ISI's active role in the Afghan jihad brought Pakistani army officers into direct contact with the radical Islamists.

The handling of jihad also indoctrinated the military and intelligence officers. At least two former ISI chiefs – General Hamid Gul and General Javed Nasir – remained actively involved with Islamic radical movements.[21] Both promoted pan-Islamism and strove for an Islamic revolution that would free Pakistan from perceived western, and particularly American, cultural and political influences. General Gul, who liked to call himself a 'Muslim visionary', succeeded General

Rehman in 1987 when the Afghan resistance had entered its most critical juncture. The most charismatic of the ISI chiefs, he openly aligned himself with the hardline Afghan mujahidin leader, Gulbuddin Hekmatyar, and right-wing Pakistani Islamic parties. He would later take credit for dismantling the Soviet Union. General Gul had worked closely with the CIA, but turned anti-American after the Geneva Accord in 1987, which paved the way for the withdrawal of Soviet forces from Afghanistan. The Accord was signed by the Pakistani civilian government led by Prime Minister Mohammed Khan Junejo against the wishes of President Zia, who believed it deprived the Afghan mujahidin of the opportunity to take over Kabul. Resentment among the military and ISI officers deepened in 1990, just one year after the Soviets pulled out of Afghanistan and the US administration imposed sanctions on Pakistan for its nuclear programme. The CIA ended its support for the Afghan rebels and its links with the ISI went cold. It was a sudden end to the strong link between the two agencies. The military leadership accused the United States of dumping Pakistan after the collapse of the Soviet Union.

Long before the Afghan war was over, General Gul had started organizing a new jihad front in Kashmir. 'It is the years of our work that has realized the armed uprising against the Indian forces in Kashmir,' he told me in early 1990 when he was commanding the country's elite armoured corps.[22]

The death of General Zia ul-Haq in a mysterious air crash in August 1988 brought an end to Pakistan's longest-serving military government.[23] It left the generals with the choice of either imposing martial law again or holding elections and transferring power to a democratically elected civilian government. They went for the second option, realizing that a perpetuation of military rule might provoke public resistance and exacerbate the turmoil in an already highly polarised society. However, the generals were not prepared to pull out completely and leave the political field solely to the politicians, particularly to the daughter of Zulfikar Ali Bhutto, Benazir Bhutto, who now led the Pakistan People's Party, which was certain to sweep the polls.

To contain Benazir, the military cobbled together the Islamic Democratic Alliance (IDA), uniting all the right-wing parties under the leadership of Nawaz Sharif. General Aslam Beg, then Chief of Army Staff, and General Gul justified the move by saying it was necessary for the viable functioning of a democratic system. The main objective, however, was to ensure the military's continued role in the new system, overseen by the generals. By creating a counterbalance in the form of the IDA, the generals constrained the new government of a political party that had led the resistance against military hegemony for ten years.[24]

The military-sponsored alliance comprised a mix of traditional power brokers, religious parties and politicians who had emerged on the scene during the 1980s under military patronage. General Zia's regime, needing a measure of legitimacy and a social base of support, had co-opted segments of Punjab's dominant socio-economic strata: influential landlords, industrialists and emerging commercial groups. The new leadership of the Pakistan Muslim League thus largely consisted of politicians who owed their political rise to the military's backing. The other important components of the alliance were the right-wing Islamic groups, including the Jamaat-i-Islami, which had been involved in the Afghan jihad against the Soviet forces and the separatist war in Indian-controlled Kashmir.

While the IDA, which carried General Zia's legacy, could not achieve any significant electoral gains in the 1988 elections in the three smaller provinces, it did relatively well in Punjab and prevented the PPP from winning an absolute majority in the National Assembly. The military reluctantly handed over power to Benazir at the centre, but prevented her party from forming the government in Punjab, the biggest and most important of Pakistan's four provinces, which was being ruled by Nawaz Sharif. Political manipulation by the ISI helped Sharif retain power in the province with the support of independent members.

Benazir Bhutto's assumption of power, touted at the time as the dawn of a new democratic era, was in fact a transition from direct to indirect military rule. The formal restoration of civilian rule in 1988 did not reduce the ISI's clout. A return to the barracks did not mean that the military's structure of control and manipulation had been dismantled. The ISI still kept a close watch on civilian rulers. The strains in civil and military relationships remained the biggest obstacle to democracy taking root in Pakistan. The Chief of Army Staff remained the power behind the scenes in alliance with the new President, Ghulam Ishaq Khan, who held sweeping powers under the Eighth Amendment in the constitution introduced by General Zia.

For the army, the new political situation offered power without responsibility. The military continued to oversee Pakistan's policies on Afghanistan and India, managing relations with the USA and controlling the country's nuclear weapons programme. The army high command's decision to rest content with dominance, rather than direct intervention, was based on a careful calculation of the advantages and disadvantages of playing arbiter in Pakistan's highly polarized and conflict-ridden political scene.

A hamstrung Benazir Bhutto found herself directly clashing with the army when she removed General Gul from the ISI. The General, who was the architect of the IDA, had never reconciled himself to even restricted civilian rule. Benazir was never trusted by the establishment and many generals made it a point not to salute her. It was in February 1990 when I met General Gul in Multan, where he was posted as the commander of Pakistan's main strike corps, after being sacked from the ISI. It was the period when the army had just concluded a major war exercise called 'Zarb-i-Momin'. The General accused Prime Minister Benazir of trying to make peace with India and questioned her patriotism. 'By conducting the exercise we have blocked her designs to undermine Pakistan's defence,' he said.

It was apparent that the generals were looking for an opportune moment to remove Benazir from power. The clash came to a head when the Prime Minister tried to retire the Chairman of the Joint Chiefs of Staff Committee, Admiral Iftikhar Ahmed Sarohi, and gave a year's extension in service to Lt.-General Alam Jan Mehsud, a senior general believed to be close to her government. The army top brass saw this as blatant interference in the army's internal affairs. Eventually, on 6 August 1990, President Ghulam Ishaq Khan dismissed her government on charges of corruption and dissolved the National Assembly. President Khan, a former top bureaucrat, was the central pillar of General Zia's military rule and represented his legacy.

Benazir's party met a humiliating defeat in the following elections, losing the government even in her home province and political stronghold, Sindh. The military leadership did not want to take any chances that time. To ensure the IDA's electoral victory, the ISI financed the election campaign of many top Alliance leaders.[25] The list, which was published in national newspapers, contained the names of some leading politicians, including Nawaz Sharif. Most of them later held important posts in the new government.

In 1988, the long-simmering political discontent in Kashmir exploded into a popular uprising against Indian control. Thousands of young Kashmiris crossed over to the Pakistani side of the Line of Control to receive guerrilla training as the Indian authorities tried to crush the insurgency by brute force. Essentially an indigenous rebellion, it soon turned into an armed struggle against Indian forces. Thousands of Kashmiri youths joined the separatist struggle, which was initially led by the independent nationalist organization, Jammu and Kashmir Liberation Front (JKLF)

The ISI used the extensive intelligence and militant network that it had built up during the Afghan war to support a new jihad against the Indian forces in Kashmir. In Afghanistan in the 1980s, jihadist cadres came from the ranks of motivated Islamists across the Muslim world who were prepared to die for the cause, as well as kill the 'communists'. The spirit saw its continuation in Kashmir, which became one of the world's hottest 'Islamic jihad' spots. The ISI's involvement increased further in the early 1990s when, in an attempt to sideline the JKLF, it started supporting the pro-Pakistani Hezb-ul Mujahideen. The move divided the Kashmiri struggle and led to internecine battles. The mid 1990s saw the increasing role of Pakistani-based militant groups. That was when Harkat-ul-Mujahideen (HuM), Lashkar-e-Taiba (LeT) and later Jaish-e-Mohammed (JeM) emerged as the main guerrilla forces in the disputed state. Those hardline Islamic groups changed the complexion of the struggle.

Most of the fighters belonging to those Islamic militant groups came from Punjab and the North West Frontier Province. They tried to give an Islamic orientation to a secular separatist movement, with disastrous consequences. While the increasing involvement of Pakistani groups kept the armed struggle alive, it also widened the division within the movement. Many Kashmiri groups resented the ISI's attempts, first to 'Pakistanize' and then to 'Islamize' the movement. Thousands of Pakistani militants had been killed in the fighting in Kashmir in more than a decade.

In November 1990, Nawaz Sharif took over as Pakistan's new Prime Minister. A scion of one of the country's richest business families from Lahore, Sharif had entered politics as the protégé of General Zia. His political career owed much to his father's close links with General Ghulam Jilani. The former ISI chief, who was appointed by Zia as governor of Pakistan's most powerful Punjab province as a reward for his role in the 1977 coup, groomed Sharif as the alternative leader to Benazir. He was appointed Punjab's finance minister in 1981 and, a couple of years later, he rose to the post of Chief Minister. Sharif was a man of very mediocre talents. He had neither charisma nor any political roots when he was chosen by General Zia to head the government of Pakistan's most powerful province.

Sharif assumed power with much greater advantages than his predecessor had enjoyed. His accession to power brought a rare harmony to the power troika – President, Prime Minister and Chief of Army Staff.

But this harmony was not to last: Sharif sought to wear down constraints on his power imposed by his old patrons – the military. The rivalry between Sharif and the army reached a peak in 1992, when Sharif picked General Javed Nasir for the post of director general of the ISI, against the advice of his most senior advisers. A born-again Muslim, the bearded General Nasir saw himself as a visionary. The General, who made no secret of his radical religious beliefs and his association with the 'Tablighi Jamaat', was widely believed to be personally associated with the ISI's adventurous policy actions during his brief tenure. General Nasir's religious zeal and maverick actions became embarrassing for the military high command, which had completely lost control over the country's premier spy agency. It was never clear whether some of the activities General Nasir engaged the ISI in had the government's sanction or whether the overzealous spymaster was exceeding his mandate.

General Nasir widened the ISI's covert operation beyond Kashmir and Afghanistan. During his tenure, the spy agency was accused of masterminding a series of bomb blasts in the Indian financial capital of Mumbai in March 1993, which killed hundreds of people. The bombing was allegedly carried out by a Bombay crime mafia, headed by Dawood Ibrahim, to avenge the demolition of the sixteenth-century Babri Mosque by Hindu extremists. Ibrahim, who was top of a list of 20 fugitives that India wanted Pakistan to hand over, lived in the Pakistani city of Karachi under ISI protection. He was also put on the global terrorist list. The allegation about the ISI's involvement in fanning cross-border strife, landed Pakistan in serious trouble.

In May 1992, the USA issued a warning that it could declare Pakistan a terrorist state. Washington's main concern was that Pakistan continued to provide material support to the Islamic militants in Kashmir and the Sikh insurgents in the Indian state of Punjab, despite Islamabad's repeated assurances that no official agency was involved there.[26] The CIA director, John Woolsey, reported that the ISI was fanning conflict in the region. In a letter to Prime Minister Nawaz Sharif in 1992, the US Secretary of State, James Baker, warned that the ISI's material support to the groups that had engaged in terrorism could lead to the imposition of a package of sanctions against Pakistan.

In April 1993, worried by the possibility of Pakistan ending up on the terrorist list, Sharif sent his foreign secretary, Akram Zaki, to assure Washington that he would not support militancy.[27] But the USA insisted on stronger action to curb groups engaging in 'terrorism'. The ISI's direct support for the militant groups was curtailed, but help to the Kashmiri insurgents continued through 'private channels', comprising Islamic parties like the Jamaat-i-Islami. Although the measure fell short of the US demand, they prevented Pakistan's inclusion on the list of terrorist states.

The ISI's involvement was not limited to India, however. Under General Nasir's instructions, the ISI violated the UN embargo on supplying arms to the warring parties in Bosnia-Herzegovina and airlifted heavy weapons and missiles for the Bosnian Muslims. In 1993, several Arab countries, including Egypt, Tunisia, and Algeria, had complained about General Nasir extending support to radical Islamic movements in their countries.[28]

The maverick General Nasir was sacked from the ISI and prematurely retired from the army in May 1993, following the dismissal of Prime Minister Nawaz Sharif's government. The army-backed caretaker administration, led by former World Bank executive Moeen Qureshi, moved to clean up the ISI and alleviate US pressure on Pakistan. Scores of officers, who had become closely linked with radical Afghan mujahidin groups during the anti-Soviet struggle, were systematically weeded out. Some eleven hundred operatives were either retired or sent back to their units in the army. The purge was largely the result of a change in Islamabad's policy of no longer aligning itself with any of the groups involved in the fratricidal war in Afghanistan that followed the fall of the communist regime of Najibullah in May 1992. The measure was also aimed at satisfying Washington. The purge may have helped restore some discipline in the ISI, but did not change its basic orientation. The agency had become deeply involved in the Kashmiri separatist struggle, and the military was reluctant to pull back support for the militants it believed were fighting Pakistan's war. Many in the military establishment contended that by engaging around half a million Indian troops in Kashmir, the 'Kashmiri freedom fighters' had ensured Pakistan's security.

The game of musical chairs continued as it was now Benazir Bhutto's turn to form the government again. She returned as Prime Minister for the second time in November 1993, just three years after her unceremonious exit. This time around she was much better placed. She had the blessing of the army, which had been instrumental in her usurpation in 1990. There was a marked difference in the situation for Benazir compared to her first term in office. This time she had a cooperative army chief, General Abdul Waheed Kakar, and a new president of her own choice: Farooq Leghari was an old Pakistan People's Party loyalist. The troika operated harmoniously in contrast to the discord that marked her first term. Learning from past experience, she tried to appease the army and toed the line on sensitive foreign policy security issues.

By 1994, the ISI was back in Afghanistan sponsoring the emerging Taliban Islamic movement. It was in mid 1993, when some three dozen Taliban got together at Kashke Nakud, near Kandahar in south-western Afghanistan, to voice their concern over the infighting among the various mujahidin factions and lawlessness in the country. Taliban is a Pashto word meaning students of a religious school or madrasa. They come from the poorest section of the population and many of them were homeless or orphans. The group, led by a former mujahidin commander, Mullah Mohammed Omar, took upon themselves the task of cleaning up their region of corrupt mujahidin commanders.

Mullah Omar, who had lost one eye in the war against the Soviet forces and had retired to become a 'Talib' (student), had already become a legend after he executed a mujahidin commander who had raped two young girls near his village of Maiwand and left his body hung on the barrel of a tank for several days. With this symbolic strike against the mujahidin's abuses of power, spontaneous expressions of support came in from all over the district, and thus the Taliban were born.[29]

In October 1994, Pakistani security officials contacted Mullah Omar for the first time, seeking help for the safe passage of a convoy of trucks transporting goods to Turkmenistan. Initially, the ISI, which had long favoured the Afghan mujahidin faction Hezb-i-Islami led by Gulbuddin Hekmatyar, was sceptical of the Taliban. But Naseerullah Babar, a retired general and Interior Minister in Benazir's government, saw the Taliban's potential as a formidable political force that could bring peace to the war-ravaged country and serve Pakistan's long-term economic and strategic interests.

The control of a friendly force in south-west Afghanistan could open the prospect for an energy and trade corridor between Pakistan and central Asia. Pakistan was keen to export gas from Turkmenistan but that would only be possible through a pipeline via Afghanistan.[30] This was probably the reason why the USA, in the beginning, was sympathetic towards the student militia. US diplomats in Islamabad believed that the Taliban could play a useful role in restoring a strong, centralized government to Afghanistan. This view was also shared privately by many relief organizations, who were frustrated by the fruitless negotiations of the UN Special Mission. They saw in the Taliban, with all their prejudices, a peculiarly Afghan solution to the problem which had defied international peacemakers for many years. All of them seemed to have been taken in by the Taliban rhetoric of an 'Islamic revolution for social justice'. There was also talk of a trade-off between peace and security on the one hand and human rights on the other.[31]

In 1995, Islamabad decided to back the movement, which by then had captured Kandahar and several other provinces. That also led to the involvement of the ISI. Dozens of intelligence agents were attached to the Taliban forces, providing them with tactical and professional support. Most of them had operated in Afghanistan during the anti-Soviet jihad and had close connections with various Afghan mujahidin factions.

Amir Sultan Tarar, who had been involved in Afghanistan since the beginning of the CIA-ISI covert operation, received a new task. Better known by his code name, Colonel Imam, he had known many of the Taliban leaders since the jihad days, which made him the ideal man for the job. Bearded and wearing a turban, Colonel Imam blended in easily with his clients and developed a close rapport with Mullah Omar. Posted as Pakistan's consul general, first in Kandahar and then in the western Afghan city of Herat, he emerged as a key adviser to the Taliban leaders and also acted as a conduit for arms and money. It was that crucial help that tilted the balance for the Taliban in their battle against the rival warlords. Colonel Imam and other ISI officers posted in Kandahar covertly worked to buy off commanders' loyalties for the Taliban. The role of the ISI increased tremendously after the Taliban seized Kabul in September 1996 and moved to establish their control over the rest of the country.[32]

The meteoric rise of the Taliban movement owed much to the backing of Islamabad and help from Pakistani Islamic parties. Thousands of Pakistani students from madrasas in the border areas were dispatched to Afghanistan in 1997 to join the Taliban forces in the battle for Mazar-i-Sharif. Madrasas in the North West Frontier Province and Balochistan were closed down for months to allow students to participate in the 'holy war'.

Pakistan's support for the Taliban was certainly not based on any ideological consideration. It was based on purely geo-strategic reasons, aimed at asserting Pakistan's influence over Afghanistan through a Pashtun movement. The main objective was to get strategic depth vis-à-vis India and isolate Iran. Pakistan's military strategists believed that a Pashtun-dominated friendly government in Afghanistan could provide strategic advantage in the country against its arch rival, India, with whom it had long been locked in bitter conflict on Kashmir.[33] They argued that lack of geographical depth and hinterland would make Pakistan's security vulnerable in the event of a war with India. The attainment of this 'strategic depth' had been a key element in Pakistan's Afghan policy since the 1980s. But the rise to power of the Taliban did not achieve this objective, as the Taliban refused to accept a client position.

Pakistan received a rude shock when the radical Islamic regime refused to recognize the Durand Line and also to drop Afghanistan's claim over a part of the North West Frontier Province. Pakistan's relations with Afghanistan had been strained since the end of British colonial rule in the Indian subcontinent. Every Afghan government had rejected the controversial Durand Line drawn by the British as an international border with Pakistan. Afghanistan was the only country not to vote for Pakistan's membership of the United Nations. In the 1950s and 1960s, the Afghan government had sponsored a Pashtun separatist movement in Pakistan's North West Frontier Province.[34]

The main objective of Pakistan's policy since the 1980s had been to establish a friendly or pliant government in Afghanistan, using ethnic and religious connections. Throughout the war against Soviet forces, Pakistan backed radical Pashtun mujahidin commanders like Gulbuddin Hekmatyar. The decision to support the Pashtun-dominated Taliban was driven by the same consideration. With its hardline conservative world-view, the Taliban regime became an international pariah. Afghanistan provided a safe haven for Islamic militants from all over the world and that had a direct bearing on Pakistan. In fact, Pakistan appeared to have provided the Taliban with strategic depth, as their influence started spreading inside Pakistani Pashtun areas, raising fears of the Talibanization of Pakistan.

Taliban rule turned the war-ravaged country into a base for Osama bin Laden. The tentacles of the al-Qaeda terrorist network extended into Pakistan, where it had strong allies among the ISI-trained Islamic militants. The country became a conduit for training aspiring militants across the world. That also created a nexus between groups fighting in Afghanistan and those operating in Kashmir. Meanwhile, Pakistan also became home to a thriving community of foreign jihadists, many of whom were veterans of the anti-Soviet Afghan war and had stayed there for the simple reason that they could not return to their countries of origin for fear of persecution. The state-sponsored jihadist culture provided them a safe haven in Pakistan.

Meanwhile, Benazir Bhutto lost the battle to maintain her authority over an increasingly radicalized society, and in October 1996 she was, after a protracted power struggle, dismissed by the President. It was the third time in eight years that an elected government had been dismissed less than halfway through its term. Weak democratic institutions, lack of a democratic political culture, politics of patronage, ineptitude of political leadership and the military's involvement in politics all contributed to the continuing crisis of democracy in Pakistan.

In the subsequent elections, former Prime Minister Nawaz Sharif was re-elected with a large majority. Sharif was determined not to lose power again and set about undermining the role of the presidency and the judiciary. He used Islamic policies to bolster his own position. Sharif introduced an Islamic sharia bill, reinforcing the Islamization process initiated by General Zia. His exploitation of religion for political purposes strengthened the Islamic orthodoxy and religious militancy. That also led to an upsurge in religion-based violence. Sharif's preoccupation with power proved to be a fatal distraction, as the country drifted towards an economic meltdown. The fiscal indiscipline brought the country to the verge of bankruptcy. Sharif had a total disregard for institutions – he neither understood nor respected nor learnt to live with the institutions of a modern state and followed a patrimonial style of government. Editors and journalists were arrested and harassed for criticizing the government. Sharif had planned to make further amendments to the Constitution, declaring himself 'Amirul Mominin' (absolute leader of the Muslims).

While suppressing civil society and democratic institutions, Sharif increased his reliance on the army to manage everything from state-owned corporations to development work. A quarter of a million troops were mobilized to conduct a long-delayed population census. Another one hundred thousand were deployed to read electricity meters and run an almost bankrupt Water and Power Development Authority, which was responsible for electricity supply and the country's huge irrigation network. At one point, army soldiers were brought in to help kill stray dogs in Sharif's home town, Lahore.[35]

Such a large-scale induction of army personnel into civilian affairs was unprecedented even in Pakistan. The growing dependence on the army created its own predicament. Increasingly tasked with administration of civilian affairs, the army top brass wanted more political power in the state. This led to tensions between the army and Sharif, who was determined not to cede power to anyone.

Sharif had picked General Pervez Musharraf ahead of two senior generals as the new army chief. He deliberately chose a man from the Mohajir minority ethnic group to head a predominantly Punjabi army, assuming that he would not be able to challenge an all-powerful Punjabi Prime Minister. But he failed to understand that the conflict with the army had a strong institutional dimension and was not simply about personalities. He erroneously assumed that the army would remain subservient to his rule once he had put in a man of his own choice at the top. For Sharif it was a game of persons. For the army it was an institutional matter.

The trigger for the eventual showdown between the army chief and the Prime Minister came in May 1999, following Sharif's peace talks with India, at which point Musharraf decided to revive the faltering campaign in Kashmir without telling the Prime Minister. The Pakistani army sent in soldiers to occupy Indian positions in the Kargil peaks, which the Indian army traditionally vacated during winter. The move led to a stand-off with India, and a terrified Sharif had almost begged President Clinton to mediate. He was forced to make a humiliating climbdown, which provoked an inevitable backlash from militants at home. By the time he tried to reassert himself by sacking Musharraf in October, it was already clear that it was, as it had always been, the radical military, not the elected government, who was in the driving seat in Pakistan.

2

VOLTE-FACE

On the morning of 11 September 2001, Lt.-General Mahmood Ahmed, the chief of the ISI, was at a breakfast meeting on Capitol Hill in Washington with Senator Bob Graham and Congressman Porter Goss, the chairmen of the Senate and House Intelligence committees. Also present there were Senator John Kyle and Pakistan's ambassador to Washington, Maleeha Lodhi. As they talked about terrorism, specifically about bin Laden, a member of Senator Graham's staff informed them about the planes hitting the World Trade Center. The meeting continued until one plane was reported heading towards Capitol Hill and evacuation was ordered. General Mahmood expressed his deep sympathy to the people of the USA before the five hurriedly dispersed.[1]

General Mahmood had been due to return that evening after completing his week-long official visit to Washington, but his departure was delayed as all the airports were closed after the terrorist attacks. He had arrived in Washington on 4 September on the invitation of the CIA chief for routine consultations with senior US officials. The CIA and the ISI, erstwhile partners in the covert war against Soviet forces in Afghanistan in the 1980s, had maintained close contact despite the low in the relations between Washington and Islamabad that had followed the USA's nuclear-related sanctions on Pakistan in 1990.

It was General Mahmood's second visit to Washington as the ISI chief. His previous trip in April 2000 followed President Clinton's short stopover in Islamabad. The visit was arranged by the CIA with a view to cultivating Pakistan's new chief spymaster. He was hugely pampered as the CIA officials tried to win his confidence.[2] At the General's request, the agency had arranged a private tour of Gettysburg, the venue of a crucial battle during the American Civil War in 1863. General Mahmood had a special interest in the battle of Gettysburg and had done his thesis on the subject at the National Defence College. He would talk endlessly on the tactics and other aspects of the battle. The CIA officials, however, were not sure whether all that effort won his cooperation. The trip went sour at the end when he received a dressing-down from Thomas Pickering, the US Under-Secretary of State, for helping the Taliban regime. He went back home angry and humiliated.[3] The incident did not help improve relations between the USA and Pakistan, which had already become strained after the return of military rule and imposition of democratic sanctions. Pakistan's patronage of the orthodox Taliban regime, which had provided a base for bin Laden and thousands of other militants from different countries, was a serious concern for the Bush administration.

General Mahmood was the second-most-powerful man in the Pakistani military junta. after General Musharraf. A stocky man with a long handlebar moustache, he was ruthless and highly ambitious. Because of his brashness and arrogance he was not very popular among his fellow officers. As the commander of the key 10th Corps based in Rawalpindi, he was one of the two coup-makers who brought Musharraf to power on 12 October 1999. His troops seized control of Islamabad and arrested the Prime Minister, Nawaz Sharif. He was rewarded for his loyalty when Musharraf appointed him director general of the ISI. During his tenure as head of the country's premier intelligence agency he had accelerated support for Islamic militant groups. The jihadist activities in Kashmir saw an unprecedented rise and Pakistan got much more deeply involved with the Taliban's efforts to expand their control in Afghanistan.

During his second stay in Washington, General Mahmood had met with senior CIA, Pentagon and National Security Council officials. Terrorism coming out of Afghanistan was the central issue of their discussions. He defended Pakistan's policy of engagement with the

Tailban and told George Tenet and other CIA officials that Mullah Omar was a pious and religious person, not a man of violence. The situation became tense when, on 9 September, two suicide bombers masquerading as journalists assassinated Ahmed Shah Masood, the leader of the rebel Afghan Northern Alliance. The leaders of the alliance blamed al-Qaeda and the ISI for the murder.

General Mahmood was watching television coverage of the Twin Tower attacks at Ambassador Lodhi's office when he received a call at 5 pm inviting him for an emergency meeting with Richard Armitage, the US Deputy Secretary of State. At 10 am on 12 September, the General, accompanied by Ambassador Lodhi and Zamir Akram, a senior official at the Embassy, arrived at the State Department. Armitage was terse as he began saying that Pakistan faced a stark choice. 'We want to know whether you are with us or not. This is a black and white choice with no grey, 'he said. The General enquired what his country could do in that situation. 'We need your country's full support and cooperation. We will tell you tomorrow the specifics about the cooperation that is required,' said Armitage and asked the General to meet him the next day.[4]

Returning to the Embassy, General Mahmood telephoned President Musharraf. Musharraf had been speaking to a group of local government representatives in Karachi when his Press Secretary had interrupted to tell him about the World Trade Center attacks. He immediately perceived the choice that he was about to be faced with. 'I took a fast decision,' he later told me, 'but I thought about it very carefully.'[5] Only afterwards did he consult his aides and senior military commanders. 'I keep to Napoleon's view that two-thirds of the decision-making process is based on analysis and information and one-third is always a leap in the dark.'[6]

The shock and anger in Washington which was relayed to him by his spy chief did not surprise Musharraf. He had also received a telephone call from Secretary of State Colin Powell, who had spelled out the situation in stark terms, telling the Pakistani President: 'The American people would not understand if Pakistan was not in this fight with the United States.'[7] Musharraf assured him of his country's full cooperation.

On 13 September, General Mahmood returned to the State Department for the second meeting. 'This is not negotiable,' said Armitage, as he handed him a single sheet of paper with a list of seven demands that the Bush administration wanted him to accept. The General, who was known for his hardline pro-Taliban position, glanced through the paper for a few seconds and passed it on to Ambassador Lodhi. Before she started reading the paper, General Mahmood replied, 'They are all acceptable to us.' The swift response took Armitage by surprise and left Pakistani officials flabbergasted. 'These are very powerful words, General. Don't you want to discuss this with your President?' he asked. 'I know the President's mind,' replied General Mahmood. A relieved Armitage asked General Mahmood to meet with Tenet at his headquarters at Langley. 'He is waiting for you,' said Armitage.[8]

General Mahmood looked glum as he was driven to Langley for a crucial meeting with the CIA officials. He later grumbled about the high-handedness of American officials. He was not at all happy with the terms for cooperation with the USA, which he had acceded to a few minutes previously. He looked like a general who had just lost a battle. Meanwhile, Ambassador Lodhi returned to the Embassy, from where she faxed the paper to President Musharraf in Islamabad. General Mahmood stayed in Washington until 16 September, discussing Pakistan's role in the 'war on terror' with American officials. But it was apparent that he was not keen to see that role implemented.

On 13 September, Wendy Chamberlain, the newly appointed US ambassador to Islamabad, met with Musharraf and conveyed a formal message from President Bush with the same list of demands which had earlier been handed over to General Mahmood in Washington. It read:

1) Stop al-Qaeda operations on the Pakistani border, intercept arms shipments through Pakistan and all logistical support for bin Laden.
2) Blanket over-flight and landing rights for US planes.
3) Access to Pakistan's naval bases, air bases and borders.
4) Immediate intelligence and immigration information.
5) Curb all domestic expression of support for terrorism against the United States, its friends and allies.
6) Cut off fuel supply to the Taliban and stop Pakistani volunteers going into Afghanistan to join the Taliban.
7) Pakistan to break diplomatic relations with the Taliban and assist the US in destroying bin Laden and his al-Qaeda network.[9]

The same evening, General Musharraf made a statement assuring the

US President of his unstinting cooperation in the fight against terrorism. He declared Pakistan would commit all of its resources in an effort coordinated with the USA to locate and punish those involved in that horrific act. President Bush responded to Musharraf's message of support by saying, 'Now we'll find out what that means. Won't we?'

Pakistan's support was important for the USA. Its geographic proximity and its vast intelligence information on Afghanistan were seen as crucial for any military action against the Taliban and al-Qaeda. Pakistan was one of the three countries – the others were the United Arab Emirates and Saudi Arabia – which had formally recognized the conservative Afghan Islamic government and the only country which had maintained diplomatic relations with Kabul. The American demands, to which General Mahmood had agreed in next to no time, required Pakistan to abandon its support for the Taliban regime and provide logistic support to the American forces. After having spent the past seven years helping the Taliban consolidate their rule, providing them with military, political and financial support, Pakistan was now being asked by the Bush administration to help the USA dislodge the Islamic fundamentalist government.

The list was clearly only the first step in testing Pakistan's resolve. Washington had also asked for a comprehensive report from the ISI about every detail it had on bin Laden, including his contacts with Pakistani and other Islamic militant organizations. Pakistan eventually negotiated with the USA that no combat missions would be carried out from its territory and, instead of blanket over-flight rights, an air corridor was assigned to US planes. Pakistan was ready to break diplomatic relations with the Taliban government immediately, but the move was delayed on American advice. The US Assistant Secretary of State, Christina Rocca, told Ambassador Lodhi that Pakistan should keep the diplomatic channel open with the Taliban until the US invasion was completed.[10] Breaking off diplomatic relations at that point, in Washington's view, would have given a clear indication to the Taliban about the exact timing of an impending US attack.

The turnaround was met with astonishment by the military. They had been actively supporting the Pashtun Taliban regime, which, according to them, provided Pakistan with 'strategic depth' against any aggression from arch rival India. The Pakistani military feared that they would lose their strategic depth in Kabul if they withdrew support from the hardline Islamic regime.

Several efforts by the USA prior to 9/11 had failed to elicit Islamabad's cooperation in the expulsion of bin Laden from Afghanistan. Musharraf's coming to power in October 1999 had reversed a secret mission plan with Washington to send a Pakistani special commando force into Afghanistan to capture bin Laden using the ISI's information. Under the plan, which was suggested by the then Prime Minister Nawaz Sharif during his visit to Washington in July 1999, the USA had agreed to provide $25 million for training a group of ex-ISI and Pakistani army officers for the operation. The detail of the operation was worked out in subsequent meetings between the ISI's then chief, Lt.-General Ziauddin, and CIA officials in Washington in September.[11] But before the plan could be implemented Sharif had been ousted from power. General Ziauddin, who was appointed as Chief of Army Staff by Sharif, was arrested after Musharraf's loyalists took over control of Islamabad. Pakistani military officials argued the plan was not realistic and would never have taken off. However, Washington continued to press the military regime to get bin Laden expelled from Afghanistan.

In January 2000, Musharraf promised senior American officials that he would meet with the Taliban supreme leader Mullah Omar and press him on the matter of expelling bin Laden. But the visit never materialized.[12] In March 2000, President Clinton made a one-day stopover in Islamabad on his way back from India. It was the first time a US president had been there since 1969. Clinton made the trip despite strong opposition from members of his administration. Washington had imposed sanctions on Pakistan after the military coup and relations between the two countries had hit a new low. During his brief one-to-one meeting, Clinton asked the General for help regarding bin Laden. The US President later told his aides: 'I offered him the moon when I went to see him, in terms of better relations with the United States, if he would help us get bin Laden and deal with another issue or two.'[13] Ambassador Lodhi, who was present at the meeting, denied that any such offer was made. 'I don't remember any moon that Pakistan was offered,' she said.

Again in May that year President Clinton reminded Musharraf to carry out his promise to visit Afghanistan and convince Mullah Omar to get rid of bin Laden. In June, CIA Director George Tenet travelled to Pakistan with the same message. Musharraf could not visit Afghanistan because of clear indications that Mullah Omar would not respond positively to any suggestion to extradite bin Laden. It was also apparent that his hardline generals, particularly General Mahmood, were not keen to push the issue too much as the Taliban prepared to launch the 'final' assault against the opposition Northern Alliance. The Arab militants were an important part of the Taliban fighting machine and their role was crucial in the coming battles. Frustrated by the inaction, Washington became openly critical of Pakistan for supporting the Taliban offensive to complete their control over Afghanistan. In December, the United Nations Security Council imposed fresh sanctions against the Taliban regime, calling for bin Laden's expulsion and forbidding any country to provide them with arms or military assistance. The latest sanction, however, did little to stop Islamabad from continuing to supply weapons and financial aid to its ally. There was a complete stalemate in US relations with Pakistan in Clinton's final year as President. The administration had little incentive to offer with congressional nuclear- and democracy-related sanctions against Pakistan. The US 'stick heavy' policy failed to force Pakistan to cooperate.[14]

Immediately after his inauguration, President Bush raised the terrorism issue with Pakistan's military ruler; in February 2001, he sent a letter to General Musharraf seeking his support in dealing with terrorism. He emphasized that bin Laden and al-Qaeda were a direct threat to the United States and its interests and that this threat had to be addressed.[15] There was, however, a clear shift in the approach of the new US administration. Instead of just using the stick, Secretary of State Colin Powell recommended providing some incentives to persuade Pakistan to cooperate. To break the logjam, the US administration moved to pursue a policy of enhanced engagement with Islamabad and also considered lifting some of the sanctions against the military government. But, because of a negative view of Pakistan on Capitol Hill, the idea of lifting sanctions could not make much headway. On 4 August, President Bush again wrote to President Musharraf registering his concern over terrorism emanating from Afghanistan and requested him to engage actively against al-Qaeda.[16]

Although Pakistan's leverage over the Taliban had weakened over the years and relations between them had become quite testy, Musharraf was not willing to pull support completely. He snapped shut a green folder containing a letter from Mullah Omar when I and a colleague from *Newsweek* arrived in the first week of February 2001 for an interview at his office in the Army General Headquarters in Rawalpindi. Mullah Omar's letter was in reply to Musharraf's message that had drawn the Afghan leader's attention to the international concern over the terrorism issue. 'I told him he must address the problems of terrorism, religious extremism and the gender issue to improve the Taliban's image,' he told us, but there was no indication from him that he was going to abandon support for the conservative regime, which he believed was in Pakistan's interest. Musharraf was visibly unhappy with the UN sanctions slapped on the Taliban regime. 'We are putting them against the wall,' he said, 'They have banned poppy cultivation. The world should understand that, since we have imposed sanctions as well, that means we are telling them to commit suicide.' On the bin Laden issue, the President suggested a middle way could be found on the issue of his extradition. 'He can be sent to any third country.' But he was not sure how it could be done.

In the event, the change came astonishingly fast in the aftermath of the 9/11 terrorist attacks. The quick about-turn surprised even the American authorities. Concern for the state of Pakistan's democracy melted away and the military government was hailed by the West as 'an exemplary country in the fight against terrorism'.

Events in Washington and Islamabad during the week following 11 September provide an interesting insight into the decision-making process in Pakistan on crucial national security and foreign policy issues. Like the policy to support the Taliban regime, the decision on the about-turn was also taken by just a few people. There were no consultations at any level when President Musharraf decided to abandon support for the Taliban and gave the American forces complete access to Pakistani territory and airspace. It was all done in the best national interest, Musharraf later declared. The military leader had offered the same argument when Pakistan got into a messy situation by supporting the Taliban.

There was no discussion with the political parties on the paradigm shift in the country's strategic policy. President Musharraf took his handpicked cabinet into his confidence almost three days after he had already consented to the US demands. On 14 September, he met with his cabinet and the National Security Council in a marathon session lasting until the early hours of the morning in which he explained why he had decided to support the US. His line was that Pakistan itself was a victim of terrorism and the Taliban government was providing refuge to the religious extremists involved in sectarian killings in Pakistan. 'We had given a long list of the terrorists who we wanted to be handed over to us. At least they should have turned over the terrorists to us.' He told the ministers that the decision to cooperate with the United States was necessary to safeguard Pakistan's nuclear assets and its Kashmir policy. He gave them the details of military and logistic support he had agreed to provide to the US forces in the planned military action on Afghanistan. There were only a few feeble voices in the cabinet expressing concern over the possible public backlash. But largely it was a tame affair.

General Musharraf did not find it hard to convince his handpicked civilian cabinet, but it was not so smooth when it came to his top commanders and members of his military junta. There was a complete division over the issue. At least four top commanders, including General Mahmood who had earlier, in Washington, signed on the dotted line, showed reservations on the decision to provide unqualified support to the United States in its war on Afghanistan. Lt.-General Mohammed Aziz, Corps Commander Lahore, Lt.-General Jamshed Gulzar Kiani, Corps Commander, Rawalpindi, and Lt.-General Muzaffar Usmani, Deputy Chief of Army Staff, were among those who opposed pulling out support for the Taliban regime. They had all played key roles in the 1999 military coup. Musharraf, however, had the backing of other corps commanders. It was a precarious situation for him.

He could certainly not backtrack. He tried to persuade Washington to delay the attack on Afghanistan and give diplomacy a last chance. He thought there was still a possibility of persuading Mullah Omar to hand over bin Laden and avoid military action. He was worried about an extremist backlash against the US attack on a Muslim country and his government's support for it. General Musharraf expressed his concern about the domestic fall out to the American ambassador during his long meeting with her on 15 September. 'These decisions are not very easy and we need understanding from the United States and also support from them, so that I can take the nation along with me in our fight against terrorism,' General Musharraf recalled telling her. He was, perhaps, more concerned about the reaction within the military.

Donning his military uniform, General Musharraf looked stressed as he appeared on state television on the evening of 19 September to explain why he had decided to side with the USA in the war on terror. His tone was highly defensive as he told his countrymen how hard he had tried to defend the Taliban against all odds. He justified his decision saying it was done to save the country's strategic assets, safeguard the cause of Kashmir and prevent Pakistan from being declared a terrorist state.

He chose the occasion to warn India to 'lay off' Pakistan at that moment of crisis. The speech was aimed at defusing domestic opposition and to assure the military that by sacrificing the Taliban, he had protected Pakistan's vital interests.[18]

In a last-ditch attempt to put off a US attack on Afghanistan, and the backlash it would provoke, General Musharraf dispatched General Mamhood to Kandahar on 17 September to persuade Mullah Omar to hand bin Laden over to the USA. 'I was trying to drill home to him that he shouldn't make the people of Afghanistan suffer for a person who's not even an Afghan, but someone who's come from outside,' General Musharraf said.[19]

When the Saudi fugitive had first settled in Afghanistan in the 1990s after his expulsion from Sudan, relations between him and Mullah Omar were not cordial. Mullah Omar would often call him 'donkey' and make fun of bin Laden among his fellows. The Taliban leader would argue that he had inherited the Saudi militant and had to treat him as a guest and protect him according to Pashtun tradition. 'He is like chicken bone stuck in our throat,' he once told a senior Pakistani diplomat.[20]. The Taliban and al-Qaeda were very different in their aims and political and religious philosophy. The Taliban represented an ultra-conservative society; their agenda was Afghan-specific. Before 11 September, the USA was not their number one enemy. Al-Qaeda, on the other hand, had a wider international agenda. Its main objective was to attack US interests wherever possible. Its cadres were not necessarily orthodox religious people.

Over the years, bin Laden had expanded his influence as the conservative Islamic forces became increasingly reliant on his financial support and foreign fighters to extend control over the rest of Afghanistan. There was a visible hardening in Mullah Omar's stance with the improvement in relations with his guest.

Islamabad seemed to be losing whatever clout it had on the Islamic fundamentalist regime. Mullah Omar was not prepared to listen to his patrons anymore. The biggest embarrassment came in early 2001 when the he snubbed Musharraf's Interior Minister, Moinuddin Haider, who sought the extradition of leaders of a Pakistani sectarian group who had taken refuge in Afghanistan. They were wanted in several cases of murder and attacks on Shia mosques.[21] The worst snub came in March 2001, when Mullah Omar rejected Pakistan's request not to obliterate statues of Buddha in Bamiyan. Pakistan had tried to use the Taliban and al-Qaeda to promote its influence in war-torn Afghanistan – only to eventually lose control over both of them. Despite international outrage and dissent within their own ranks, hardline Taliban extremists systematically destroyed Afghanistan's pre-Islamic heritage.[22]

Some Taliban sources later associated the decision to blow up Afghanistan's ancient Buddhist statues with the growing influence of bin Laden. The military commanders who supported the decision were believed to have strong links with the al-Qaeda leader. They had fought together against the Soviet forces and that bond was further strengthened over the years during his stay in Afghanistan. The Taliban's growing dependence on Arab fighters who, along with Pakistanis, constituted the most crucial part of its war machinery had caused an increase in bin Laden's influence. The terrorist training camp funded by him had expanded with new recruits from across the Islamic world. Many of those trained there were assigned to the 55th Brigade, a unit bin Laden had created to help the Taliban fight its Afghan opponents.

General Mahmood arrived in Kandahar on 17 September 2001 and met with Mullah Omar without any aides. A senior Pakistani foreign ministry official who accompanied the ISI chief said he was surprised when the ISI chief asked him to stay outside and insisted on meeting the Taliban supreme leader alone. No one knew what transpired in the meeting, but he reported back to General Musharraf that 'he was encouraged by Mullah Omar's response.' General Musharraf said that Mullah Omar seemed to show 'a little bit of flexibility'.[23]. The flexibility Mullah Omar had indicated was not enough to meet the American demand of surrendering bin Laden. He had only agreed to form a court comprising Islamic religious scholars to try him, provided America was prepared to present evidence of his involvement in the terrorist attacks. But the trial never took place.

A few days later, General Mahmood sent a delegation of religious scholars to Mullah Omar. Interestingly, the delegation comprised hardline pro-Taliban clerics headed by Mufti Nizamuddin Shamzai, who later issued a *fatwa* (religious edict) for jihad against the American-led coalition forces. While he himself led violent protests against the Musharraf government, one of his sons went to Afghanistan to fight on behalf of the Taliban. There was a strong suspicion that the ISI chief may have been involved in deception. Some officials suggest that he had told Mullah Omar to remain steadfast and not to succumb to American pressure.[24]

As Pakistan's desperate diplomatic efforts failed to make Mullah Omar change his mind, by the end of September American forces were making final preparations to launch an attack on Afghanistan. They had already acquired three air bases in Pakistan close to Afghanistan and set up a command post at the air force base in Jacobabad in the southern Sindh province. The American military build-up and the presence of US troops in Pakistan had fuelled public anger. Thousands of people, largely supporters of hardline Islamic organizations, poured into the streets of Pakistan's main cities.

It was a tricky situation for the USA when it decided to go for military action against bin Laden and the Taliban regime in Afghanistan. For Washington, the factors that made the ISI valuable also made it suspect. Not only had Pakistan turned a blind eye for years to the growing ties between bin Laden and the Taliban; the ISI had also relied on al-Qaeda camps for training Kashmiri militants. The agency had maintained an indirect but long-standing relationship with Osama bin Laden. The connection came to light in August 1998 when the USA launched a cruise missile attack against al-Qaeda camps near Khost in Afghanistan in response to the bombings of two US embassies in East Africa. The casualties included several members of a Pakistani-backed Islamic militant group, HuM, who were training in the camps.

In some cases, ISI agents also facilitated Arab militants travelling to Afghanistan to wage jihad. It was widely suspected that bin Laden escaped the attack because of a tip-off from the ISI.[25] However, there had not been any evidence of the agency ever being directly involved in al-Qaeda terrorist activities against the USA. In fact, the ISI cooperated with the CIA and the FBI on several counter-terrorism operations in the 1990s. The agency was instrumental in the 1995 capture in Islamabad of Ramzi Yousuf, the mastermind of the first World Trade Center bombing in 1993, and the arrest in Pakistan in 1998 of Aimal Kansi, who had shot dead two CIA employees outside the agency's headquarters in Langley, Virginia in 1993.[26]

With its deep involvement in Afghanistan, the ISI had the most extensive intelligence data on that country and the Taliban. When Pakistan changed its course, it also brought about a reversal in the ISI's role. The ISI was back together with the CIA for a new war, very different from the one that they had fought in the 1980s. It was not the convergence of interests that fostered the alliance this time, but a forced relationship. The agency was now required to undo the politics of militancy, which it had actively promoted for almost a quarter of a century. It had never been easy for the agency to completely break its association with the Islamists.

With General Mahmood at the helm of the powerful ISI, President Musharraf would have had a difficult time pushing his new US-backed Afghan policy. There was no way Pakistan could have delivered what the Americans were demanding, with some top generals not in full agreement. General Musharraf was also not very happy with General Mahmood's arrogant style, and for not consulting him before agreeing to Armitage's seven-point demands. Though the President would have given his consent, he did not like being bypassed. A new policy needed a new team.

On 7 October 2001, just three weeks after his decision to join the US war on terror, Musharraf sacked General Mahmood and sidelined three other top generals known for their hardline Islamic views in a major shake-up of the army top brass. Initially, Musharraf just wanted to remove General Mahmood from the ISI and offered to elevate him to the post of Chairman of the Joint Chiefs of Staff Committee, which he refused. General Aziz reluctantly accepted the job. 'I just want to know whether it is your own decision or are you doing it because America wanted it?' General Aziz asked his boss. General Musharraf replied that it was his decision.[27] General Usmani simply resigned after being superseded by the appointment of General Mohammed Yousuf to the newly created post of Vice Chief of the Army Staff and General Gulzar Kiani as Quarter Master General. Ironically, in his new position of Chairman Joint Chiefs of Staff Committee, General Aziz coordinated with the Pentagon for logistical support for 'Operation Enduring Freedom' in Afghanistan.

The changes coincided with the launching of the joint US-British military operation in Afghanistan, and were seen as a part of General Musharraf's plan to appoint to key positions those officers who would support his pro-West policy shift. The shake-up in the army high command changed the entire composition of the junta, which had ruled the country since seizing power in October 1999 and consolidated General Musharraf's position as the sole power centre. In the past, every decision taken by the cabinet and the National Security Council had to be stamped by the powerful coterie of generals. The top brass now bore a totally new and liberal image, tailored to the requirement of the new situation with Pakistan trying to cut its umbilical cord with militant Islam and the Taliban.

With no peer, Musharraf could now operate much more freely. The removal of the hardline generals from the decision-making process came as a great relief to the USA as well. Within a few weeks of 11

September, Musharraf had swept aside five of his top 13 generals. 'The critical element of strategy are timing, space and strength,' he told me in January 2002, appearing much more relaxed and basking in his new-found international role. 'No democratically elected government could have moved so quickly,' he added.[28]

General Mahmood's removal was important, but it did not solve all the problems. Many senior officers harboured strong anti-American sentiments and obviously resented Pakistan fighting what they described as 'America's dirty war'. 'I hate to work with the Americans,' a senior ISI brigadier told me. 'I wish they get bogged down in Afghanistan.' Some of them refused to accept that al-Qaeda or Muslims were responsible for the 11 September attacks. It was going to be very difficult for them to break their associations and change their opinions after collaborating with militant Islamists for so long.

Musharraf chose Lt.-General Ehsan ul-Haq, a moderate officer with a strong intelligence background, as the new ISI chief. A Pashtun from Pakistan's North West Frontier Province, he had earlier served as head of Military Intelligence and was known for his middle-of-the-road views. One of his first jobs was to revamp the agency and to weed out those officers who had a long association with the Islamic militants. General Haq signalled a significant change in course, disbanding two major units of the ISI that had close links to Islamic militants in Afghanistan and Kashmir.

The move was seen as one of most significant shifts emerging from Musharraf's decision to align his country with the USA and to reduce ties with Islamic militants there and in Kashmir. The measure resulted in the transfer of perhaps 40 per cent of forces assigned to the ISI, which drew most of its manpower from the military. The action also served a major purpose of purging the 'Taliban cell' set up in the intelligence agency by General Mahmood. The American intelligence officials reportedly helped in compiling a list of suspect pro-Islamic officers who were to be removed from the organization. Despite the massive changes, the ISI's links with the Islamists were never successfully severed. They found it difficult to leave the old linkages behind. Nevertheless, the ISI helped tilt the balance in the battle in Afghanistan. The withdrawal of the ISI's support catalysed the swift fall of the Taliban regime. The agency, which had been deeply involved with the Taliban from its inception, guided the American forces in ousting its own creation.

Unlike his predecessor, General Haq kept a low profile, but became a key member of Musharraf's inner coterie. The ISI had assumed a much greater importance not only because of its new-found role in the US-led war on terror, but also because of its growing involvement in domestic politics. General Haq kept the Americans happy by capturing hundreds of al-Qaeda fugitives, but there was also huge scepticism over his efforts to curb home-grown Islamic militants, who continued to operate unabatedly, despite the apparent ban on their activities.

Though the changes in the military hierarchy had placed General Musharraf firmly in the driving seat, his position still appeared quite tenuous as he faced a strong challenge from the country's powerful Islamic groups who were out on the streets violently protesting against his pro-US policy. This was problematic for Musharraf, as these groups had significant influence among the rank and file of the army. Musharraf hoped for a quick end to the war, but his standing became more precarious when civilian casualties from the American air raids rose. The reaction from the extremist religious parties was swift and deadly. Thousands of people took to the streets in the western city of Quetta, close to the Afghan border, destroying and looting banks and torching UNICEF offices. The army was called out in Islamabad, the capital, and other cities to control violent demonstrations.

Armed with anything from locally made rifles to machine guns, thousands of Pakistani tribesmen streamed into Afghanistan in response to the Taliban's call for jihad. In the last week of October 2001, Sufi Mohammed, a radical Islamic cleric, crossed the border with 10,000 volunteers, including madrasa students, to fight against US-led coalition forces. Pakistani forces turned a blind eye to the hordes of volunteers crossing the border. 'They should go to Afghanistan rather than disrupting civil life here,' declared an Interior Ministry spokesman.[29] More than 5,000 Pakistani jihadists died fighting for the Taliban. Thousands of others were taken prisoner by various Afghan warlords.

What worried the military government was the danger of a spillover effect of the Afghan war into Pakistan. Islamic zealots seeking revenge for the American bombings in Afghanistan massacred 18 innocent Christian worshippers in a Bahawalpur church. This barbaric action was apparently inspired by the rhetoric of war between 'Islam and Christianity' emanating from the radical Islamists. The carnage gave a violent turn to the anti-American agitation and brought the war into Pakistani territory. The situation became even more explosive as hundreds of thousands of Afghans fleeing the American bombings poured into Pakistan. Strong support from the moderate and pro-West liberal political parties like former Prime Minister Benazir Bhutto's Pakistan People's Party and the Muttahida Qaumi Movement helped the military government to contain the Islamic forces. The protests were confined to the Pashtun-dominated region of the North West Frontier Province and Western Balochistan. This outrage against the US attack on Afghanistan consequently led the Islamic parties to sweep the parliamentary polls a year later in the two border provinces having close ethnic proximity with Afghanistan.

General Musharraf had two major concerns as the US-led coalition forces launched military strikes in Afghanistan: the war had to be short and targeted, so as to avoid collateral damage; and there should be a friendly post-operation political dispensation in Afghanistan. He suggested working with what he called the 'moderate Taliban'. In a television interview in November 2001, Musharraf argued that the moderate Taliban was willing to bring about a change and it should be accepted in a future administration. He repeatedly sought assurances from the US administration that the Northern Alliance, which had a strong anti-Pakistan stance and close ties with India, would not be permitted to enter Kabul.[30]

After putting up stiff resistance, the Taliban regime collapsed in the second week of November. The quick fall came as a surprise to the US military authorities who expected the war to drag on for months if not years. The Taliban first lost Mazar-i-Sharif to the Northern Alliance where thousands of their soldiers were made prisoners. A large number of them were Pakistanis. Within a few days, Taliban forces had fled Kabul in the dead of night without a shot being fired. The next day the Northern Alliance triumphantly entered Kabul to the utter embarrassment of President Bush who had asked them to stay out of the Afghan capital. He had done so on the urging of General Musharraf who had warned that revenge killings would ensue if Kabul fell to the Northern Alliance. The US and Pakistani leaders had agreed to put in place a representative government in Kabul and declare it a demilitarized city. Getting the American President to agree to his request was seen as a major diplomatic success for the Pakistani military leader.

Pakistan was not happy when the anti-Taliban alliance took over control of the city, and there was a visible estrangement in Islamabad's relations with the new political regime installed in Kabul. Long-term ties with the Taliban made Pakistan wary of the new internationally supported Afghan government. However, Pakistani intelligence agencies maintained some degree of cooperation with the Taliban elements fleeing the fighting. While the Pakistani military establishment was eager to reassert its influence in Kabul, it was not possible in the new power equation that emerged in the post-Taliban Afghanistan. In December 2001, after much haggling at a conference in Bonn, the rival Afghan factions agreed to a new interim set-up in Afghanistan headed by a Pashtun Afghan leader Hamid Karzai.[31]. The arrangement diminished the role of the Northern Alliance, but it remained the most powerful part of the government, controlling the ministries of defence, interior and foreign affairs.

Meanwhile, thousands of retreating Taliban officials and fighters found refuge in the North West Frontier Province and Balochistan. Intense US bombing of their mountainous hideouts in Afghanistan forced bin Laden and hundreds of his fighters to flee into Pakistan, leading to a new and prolonged phase of the anti-terror war on Pakistan's territory. The vast lawless tribal border regions made Pakistan attractive to jihadist recruits and militants seeking refuge. It also provided a base for operations against US-led coalition forces in Afghanistan. Pakistan became the backyard of America's war on terror and its war in Afghanistan.

Musharraf's support for the US war on terror brought huge economic and political dividends to his country. From a pariah state, Pakistan became the centre of focus of the international community. Never before had so many head of states travelled to Pakistan as they did, in the few weeks after 11 September. Pakistan was, once more, the USA's strategic partner. The military government did not negotiate any economic aid package in return for its cooperation with the USA. Musharraf thought it was quite unbecoming at that time to be talking of money. 'I made it a point not to be talking on these issues, but yes, an indication of cooperation and assistance to Pakistan, understanding our internal problems, that was there.'[32]

The economic aid and concessions from the USA and other western countries to Pakistan increased considerably after the collapse of the Taliban regime. These included a $1 billion loan write-off, $600 million in budgetary support and debt rescheduling. Such a rescheduling had taken place many times in the past, but the scale of concession allowed in the post-9/11 period, particularly in December 2001, largely a payback to General Musharraf for his cooperation in the war on terror, was extraordinary. The $12.5 billion debt rescheduling was not only far larger than any in the past, but the terms of the agreement were also much more favourable. Basically the entire bilateral debt of the consortium countries was rescheduled for a far greater period than in the past. The lifting of sanctions and direct economic support from the USA helped ease Pakistan's financial difficulties. For Pakistan, it was almost a return to the 1980s when massive western aid had poured into the country following the Soviet invasion of Afghanistan.

Pakistan was repaid handsomely as a consequence of its role as the frontline state in the US war on terror. The World Bank, the IMF and numerous other donors were back to help out Pakistan. Even USAID, which had pulled out almost a decade ago after the USA enforced nuclear-related sanctions in 1990, returned to Pakistan.[33]. Another consequence of 9/11 was the huge increase in remittances, particularly from Pakistanis living in the USA. All those factors led to a turnaround for the Pakistani economy, which had been in dire straits before General Musharraf's volte-face on Pakistan's policy towards Afghanistan.[34]

While General Musharraf provided the US-led coalition with active support in the war in Afghanistan, the break with the constituency that backed the conservative Taliban had yet to come, exposing a paradox in his policy. He tried to walk the fence; combating al-Qaeda while seeking to avoid direct confrontation with the Taliban remnants and Islamic militants. Pakistan rejected repeated requests by Washington to allow US combat troops to be deployed in the tribal areas, saying their presence would provoke the fiercely independent population. 'We don't want the American forces to operate over here as they are doing in Afghanistan,' said a senior military official.[35] Pakistani military authorities also refused to let US officials make direct contact with local tribal leaders. 'The Americans want to distribute money to the tribal chiefs as they did in Afghanistan,' said the official. 'We don't want them to breach our sovereignty.' The issue remained a constant cause of friction between Islamabad and Washington. US officials would often accuse their ally of not doing enough.

However, the CIA and FBI operated freely in the country. There were also a limited number of US military personnel assisting Pakistani forces involved in the hunt for al-Qaeda fugitives. As the operation proceeded, Pakistani officials said that the number of American personnel involved in the search operations was not more than a dozen and that they were just helping Pakistani troops with communication and intelligence. But the involvement of even a limited number of

American personnel in raids became a politically sensitive issue. As was becoming increasingly clear to Musharraf, the benefits of the US embrace came with a heavy price tag.

3

INSIDE JIHAD

ARMY OF THE PURE

On 12 January 2002, Musharraf made another about-turn when he declared that no Pakistan-based organization would be allowed to indulge in terrorism in the name of religion. In a televised speech lasting well over an hour, he unequivocally condemned all acts of terrorism, including those carried out in the name of freeing Kashmir's Muslim majority from Indian rule.

He banned five Islamic extremists groups including Lashkar-e-Taiba (LeT) and Jaish-e-Mohammed (JeM), the two most powerful jihadist organizations. 'No party in future will be allowed to be identified with words like Jaish, Lashkar or Sipah,' he warned.[1] This declaration was acclaimed as an *ipso facto* renunciation of jihad as a state policy. From a western perspective, Musharraf's landmark speech positioned him as the kind of leader in the Muslim world the West had been desperately seeking.

The speech marked a departure from the policy of supporting pan-Islamism and the process of Islamization. Musharraf strongly asserted that the state should exercise a monopoly over external policy and it should be determined, not by Islamic solidarity, but by the country's national interests. He vowed to suppress Islamic extremist groups challenging the authority of the state and rein in radical madrasas.

For Musharraf, the 12 January declaration was more important than his decision to support the US war on Afghanistan. 'This sets a direction for the country, that was a response to a terrorist attack,' the General told me a week after his decision that brought him into direct conflict with the militant groups once sponsored by his intelligence agencies.[2] But he found it hard to root out a deeply entrenched jihadist culture nurtured by the state for more than two decades.

The first Pakistani jihadist group emerged in 1980 when thousands of volunteers, mainly students from religious seminaries, joined the anti-Soviet resistance in Afghanistan. By 2002, Pakistan had become home to 24 militant groups.[3] Highly disciplined paramilitary organizations operated in every neighbourhood, pursuing their own internal and external agenda. The largest among them were LeT, JeM, Harakat-ul-Mujahideen (HuM) and Harkat-al-Jihad-al-Islami (HJI). All these paramilitary groups, originally from the same source, had similar motivations and goals, and recruited from the same kind of people (often unemployed youth from Punjab and the North West Frontier Province). The only difference was in patronage: HuM and HJI were both strongly linked with the Taliban, whilst LeT had strong links with Wahabi groups in Saudi Arabia.

These militant organizations were not clandestine nor had they sprouted surreptitiously. Their growth, if not actually sponsored, had certainly been looked upon with favour by the state.[4] Their activities were not secret, and found expression in graffiti, wall posters and pamphlets all over the country, inviting Muslims to join forces with them. They also carried addresses and telephone numbers to contact for training. 'Jihad is the shortest route to paradise,' declared one of the many exhortations. 'A martyr ensures salvation for the entire family.' Every jihadist organization had funds to help families of 'martyrs'. Although money was not the primary motivation of jihadists, it was essential to sustain the culture of jihad.[5] The state's patronage helped the jihadists to raise funds at public places. The militant groups had developed a powerful propaganda machinery. Their publications had gained a large readership and their messages were also available on video and audiotapes.

During the 1980s and 1990s, the objective of jihadist movements in Pakistan was not, like that of Arab Salafists such as bin Laden, the establishment of a global Islamic caliphate. Their objectives were more in line with the regional strategy of the Pakistani military establishment: the liberation of Kashmir from India and the installation of a Pashtun Islamist government in Afghanistan. Almost all the Islamic militant groups served as instruments of Pakistan's regional policy. The army needed them as much as they needed the army. After 9/11, Pakistan's support for the American-led war on terror pitted it against its former clients. Although as the following chapter shows, this did not mean that support for them in the state security apparatus was completely withdrawn.

The Wahabi-inspired LeT, the most radical face of jihad in Pakistan, was also more amenable to the ISI than any other militant outfits. After the 2002 ban, it reduced its public visibility. Instead of challenging Musharraf's military led government, it agreed to work within new parameters and restrict its activities to a 'controlled jihad' in Kashmir while keeping a low profile inside Pakistan. However, this tactical truce was a strained one. Islamist groups, even government-friendly ones like LeT, were becoming radicalized by the ideological currents of the region. Increasingly, their ambitions exceeded the goals of the ISI. Even in 2000, the founder of LeT, Hafiz Mohammed Saeed told me that he saw the struggle in Kashmir as 'the gateway to the liberation of Indian Muslims'. He went on: 'We believe in a clash of civilizations and our jihad will continue until Islam becomes the dominant religion.'[6]

A former university professor, Hafiz Saeed is not a charismatic man; he comes across as shy and self-effacing, not the ingredients that militant leaders are generally made of. Short and chubby, his long beard dyed with henna, when I met him in January 2001 he was always surrounded by his young followers. For him, killing infidels and destroying the forces of 'evil and disbelief is the obligation of every pious Muslim'.[7] The horrors of the partition of India in 1947, which uprooted his family from their home in Simla, left a huge imprint on Hafiz Saeed's personality. Millions of people were massacred in the communal violence that followed the creation of the new Muslim state. Thirty-six members of his family were killed while migrating to Pakistan. There his family settled in the central Punjab district of Sargodha.[8]

Farm land allotted by the government, and hard work, brought prosperity to the family. Hafiz Saeed's parents were very religious. His mother taught the Qur'an to her seven sons. Five of them were still alive. Hafiz Saeed received his primary education in the village. After

graduating from the University of Punjab he joined the King Abdul
Aziz Islamic University in Riyadh where he also taught for many years.
During his stay in Saudi Arabia he developed close links with Wahabi
clerics. After returning to Pakistan, Hafiz Saeed took up a teaching
job at the Department of Islamic Studies at the Lahore University of
Engineering and Technology. His two brothers lived in America. One
was head of an Islamic centre and the other pursued an academic
career. Hafiz Saeed himself had never travelled to the USA or any
other western country.[9]

In the early 1980s, Hafiz Saeed joined the mujahidin war in
Afghanistan which also brought him into close contact with Abdullah
Azzam and Osama bin Laden. Their 'dedication to jihad' inspired
him immensely. 'Osama was a man of extraordinary qualities,' he
recalled.[10] Azzam, a Palestinian who had worked as a professor of
Islamic jurisprudence at the University of Jordan in Amman had a huge
influence on Hafiz Saeed. The Palestinian scholar arrived in Pakistan
soon after the invasion of Afghanistan by Soviet forces and took up a
teaching position at the Islamic University of Islamabad. But his stint
was short. He shifted to Peshawar and emerged as the main jihadist
ideologue. With Saudi finance he recruited volunteers for the Afghan
jihad from all over the Arab world. He was assassinated in a bomb
attack in Peshawar in 1989.

Azzam helped Hafiz Saeed establish Markaz Dawal al-Irshad
(MDI), an organization for Islamic preaching and guidance which was
ideologically affiliated with Wahabi Ahle Hadith. In the tradition of
the reformist Sunni movements, the MDI sought to purify society and
Islam of 'outside influences'. Its sprawling headquarters in Muridke on
the outskirts of Lahore housed a university, a farm, a clothing factory
and a carpentry workshop. The objective was to create a model
Islamic environment removed from any state interference.[11] In 1994,
the movement set up a network of schools across the country with the
objectives of promoting the Wahabi version of Islam and preparing the
students for jihad. The MDI observed a strict educational philosophy
that was directed towards developing a jihadist culture and to produce
a reformed individual, who would be well versed not only in Islamic
moral principles, but also in science and technology. The teaching
was aimed at producing an alternative model of governance and •
development.[12] These schools, located in the poorer urban and rural
neighbourhoods, attracted children of families who could not afford a
better education. The organization encouraged its supporters to have

large families, so that more volunteers were available for jihad.

Hafiz Saeed founded LeT in 1990, soon after the withdrawal of Soviet forces from Afghanistan, as a military wing of the MDI to wage jihad against the Indian authorities in Kashmir. The LeT announced its arrival on the Kashmir jihad scene on 5 February 1993 with a ferocious attack on an Indian military force in Poonch district that killed at least two soldiers. Two of the guerrillas were also killed. Since then the outfit has been responsible for hundreds of guerrilla raids in the disputed territory. Within a short span, LeT emerged as the fiercest militant organization – it possessed not only thousands of well trained and highly motivated fighters, but also a huge propaganda network. Its several publications in different languages had a circulation of hundreds of thousands. Its main publication, *Al-Dawat*, had more than 80,000 copies printed and sold at major bookshops across the country.[13]. LeT had worked in close coordination with the ISI, which also provided support to launch the militants across the border.

LeT was an extremely secretive organization. Except for the top leadership, the identity of its members was not disclosed. Since its inception in 1990, it has produced thousands of highly trained fighters, who have given a new dimension to the guerrilla war in Kashmir. The earliest fighters were trained in various camps in Afghanistan. But after 1992 the camps were shifted to remote regions of Azad Kashmir (Free Kashmir) and the mountainous tribal regions of the North West Frontier Province close to the border with Afghanistan.

The procedure was simple. Any jihadist aspirant could enroll himself for training at one of hundreds of LeT centres operating openly across the country. The volunteers, most of them in their teens, were then taken to various camps for military training, conducted in two stages. At the initial level they were given basic weapons training for three weeks. The second stage of rigorous guerrilla training was restricted to those who were fully committed to jihad and were practising Muslims.[14]

At the camp, volunteers began their day with the call to morning prayers. They were then kept busy in gruelling physical and military exercise until dusk. Part of the training, included religious instruction, Qur'anic lessons and adherence to prayers. The trainees learned to transform their lives in line with the teaching of Islam. To be in the ranks of the 'soldiers of Allah', growing a beard was mandatory, shalwar (loose trousers) had to be hiked above the ankle, and watching television and listening to music were banned. Individualism was curbed, beginning with the sharing of food and drinks from the same utensils.[15]

After the initial training, the would-be mujahid was sent back, usually to his home town, and kept under observation by senior LeT officials for a couple of months. His conduct was closely watched as he performed routine organizational duties. He was supposed to collect funds, organize propaganda meetings and practise the preaching of Islam in his home and neighbourhood. Only a select number of volunteers were chosen for the extended programme. They returned home completely transformed after the course. They kept their hair long and stopped cutting their beards. They were identified by new names, mostly the surnames of companions of the Prophet Mohammed or of the earliest Islamic heroes.[16] Between 10,000 and 30,000 young men were trained at LeT camps.

The extended training, however, did not ensure that a volunteer would be sent for combat operations. Thousands of trained guerrillas anxiously awaited their turn to cross into Kashmir, but not everyone was given the chance. 'I pray to Allah that my turn [to go to Kashmir] comes soon, 'said Abu Mohammed, a young college student who had already completed the second level training. Hafiz Saeed often said that he would not put a weapon in the hands of any young recruit who was not secure in his faith. To be a combatant one had to be a pious person.[17]

LeT, unlike some of the other jihadist groups, drew its recruits from universities and colleges as well as from among unemployed youth. The traditional Islamic madrasas provided only ten per cent of the volunteers.[18] Influenced by radical Islamic literature, many university and college students joined the group. 'Those coming from educational institutions are much more motivated and conscious of what they are doing,' said Naveed Qamar, an LeT activist and graduate of the University of Engineering and Technology, Lahore. The top leadership of the group, including Hafiz Saeed, had been on the faculty of that university. A large number of LeT activists also came from the working class or were school drop-outs. In the countryside, LeT recruits were largely from families which were influenced by Wahabi Islam.[19]

The majority of LeT recruits came from Punjab, particularly from Lahore, Gujranwala and Multan where Ahle Hadith had its strongholds. In some central Punjab district villages LeT had considerable influence because of support for the Kashmir jihad. Gondlawala, a small dusty village, is now called Pind Shaheedan (the village of martyrs) because at least one person from every family had fought or died in the Kashmir jihad, mainly as an LeT fighter. The group's increasing influence was indicated by the fact that the villagers would accept its arbitration in local and even in domestic disputes.[20] In recent years, LeT had started attracting an increasing number of volunteers from Pakistan's southern provinces of Sindh and Balochistan where Wahabi influence had increased. Muslims from other countries, including Britain, had also joined LeT. Shamshur Rehman, an Afghan, was the chief commander of LeT when he was killed in Badgam district in Kashmir in May 1995 in an encounter with Indian security forces.[21] Several foreign militants were believed to have received training at LeT camps in Pakistan. Among them were Guantanamo Bay inmates David Hicks and French terrorist suspect Willie Brigitte, who were accused of planning attacks in Australia.[22]

LeT gave a new and more violent dimension to the Kashmiri struggle by launching *Fidayin* raids against Indian forces and military installations. The term 'Fidayin attack' was used by the LeT leadership for target operations well inside the Indian military bases.[23] 'A Fidayin is one who must complete his mission even in the worst circumstances,' explained Abdullah Muntazir, an LeT spokesman. He insisted that the concept of Fidayin was different from that of a suicide bomber, who blew himself up to kill others. 'We consider suicide attacks un-Islamic. Many Fidayin come back alive after completion of their missions,' said Muntazir. The Fidayin attacks had brought an unprecedented ferocity to the Kashmir jihad.

A Fidayin is chosen from among the best and most courageous fighters and not every guerrilla meets the tough criteria. An other-worldly level of devotion to the cause is required, as I discovered when I met a Fidayin recently returned from his mission. His thin frame, gentle eyes and polite manners gave not the slightest indication of his being a guerrilla fighter. The young bearded militant, who used the *nom de guerre* of Abu Ukrema, had just returned from Kashmir when I met him at the LeT headquarters in Lahore in January 2001. Abu Ukrema walked with a limp because of a bullet wound, received during an encounter with the Indian troops. 'I will return to the fighting as soon as the bullet is removed and the wounds are healed,' he told me. 'It is my desire to become a martyr.' His face lit up as he narrated how he and his fellow guerrillas had destroyed an Indian army post after a fierce gun battle which lasted several hours and left many soldiers dead.

Martyrdom is not mourned as it is considered to be the sole

guarantee of entry to paradise. LeT local officials visit the house of the martyr to offer congratulations to the family. Sweets are distributed to celebrate the death. The occasion is also used to solicit new recruits. Emotional speeches are delivered and then the martyr's testament, which often exhorts their kin to strictly observe the Islamic tenets and be prepared to give their lives in the way of Allah, is read in public. The men are implored neither to listen to music nor to watch films. They are asked to destroy their television sets because they 'spread the Hindu culture of singing and dancing'.[24] LeT's sectarian tilt and ultra-orthodox ideology distinguish it from other Pakistani radical Islamists. Some other militant groups even accuse it of undermining the Kashmiri jihad by promoting sectarian division.[25]

LeT's main stress was on jihad against Hindus, who it regarded as the worst polytheists, and against Jews who it claimed were 'singled out by the Qur'an as the enemies of Islam'. LeT leaders maintained that Hindus and Jews were their main targets because they were 'the enemies of Islam and Pakistan'.[26] A party document, 'Why are we waging jihad', argued that jihad was the only way to avenge history and re-establish the lost glory of Islam. It vowed to take back Spain, where Muslims had ruled for 800 years, and to re-establish Muslim rule in India. It said that LeT was fighting to liberate not just Kashmir, but the whole of India. It was one of the reasons why LeT's attacks against Hindus had been so savage. In many cases the victims were beheaded. In December 2000 LeT extended its jihad from Kashmir to mainland India.

It was just before dark on 3 December 2000 when two of LeT's gunmen sneaked inside Delhi's Red Fort, which housed an Indian military unit and a high-security interrogation cell used both by the Central Bureau of Interrogation and the army.[27] The fort, built by Mughal Emperor Shahjahan in the seventeenth century, sits on the edge of the Indian capital's old town and has a huge symbolic value for India. Traditionally, the Prime Minister hoisted the national flag here on Independence Day, and part of this historic landmark was opened to tourists in the daytime. A fierce firefight broke out after armed intruders stormed the security barracks, killing three guards. LeT claimed responsibility the next day, declaring that the guerrillas who were involved in the deadly attack were safe at an undisclosed location.

The audacious raid on the Red Fort was the first operation against an Indian military installation inside India by an Islamic militant group involved in the Kashmiri struggle. 'The action indicates that we have extended the jihad to India,' Hafiz Saeed declared when I met him a month after the incident. The attack on the Red Fort signalled a new and more aggressive phase in jihadist activities.

It was incidents such as this which brought LeT to the US State Department's attention and, in 2002, it was placed on the USA's list of terrorist organizations. Musharraf, having declared his support for the war on terror, had little choice but to ban it. But the ban had little affect on LeT's power. Before it was even announced, the LeT leadership had shifted their base to Indian-controlled Kashmir. This relieved some of the political pressure from Musharraf as it made it more difficult to claim that the Pakistani government was behind the Fidayin attacks. While an entirely new Kashmiri leadership was appointed to run the military wing, in Pakistan the outfit started working under the banner of its political wing, Jamaat-ud Da'awa, with Hafiz Saeed as its head. The new organization ostensibly restricted its role to preaching, education and social welfare. But in reality it never ceased working in support of the Kashmiri jihad.[28]

LeT leaders admit that the proscription slowed down their operation in Kashmir, but it certainly didn't stop it; a large number of its militants were still based in its camps in Muzaffarabad in Pakistani-controlled Kashmir. After initial restraint, LeT was back recruiting volunteers and its donation boxes had reemerged at public places and mosques. In a speech on March 2004, Hafiz Saeed had declared that more than 7,000 new volunteers had received military training at LeT camps in the previous six months. The first congregation of Jamaat-ud Da'awa held in November 2002, after the government's action against LeT, attracted more than 100,000 people.

It was apparent that Jamaat-ud Da'awa was just a cover to avoid international scrutiny. Neither its militant infrastructure nor its propaganda machinery had stopped functioning. The group continued to publish several magazines and run a website. Interestingly, no LeT activist was arrested in the government's crackdown on Islamic extremists. After being detained for a few months, Hafiz Saeed was freed by a High Court order in December 2002 and then moved freely around the country, mobilizing Muslims for jihad. 'For us jihad is sacred like praying and fasting that cannot be forsaken under any condition,' he declared at the end of his detention. 'Ours is not such a cowardly party as to bow down before the US pressure for halting support to jihad.[29] The Pakistan government placed Jamaat-ud Da'awa on the 'terror watch list' in 2003, but the action did not affect its activities, which included running a huge network of hospitals and schools.

While continuing the struggle in Kashmir, LeT had its own reason not to take on the government. 'Our main objective is to wage jihad against non-Muslims,'explained Yahya Mujahid, a spokesman for the group.[30] Indeed, unlike other militant groups such as JeM and HuM, LeT has never used its military skills within Pakistan nor did it involve itself with any sectarian or ethnic organizations. The case of LeT was indicative of Islamabad's continuing flexibility towards those organizations which had restricted their activities to Kashmir and did not indulge in terrorism at home. Pakistani authorities defended their stance saying that LeT did not present any threat to the country's internal security, so there was no need to crackdown on it. According to them the organization strictly controlled its cadres and none of its members had ever indulged in any act of terrorism inside the country.

Contrary to this claim, there is strong evidence of LeT activists providing shelter to al-Qaeda fighters fleeing from Afghanistan. Abu Zubaydah, a close associate of bin Laden, was captured in 2002 in a house in the Pakistani central city of Faisalabad rented by a LeT member. But its leaders deny any association with the terrorist network. They maintained there was a fundamental difference between them and bin Laden's views on 'jihad'. 'We do not agree with his call to overthrow the rulers of Muslim countries. Islam does not allow waging jihad against Muslims,' said Yahya Mujahid.

As well as the desire to avoid unnecessary confrontations, Islamabad's attitude towards LeT also reflected the desire to keep militancy alive until India agreed to a resolution of the Kashmir dispute. Despite an improvement in relations between India and Pakistan as a result of the peace process launched in January 2004, there has not been any substantive move on the thorny issue of Kashmir. Islamabad believed that a complete cessation of militancy in Kashmir would remove pressure on India to make any concessions.

Though its main concentration has been in Kashmir, LeT has expanded its network to several other countries. Its members were active in India, Burma, Chechnya, and Bosnia and according to some reports have also been fighting against the American forces in Iraq. In April 2004, coalition forces reportedly arrested a Pakistani Islamic fighter who was identified as Danish Ahmed. A former LeT commander in Kashmir, he was captured by British forces in Basra and later handed over to the American intelligence authorities. Ahmed is believed to be among hundreds of Pakistani volunteers involved in the Iraq war. Most of them came from religious schools run by MDI. Virulently anti-American, the party has declared that it was mandatory for Muslims to join the mujahidin fighting against the American forces in Iraq. 'Islam is in grave danger and the Iraqi mujahidin are fighting for the return of its glory. They are fighting the forces of evil in an extremely difficult situation,' Hafiz Saeed declared in his sermon at a Lahore mosque in June 2004.[51]

Though LeT refrained from indulging in terrorist activities inside Pakistan, its leaders became increasingly critical of Musharraf's pro-American policies and move to reform the madrasas. 'Most of our leaders are lapdogs of Americans,' declared *Majjalutul Dawa*, a publication of Jamaat-ud Da'awa.

Despite being seen as a 'tame', controllable force, LeT is more powerful than ever, and looks set for confrontation with the government on issues which go beyond Kashmir. Simply by carrying out its recruiting, fundraising and military activities, it contributes to the radicalization of Pakistani society. Nonetheless, for as long as the Kashmiri issue remains unresolved, the government seems prepared to embrace it.

Unlike Kashmir, Afghanistan is an area where the government's objectives and those of their erstwhile jihadist allies became very different after 9/11. However, precisely because of the extent of cooperation between the Taliban, the ISI and Pakistani jihadist groups in the 1980s, Musharraf has found it very difficult to get the state security services to effectively implement his policy about-turn. Taliban-sympathising jihadist groups, such as HuM and JeM, are now increasingly powerful on the ground in the treacherous border regions between Afghanistan and Pakistan.

The extent of Taliban/ISI/jihadist cooperation was revealed during the Indian hostage crisis of 1999, the resolution of which I witnessed first hand. I sat at Kandahar airport with a group of reporters, photographers and TV crews just 500 metres from an Indian Airlines Airbus, the only functional aircraft there. Black-turbaned Taliban soldiers guarded the plane with more than 155 passengers on board as negotiations between the hijackers and UN officials dragged on. Conditions inside the plane were stifling. The body of a passenger killed by the hijackers lay in a pool of blood.

Armed with grenades, pistols and knives, five men had seized flight IC 814 about 40 minutes after it took off from Kathmandu, Nepal on a scheduled flight to New Delhi on 24 December 1999. The plane had made stops in India, Pakistan and the United Arab Emirates before landing in Afghanistan. The hijackers, who called themselves Kashmiri freedom fighters, had demanded the release of three top Islamic militant leaders from Indian prisons. Some of the hooded hijackers would climb down occasionally to receive supplies or talk to officials. The Taliban officials were visibly warm towards them.

Interestingly, the Taliban leaders, who in the past had scorned foreign journalists and deemed photography as un-Islamic, were overly amiable, providing them with facilities. There were no restrictions on TV cameras and photography. The conservative Islamic administration appeared extremely keen to have international publicity for the event. Scores of media persons from the world over had descended on the spiritual headquarters of the regime as the hijacking drama unfolded.

The eve of the new century brought an end to the hostages' eight-day ordeal when the Indian Foreign Minister, Jaswant Singh, arrived with the three men whose freedom was demanded by the hijackers. Among them was a short, stocky man with an unkempt black beard. A former leader of HuM, Masood Azhar was captured by the Indian authorities in 1994 and held in prison on terrorism charges. Along with him was a tall heavily built young man. A Pakistani-born British national, Ahmed Omar Saeed Sheikh had been detained in Delhi's high security Tihar prison for many years on charges of kidnapping three foreign tourists.

The hijackers stepped down triumphantly from flight IC 814, their faces still covered, as Indian officials handed over the freed militants to the Taliban authorities. Mullah Wakil Ahmed Muttawakil, the suave Foreign Minister of the Taliban regime, won international praise for his 'deft handling' of the hijacking episode. But the real-life drama was taking place at the far end of the tarmac. The freed militants were warmly greeted by Mullah Akhtar Usmani, the chief of Taliban forces in Kandahar, and dozens of other senior officials of the fundamentalist regime. They were joined by two of the hijackers, one wearing a western suit and the other in safari dress. 'Are you satisfied now?' a smiling Mullah Usmani asked the two men. 'Indeed,' replied one of them excitedly. They were whisked away in a window-blackened vehicle to an unknown destination. The three other hijackers also vanished from the scene.[32]

'Everything had gone amazingly smoothly due to the Taliban's excellent political acumen and superb handling of the situation,' Azhar later recalled. It was the first time that a Pakistani-based militant group had successfully used hijacking as an instrument of terror. The well-planned action was carried out by HuM: a group similar to LeT, but which drew its recruits from less well-educated, unemployed youth, often from the North-West Frontier Province. HuM was formed by former members of Harkat-ul-Ansar (HuA) after it was put on the State Department terrorist organizations list in 1994.

The group could not have succeeded without backing from the Taliban government and its Pakistani patrons. In fact, Afghan sources, including Muttawakil, who had surrendred himself to US forces after the fall of the Taliban regime, revealed that the hijackers were taking instructions from Pakistani intelligence officials present at the airport.[33] The hijacking was followed by an extension of militant operations well inside India. Ironically, all its jihadist 'assets' who had figured in the incident returned to haunt Pakistan with the turn of events a few years later.

It was late in the evening on 7 January 2000 when Azhar resurfaced at Al-Rasheedia mosque in Karachi's central district. Surrounded by some two dozen men dressed in camouflage-style uniforms and brandishing automatic rifles, he triumphantly declared that his freedom was a defeat for India. 'I have come here because it is my duty to tell you that Muslims should not rest in peace until we have destroyed America and India,' thundered the militant leader, his head wrapped in a chequered scarf. Some 10,000 people who had gathered there after evening prayers greeted him with chants of 'Allah o Akbar' (God is the greatest) and 'Death to India'. 'I will not rest in peace until I wrest Kashmir from India.'[34] There was no effort from the government to detain Azhar or even to stop him from making an inflammatory speech. It was quite apparent that he enjoyed state protection.

Born in 1968 in the southern Punjab district of Bahawalpur, Azhar was the third of 12 children of a schoolteacher. He grew up in an intensely religious atmosphere and most of his family members had been associated with radical Islam.[35] Azhar received his Islamic religious education at one of Pakistan's largest and most influential Islamic seminaries, Jamia Ulumia Islamia, also known as Jamia Binoria, in Karachi, before joining the institution as a teacher. Run by a trust established by Islamic scholar Yousuf Binori in the 1950s, the school had been transformed into a centre for jihad in the 1980s during the anti-Soviet war in Afghanistan.

The seminary was the bastion in Pakistan of the fundamentalist Deobandi movement, which developed in the nineteenth century. A branch of Sunni Hanafi Islam, the creed is named after a great religious seminary established in 1867 in the Indian village of Deoband near Delhi. The founders of the seminary drew their spiritual guidance from Shah Wali Ullah, an eighteenth-century Islamic scholar who endeavoured to bind together different Islamic schools of thought. The movement, which was purely a South Asian phenomenon, sought to revive puritan Islam, but became radicalized with the call for jihad against the Soviet occupation of Muslim Afghanistan.

The first squad of Pakistani jihadists came from this institution in 1980,[36] and in the next two decades thousands of its students participated in 'holy wars' in Afghanistan and Kashmir. Many of the Taliban leaders were graduates of this institution. They would often consult Mufti Nizamuddin Shamzai, a widely respected cleric and dean of the school, on matters relating to Islamic sharia.

Azhar's journey into jihad started during his stay in Jamia Binoria. In the mid 1980s he went to Afghanistan to fight along with the mujahidin in the eastern Khost province. There was no going back for him from there. It was in Afghanistan that he decided to dedicate his life to the cause of jihad. He joined HuM, one of the most powerful jihadist groups involved in the Afghan war. Because of his weak physical condition he was assigned propaganda and organizational work. With his fiery speeches he soon made his mark on the movement. Audio cassettes of his speeches were used to motivate Muslims to join the jihadist cause. He was also a powerful writer and in the 1980s edited a magazine called *Sadai Mujahid* ('Voice of Mujahid'). He soon rose up the group's leadership ladder.

One of his tasks was to mobilize support in other countries and, during the 1990s, he made trips to several European and African countries. Some reports suggest he followed Osama bin Laden to Sudan in 1992 and fought in Somalia along with Arab fighters, most of them former Afghan war veterans, for the local warlord, Aided. He was also said to have been involved in the training of militants in Yemen before he was sent to organize the party's jihadist network in Indian-controlled Kashmir.[37] Captured by Indian forces in February 1994 for travelling on a forged Portuguese passport, he was tried on terrorism charges. He was acquitted in that case, but remained in jail for more than six years. He made an attempt to escape by digging a tunnel, but was caught and put in a high security prison in Srinagar. During his six-year detention in Indian jails, Azhar, still in his mid thirties, wrote numerous articles on jihad, often referring in his writings to Africa.

It was in July 1994 that Ahmed Omar Saeed Sheikh, then a student at the London School of Economics, was sent to Delhi by the HuM leadership with a mandate to kidnap a group of western tourists and demand as ransom the release of Azhar and some other militant leaders. Sheikh succeeded in kidnapping one American and three British nationals from a hotel in New Delhi, but the hostages were rescued by the police from a house in Sharanpur town in Uttar Pradesh. Sheikh was captured after a shoot-out in which one policeman was killed. It took another five years and the hijacking of an Indian Airlines jet to earn his and his mentor's freedom. The two probably met face to face for the first time in the plane which took them to Kandahar.

The son of a wealthy Pakistani businessman who had migrated to Britain for a better economic future, Sheikh fitted the profile of a classic politically aware Islamic militant. His passage to militancy started in 1992 when he watched a series of documentary films about the oppression of Muslims following the break up of the former Yugoslavia. In the wars in the Balkans in the 1990s, thousands of Muslims were brutally murdered in scenes of violence not seen in Europe since the Second World War.[38]

A story gained prominence regarding Sheikh's path to extremism: moved by the plight of Muslims, it said that Sheikh travelled to Bosnia with an organization known as 'Convoy of Mercy'. The purpose of the visit was to provide humanitarian help to the victims of ethnic cleansing. But the people he had met and the things he saw during the trip radicalized him.[39] After his return, he dropped out of the LSE and headed to a training camp in Afghanistan where he established links with HuM. Equally important in terms of what happened next, he was recruited by the ISI in London before leaving for India.

On returning home, Azhar broke away from HuM and decided to form his own group. On 30 January 2000, flanked by his teacher and mentor, Mufti Nizamuddin Shamzai, and some other senior clerics of the Jamia Binoria, Azhar announced the formation of a new militant outfit, Jaish-e-Mohammed (JeM). The decision shocked Pakistani jihadist circles. Backing for the new party by Shamzai and other Deobandi clerics, who were considered to be very close to Pakistan's military establishment, raised many questions. Jamia Binoria had played a key role in promoting a state-sponsored jihadist culture and their support for the new militant outfit led to speculation that it was done at the behest of the ISI.

The new guerrilla group was more ambitious than any seen before, and heralded its emergence on the jihadist scene by launching a number of spectacular attacks against the Indian forces in Kashmir in mid 2000. Most of its cadres came from rural areas, small towns and from the madrasas. JeM also recruited among emigrant Kashmiris and Punjabis in Britain. One of them, Mohammed Bilal, a young man from Birmingham, drove a car full of explosives into an Indian army base in Srinagar on 25 December 2000. Pakistani and Kashmiri expatriates in Britain and other countries were the source of funding for the group.[40]

In addition to guerrilla activities in Kashmir, JeM continued to have close ties to the Taliban regime in Afghanistan. Several of Azhar's close family members were in government jobs in Kabul. Hundreds of JeM activists received training in camps in Afghanistan, bringing them into contact with al-Qaeda. The group's newspaper, *Zerb-i-Momin*, became a mouthpiece of the Taliban regime and was widely read among the officials.

The weekly newspaper, published from Karachi in both Urdu and English, sold about a quarter of a million copies across Pakistan. It represented a new breed of jihadist journalism which saw huge growth during the 1990s. With the rise to power of the Taliban in Afghanistan, these publications received a massive boost and became very vocal and proactive in favour of what could be described as 'Talibanization of mind and soul' in Pakistan. More than two dozen publications representing various militant outfits had a combined circulation of around one million. They propagated a militant Islamic and anti-western world-view. *Zerb-i-Momin* did not publish pictures of human faces in line with the Taliban's fundamentalist interpretation of Islam. Instead, it printed images of Islam's holy places or of weapons. It regularly published news about al-Qaeda and Taliban activities. *Zerb-i-Momin* continued its publication even after the proscription of JeM. The group also published an Urdu-language daily newspaper from four cities; *Islam* had a nationwide circulation of more than 100,000.

JeM had expanded its activities in Afghanistan through the Al-Rasheedia Trust founded by Maulana Abdul Rasheed, a leading Pakistani cleric associated with Jamia Binoria. The Trust, which had funded JeM's jihadist activities, established a network of mosques and madrasas in Afghanistan. The American administration in 2002 placed the Trust on the list of organizations supporting and financing terrorism. Pakistan had also frozen its funds and put a ban on it, but this action was later suspended on the orders of the High Court.

After 9/11, JeM signalled their anger at Pakistan's break with the Taliban by raiding the Kashmir state assembly building in Srinagar in October 2001, killing 35 people and later launched a suicide attack on an Indian military base in Srinagar. The attack brought the Pakistani military regime under tremendous international pressure to act against the militant organizations. The incident, which occurred a few weeks after 9/11, forced Musharraf to denounce the raid as a 'terrorist action'.

A few weeks later, JeM struck again, this time extending its operations inside India. It was just before noon on 13 December 2001 when a group of gunmen wearing military-style fatigues broke through tight security and burst into the area in front of the Indian Parliament building. One of the men was wearing explosives strapped to his body and blew himself up soon after breaking in. There were about a hundred members of Parliament inside the House as an intense gun battle between the attackers and security guards raged on for thirty minutes.[41] The Indian Prime Minister, Atal Bihari Vajpayee, was being driven towards Parliament at the time of the assault. He immediately turned back. The gun battle left five attackers and seven guards dead and 15 others injured. A JeM spokesman immediately claimed responsibility, but its leaders later backtracked, apparently under government pressure from Pakistan. Pakistan placed Azhar under protective custody but refused to hand him over to India, saying there was no evidence of his involvement in the Parliament attack. On 12 January, Musharraf banned JeM after the US Department of State placed them on its list of terrorist groups. But the action did not affect their activities. Even before the ban, JeM had started operating under a new banner, Jamaat-e-Furqa. Azhar was released by a court order a few months after his detention. But the group retaliated against the ban by launching a series of terrorist attacks across Pakistan targeting western nationals, Christians and Shia Muslims. Many of its activists subsequently became foot soldiers for al-Qaeda operations in Pakistan. The Pakistan government had chosen to ignore Azhar's involvement in all this: he was detained only for a few months under the Maintenance of Public Order. Since then he has maintained a low profile.

JeM activists returning from Afghanistan after the fall of the Taliban regime were responsible for a suicide attack on a Christian church in Islamabad's high-security diplomatic enclave which killed several people, including two Americans, in March 2002. The group was also responsible for attacks on Shia mosques in different parts of Pakistan. These kinds of sectarian attacks inside Pakistan marked it out as differing in strategy from other hardline Sunni groups such as Sipah-e-Sahaba Pakistan (SSP) and Lashkar-e-Jhangvi (LeJ), though in reality their memberships often overlapped. JeM was also involved in a December 2003 plot to assassinate Musharraf. The plan was apparently conceived by Ahmed Omar Saeed Sheikh and Amjad Hussain Farooqi, the two main characters who figured in the December 1999 hijacking of an Indian Airlines plane.

Sheikh apparently never went back to Britain after his release in Kandahar and instead joined his mentor, Azhar. Sheikh had established links with al-Qaeda soon after his release, and Pakistani intelligence agencies believe he had travelled to Afghanistan several times since then. The 28-year-old Londoner was believed to have met with bin Laden during his last trip to Afghanistan at the time of the US invasion. Just after the Taliban were ousted, he returned to Pakistan, having shaved his beard to escape capture.[42] He was furious with his former patrons for helping the American forces in the invasion of a Muslim country. Only a few weeks later, he was arrested for his role in the kidnapping and murder of *Wall Street Journal* reporter Daniel Pearl.[43]

Farooqi was a close associate of Sheikh's and the main coordinator of the group that met in Islamabad in 2001 to plot Musharraf's murder. The militants made several plans, but the two most serious ones, which were carried out within a span of two weeks in December 2003, had nearly succeeded. The plot revealed the nature of the terrorist coalition that had emerged in Pakistan after 9/11. Farooqi represented just one more link in this new alliance, confirming the worst fears about al-Qaeda's successful merger with Islamic extremists in Pakistan, one that made them difficult to identify and segregate.

In his mid thirties, Farooqi had fought against Soviet forces in Afghanistan and during Taliban rule he ran a guerrilla training camp in Afghanistan for Pakistani militants. A former activist of HuM, he had joined Azhar and served as his bodyguard, developing close ties with al-Qaeda through Khalid Sheikh Mohammed, bin Laden's chief of operations. Farooqi was the key suspect in almost every terrorist attack in Pakistan after 9/11. One of the country's most wanted terrorists, he had a half-million-dollar price on his head. He was killed in a firefight with security forces in southern Pakistan in September 2004.[44]

One of the suicide bombers involved in the Christmas Day attack on

Musharraf was a young Islamic militant who had recently been freed from an Afghan prison. Twenty-three-year-old Muhammad Jamil had fought in Kashmir before moving to Afghanistan where he received guerrilla training at an al-Qaeda camp in Rishkor, south-east of Kabul. The sprawling compound, which now houses the Afghan army, had previously served as the main training centre for militants from Pakistan and other countries. The volunteers were given standard 40-day or three-month guerrilla training here. Jamil was captured fighting for the Taliban regime by the opposition Northern Alliance forces in 2000. After spending some three years in an Afghan jail, he was finally released by President Hamid Karzai in April 2003. Pakistani intelligence agencies, with their long association with militant groups, cleared the young man of any anti-state activities and allowed him to rejoin the militant camp in his home town of Kotli in Pakistan's semi-autonomous state of Azad Kashmir.[45]

Jamil's links with the ISI were revealed during his detention at Baharak jail in Afghanistan's Panjshir valley, where he told his captors that he was a Pakistani army officer. He repeated the claim when paraded before foreign journalists. Pakistani authorities rejected the statement saying it was extracted under duress. But there is no denying his contacts with the Pakistani spy agency, which had facilitated the recruitment of thousands of youths to fight in aid of the Taliban regime. Intriguingly, the Kotli camp, run by JeM, had continued to function under ISI supervision despite Musharraf's orders to close down all such facilities. (When Musharraf learned that it was still functioning, he sacked Major-General Khalid Mahmoud, then the director of the ISI's Kashmir cell.)

JeM had developed a substantial following among the soldiers and lower-ranking military officials. Those radical contacts were extremely useful in the December attacks on Musharraf. Some two dozen air force personnel were part of a clandestine JeM cell, which was involved in the 14 December attempt to blow up the presidential convoy. Members of the cell lived in a residential colony near the Chaklala air base right in the heart of the Rawalpindi garrison, and met regularly with jihadist leaders without being spotted by intelligence agencies. One was Mushtaq Ahmad, who was instructed to plant the explosives under the bridge over which Musharraf's cavalcade passed on 14 December. A high-tech jamming device fixed in the President's car delayed the detonation by a few crucial seconds that allowed the cavalcade to cross before the explosion. It was not clear whether it was inefficiency or a deliberate oversight on the part of the intelligence agencies that they did not notice such a large quantity of explosives tied to the bridge along the high-security presidential route. Ironically, it was Indian intelligence that had warned Musharraf of the first attempt to kill him by blowing up the bridge. Mushtaq was handed a death sentence in a secret trial in November 2004, but mysteriously escaped from the detention centre inside the top-security Chaklala air base.

Some other Islamic militant groups that had earlier been aligned with the ISI also turned to jihad after being proscribed by the government. These included HuM and HJI, both of which had a long history of involvement in Afghanistan and were closely associated with al-Qaeda. They felt betrayed by Musharraf's U-turn.

I met Khalil in January 2000, a few months after the USA had put HuM on the State Department's list of terrorist groups for its involvement in the Indian Airlines hijacking. Sitting cross-legged in a stuffy room with peeling walls, HuM warrior Fazalur Rehman Khalil epitomized this sense of disappointment as he nostalgically remembered the days when the mujahidin were armed and trained by the CIA and the ISI to fight against Soviet forces in Afghanistan. 'We received all kinds of support. We defeated the Russian forces with Stinger missiles supplied by the United States,' the veteran warrior recalled.

A small ramshackle building in a crowded neighbourhood in Rawalpindi served as HuM's headquarters. Toting automatic rifles, a number of young bearded militants kept a close vigil on visitors. Inside, the walls were adorned with large propaganda posters carrying pictures of Islam's holy places, the Qur'an and Kalashnikovs. Sporting a white skull cap and a long beard, Khalil wondered why his group was pronounced terrorist. 'We have asked the Americans a number of times to tell us our crimes before announcing the punishment. There is no evidence against us.' He accused the Americans of pursuing a policy of intimidation. 'We don't understand the definition of terrorism. Those who are fighting with small rifles are terrorists and those who are dropping bombs are not.'

Khalil spoke fondly about his association with bin Laden. 'He is a brother Muslim. I have known him since the days of the Afghan jihad when he was considered a friend, a mujahid and a hero by the Americans,' he smiled. 'Now the Americans have changed their glasses and call him a terrorist.'

Like hundreds and thousands of his peers, Khalil had fought against the Soviet forces in Afghanistan until he saw what he called the myth of Soviet power shatter before his eyes. Though the days of the Afghan struggle were over in 1989 for Khalil and hundreds like him, the jihad was not. The holy warriors, hardened on the battlefields of Afghanistan, found another cause to fight for – the cause of Kashmir's liberation from India. Following the collapse of the Soviet Union in 1990, which was seen by the Islamists as the 'triumph of jihad', hundreds of militants fanned out in 1990 to new destinations.

Khalil was a student at a madrasa, Jamia Naumania, in Pakistan's North West Frontier Province when, at the age of 16, he was induced into jihad. After the Soviet invasion of Afghanistan, the madrasa he attended had become the centre of jihadist activities by a fatwa calling Muslims to join the war against communism. Without telling his parents, Khalil left home in Dera Ismail Khan in 1981 to join the mujahidin in Afghanistan.[46] For three years he had no contact with his family. He fought alongside an Afghan mujahidin group led by Younus Khalis and Commander Jalaluddin Haqani in the eastern Afghan provinces of Khost and Paktika.[47] It was also the period when he first came into contact with bin Laden. Their relationship proved to be long lasting.

In 1984 Khalil, along with another militant leader Saifullah Akhtar, founded Harkat-al-Jihad-al-Islami (HJI), the first Pakistani-based jihadist outfit. But just a few years later he broke away to form his own group, Harkat-ul-Ansar (HuA). By 1990, HuA had emerged as one of the most feared militant groups fighting in Kashmir. A large number of its cadres came from the Deobandi madrasa network in the North West Frontier Province. Espousing pan-Islamic ideology, the group believed in violent means to liberate Kashmir from India and make it a part of Pakistan.

About sixty per cent of HuA's initial 1,000 members came from northern Pakistan and Afghanistan. In later years, the ethnic composition of the organization changed with new recruits coming from Pakistani-controlled Azad Kashmir as well as Punjab and Karachi, many of them school drop-outs and jobless youths looking for some meaning in their lives. Many of them were inducted by roaming jihadist recruiting cells who, after delivering sermons in local mosques, invited the worshippers to join the jihad. Although HuA and later HuM, which it merged with, believed in Taliban-style fundamentalist Islam, it did not require its cadres to go through the same kind of religious training as conducted by LeT.

In its April 1995 report to Congress, 'Patterns of Global Terrorism', the US State Department associated HuA with terrorist activities for the first time. The report said that HuA had several thousand armed members, trained in the use of light and heavy machine guns, assault rifles, mortars, explosives and rockets. The same report also accused the group of having links with the hitherto little-known 'Al-Faran' organization which had captured western tourists in Kashmir in July 1995. One of the hostages was beheaded, another managed to escape, and the fate of the rest remains unknown. Kashmiri militants privately acknowledge that the hostages are no longer alive.

On 1 October 1997, the US Secretary of State, Madeleine Albright, submitted to the US Congress a list of 30 international terrorist organizations, which Washington had decided to bring under the purview of the Anti-Terrorism and Effective Death Penalty Act, 1997. HuA was one of the groups on the list. After being blacklisted by the US administration it resurfaced under a new banner, HuM. The new group was immediately put on the terrorist watch list by Washington. The State Department report for 1997, released in 1998, accused Pakistani officials of supporting Kashmiri militant groups, including HuM.

The rise of the Taliban gave a huge boost to Pakistani militant groups like HuM. Afghanistan became a base for their operations. Their leaders shared common origins, personnel and especially patrons. Most HuM activists came from the same seminaries in the Pakistani border region that the Taliban movement had emerged from. These groups were heavily backed by the ISI, which also patronized the Taliban. Both were important in furthering Pakistan's strategic interests – to extend Pakistani hegemony over the neighbouring state.

More than 10,000 Pakistani militants were believed to have received training in camps run by al-Qaeda and other jihadist groups during Taliban rule.[48] The evidence of their close connection with bin Laden emerged in August 1998 when scores of Pakistani militants were killed in a US cruise missile attack on an al-Qaeda camp in the Afghan southeastern border town of Khost. A day after the attack, Khalil vowed to take revenge for the death of his activists. 'The US has struck us with Tomahawk cruise missiles at only two places, but we will hit back at them everywhere in the world, wherever we find them. We have started a holy war against the US and they will find no place to hide,' he declared.

Khalil was at the meeting in Afghanistan in February 1998 at which bin Laden announced the formation of an International Islamic Front against 'Jews and crusaders'. He was also a signatory of the ruling issued by the group which had stated that it was the duty of all Muslims to 'comply with God's order by killing Americans and their allies'.[49]

On 29 September 2001, Pakistan's government banned HuM, but its activists soon regrouped under new banners, Jamaat-al-Ansar and Harkat-ul-Mujahideen-al-Alami. They retained their links with the Taliban despite the shift in Pakistan's policy.

Khalil led hundreds of his fighters into war against the US forces. He returned home in January 2002, after the fall of the Taliban regime, and continued his jihadist activities despite the ban on his organization. HuM continued supporting the Taliban and al-Qaeda remnants operating from their bases on the Pakistan-Afghan border. Khalil was detained by Pakistani police in August 2002, only to be let out a few months later. He was arrested again in 2004 after HuM activists were found to be involved in a failed attempt to assassinate Musharraf. Pakistani security forces suspected that HuM activists operating in small cells were responsible for many terrorist attacks in the country after 9/11.

HJI, led by Saifullah Akhtar, was another jihadist organization which had a vast network within the country and outside. The group constituted a significant part of the Taliban forces in Afghanistan and its fighters were known as Punjabi Taliban (because most of its fighters came from Punjab). HJI described itself as the second defence line of every Muslim country and claimed to have links with radical Islamic movements in around 24 countries including Chechnya, Britain and a number of Central Asian states.

Like most other Pakistani jihadist leaders, Akhtar was the product of an Islamic seminary. A Pashtun from the Waziristan tribal region, he received his elementary education at Darul Uloom, Wana before moving to Jamia Binoria in Karachi for higher Islamic education. He taught there briefly before joining the Afghan mujahidin in 1980. Akhtar spent a large part of his jihadist life in Afghanistan, first fighting the Soviet forces, then as a key commander of the Taliban forces. His headquarters in Kabul, known as Darul Irshad, became the main centre for Pakistani militants. More than 50 of his men were killed when American jets bombed it in November 2001.

The group's connection with Islamist elements in Pakistan's army was revealed in 1995, when Akhtar was implicated in a right-wing coup plot. It was late evening on 8 September 1995, when Pakistani customs guards stopped an army vehicle outside Kohat town in the North West Frontier Province for a routine check. The search found a huge cache of arms stored in the back cabin. Smuggled from the Dara Adam Khel tribal area, the weapons were ostensibly being supplied to Islamic militants fighting in Kashmir. The case was immediately reported to the army authorities.[50]

The attempt initially looked like a maverick operation by some zealots in the army to support Kashmiri freedom fighters, but subsequent investigations led to startling revelations. The weapons were actually meant for a group of rebel army officers plotting an 'Islamic revolution' in the country with the help of some other Islamic militant groups.

At the centre of the coup plot were Major-General Zaheerul Islam Abbasi and Brigadier Mustansar Billah and a group of middle-ranking army officers. The rebels, who had close ties with some Islamic militant groups and hardline Muslim clerics, had conspired to eliminate the top military and civilian leadership and establish an 'Islamic dictatorship' in the country. They had planned to storm a corps commander meeting at Army General Headquarters in Rawalpindi and take over the military command. General Abbasi was to declare himself 'Amirul Mominin' (the supreme leader of the faithful) and turn Pakistan into a theocratic state. One of the main accomplices in the plot was Saifullah Akhtar.

Major-General Abbasi, who was posted as Director Infantry at GHQ, had a controversial record. As a Brigadier he was posted in the late 1980s as Pakistan's military attaché in Delhi from where he was expelled on espionage charges. The bearded General, who was known for his extremist religious views, was at the end of his career after having been overlooked for promotion. Brigadier Billah, who sported a long unruly beard, had more radical religious beliefs. He was never considered professionally sound and was consigned to an obscure post at GHQ. The conspirators were highly influenced by Lt.-General Ghulam Mohammed Malik, a former commander of the 10th corps in Rawalpindi who had retired just a few months earlier. Although the General did not have any direct role in the coup plot, most of the rebel officers idolized him because of his radical Islamic views.

A military court handed down jail sentences to General Abbasi and the other accused, but Akhtar was mysteriously freed and allowed to join the Taliban forces then closing in on Kabul. Akhtar's name resurfaced in 2004 when he was arrested in Dubai in connection with a plot to assassinate Musharraf.

There are differences between the various groups. Some, such as LeT, are more focused on India (though they all share the Kashmiri cause as a rallying point). Others, like HuM, are more involved in Afghanistan: some have closer links with transnational jihadists; others, such as JeM, are more concerned with purifying Pakistan itself. They share a common culture and anti-western world-view. They draw their footsoldiers from the ranks of the lower middle class, their ideology from radical clerics and their direction from a nuclei of battle-hardened leaders with serious ISI connections. As they evolve, regroup and reposition themselves in response to domestic and international pressures, one thing becomes clear: the more powerful groups, which are the more radical ones, have outgrown their handlers.

4

NURSERY
FOR JIHAD

Sporting white turbans, the young men listened in silence to the concluding sermon at the graduation ceremony. 'Being watchmen of your religion, you are naturally the first target of your enemies,' declared a frail, black-turbaned Maulana Samiul Haq. His long grey beard coloured with henna, the fiery cleric was head of Pakistan's leading institution for Islamic learning, Darul Uloom Haqqania. Situated in the town of Akora Khattak on the Grand Trunk Road near Peshawar, the radical seminary, often described as the University of jihad, in September 2003 turned out another class of young Pakistanis and Afghans ready to wage a holy war against the enemies of their religion.

Banners showing Kalashnikov rifles and tanks adorned the walls of the seminary. Some posters carried slogans in support of bin Laden and holy war. 'It is your sacred duty to defend your faith before everything else,' exhorted Haq, a member of Parliament and the leader of an alliance of six Islamic parties that ruled the North West Frontier Province. In his mid sixties, the cleric took pride in having met bin Laden. 'He is a great hero of Islam,' he told me a week after 9/11, showing off photographs of himself posing with the Saudi militant.

Thousands of students, teachers and religious leaders assembled within a tented ground inside the sprawling campus broke into frenzied chants of 'jihad, jihad' and 'Allah is the greatest', as a message from the Taliban's fugitive supreme commander, Mullah Mohammed Omar, was read out to them. The school's support for radical Islamic movements was not a secret. It had been the cradle of the Taliban militia that ruled Afghanistan for more than five years. Many of its leaders, including several cabinet ministers, had graduated from the school. It had also been a recruiting centre for dozens of Pakistani militant groups fighting Indian forces in Kashmir. Many of the school's three thousand students were from Afghanistan and former Soviet Central Asia.[1] Some had taken part in the 'holy wars' in Afghanistan and Kashmir. 'Jihad is an essential part of Islam,' Haq asserted.

The proliferation of jihadist organizations in Pakistan over the previous two decades had been the result of a militant culture espoused by radical madrasas like Darul Uloom Haqqania. Thousands of madrasas across the country became hubs for militancy and religious extremism, having a spill-over effect and presenting a serious threat to Pakistan's internal security. Pakistani madrasas were once considered centres for basic religious learning, mostly attached to local mosques. The more formal ones were used for educating clergy. The development of simple, sparse religious schools into training centres for Kalashnikov-toting religious warriors was directly linked with the rise of militant Islam. Many of the religious parties operating the madrasas turned to militancy courtesy of the US-sponsored jihad in Afghanistan. From waging jihad against infidels in that foreign land, taking on perceived enemies of Islam at home was just a small step away. The influx of huge sums of money and a growing sense of power transformed the mullah's image from that of a docile and humble man to a mafia thug with a four-wheel-drive Jeep and armed bodyguards. The influence of mullahs with local Pakistani leaders had also become formidable. Successive governments ignored their activities out of political expediency and also because most of the foreigners supporting them were 'brotherly Muslim' countries.

The Islamic revolution in Iran in 1979 opened up the first wave of foreign funding for madrasas in Pakistan. Fearful of growing Iranian influence and the spread of revolution, Kuwait, Saudi Arabia, Iraq and some other oil-rich Muslim countries started pumping money into hardline Pakistani Sunni religious organizations willing to counter the supposed Shia threat.[2] Millions of dollars were poured into setting up madrasas across the country, particularly in Balochistan province, bordering Iran. The Islamization process started by General Zia ul-Haq's regime in 1979 also contributed to the mushrooming of madrasas. For the first time in Pakistani history, the state started providing financial support for the expansion of religious education from Zakat and Ushr funds.[3] The Islamization of education and levying of Islamic taxes had a profound long-term effect.

Zakat, one of the five pillars of Islam, had been treated as a private matter in most Muslim states. General Zia's regime broke with that tradition by deducting it from bank accounts each year during the Islamic holy month of Ramadan.[4] The substantial amount raised by Zakat was used to finance the traditional religious schools, most of them belonging to the Deobandi movement, which is akin to Saudi Wahabism. Zakat did little to improve the lot of millions of Pakistanis living in abject poverty. The only visible consequence was the transformation of the religious landscape of the nation. The foreign and government-funded madrasas also became the main centres for spreading sectarian hatred. Saudi Arabian patronage, especially of more radical Ahle Hadith madrasas, played a major role in worsening the situation.

Madrasas also had a key place in Pakistani religious and social life. Most of the seminary students came from the poorest sections of Pakistani society and were provided with free religious education, lodging and meals. The influx of the impoverished rural population to the madrasas was a major reason for their growth, with Punjab and the North West Frontier Province having the highest number of religious seminaries. Divided along sectarian and political lines, religious seminaries were largely controlled by the two main branches of Sunni Islam in South Asia – the Deobandi and the Barelvi. Ahle Hadith or Wahabi Muslims had their own schools, as did the Shias. The religious doctrinal differences among these sects were irreconcilable. Most of the madrasas were centuries apart from the outside world. Generally the students were poor, from broken homes, or were orphans. Conditions in schools were regularly condemned by human rights groups as crowded and inhumane. The students were often subjected to a regimen as harsh as any jail, and physical abuses were commonplace. In many schools, students were put in chains and iron fetters for the slightest violation of the rules. There were almost no extracurricular activities and television and radio were banned. Teaching was rudimentary and students were taught religion within a highly rigorous and traditional perspective, giving them a deeply retrograde world-view.

At the primary stage, madrasa pupils learnt to read, memorize and recite the Qur'an. Exegeses of the holy script and other branches of Islamic studies were introduced at the higher stages of learning.[5] Though the focus was on religious learning, some institutions also taught elementary mathematics, science and English. The most dangerous consequence of the content and style of teaching in religious schools was that the people that emerged could do nothing apart from guide the faithful in rituals that demand no experts. Job opportunities for madrasa graduates were few and narrow. They could only work in mosques, madrasas, the parent religious sectarian party, or its affiliate businesses or organizations.

The education imparted by traditional madrasas often spawned factional, religious and cultural conflict. It created barriers to modern knowledge, stifled creativity and bred bigotry, thus laying the foundation on which fundamentalism – militant or otherwise – was based. Divided by sectarian identities, these institutions were, by their very nature, driven by their zeal to outnumber and dominate rival sects.[6] Students were educated and trained to counter the arguments of opposing sects on matters of theology, jurisprudence and doctrines. Promoting a particular sect inevitably implied the rejection of other sects, sowing the seeds of extremism in the minds of the students.[7] The literature produced by their parent religious organizations promoted sectarian hatred and was aimed at proving the rival sects as infidels and apostates. The efforts by the successive government to modernize madrasa curricula and introduce secular subjects failed because of stiff resistance from the religious organizations controlling the religious schools.

The rise of jihad culture since the 1980s gave madrasas a new sense of purpose. As a result, their numbers multiplied and the clergy emerged as a powerful political and social force. At independence in 1947, there were only 137 madrasas in Pakistan; in the next ten years their number rose to 244. After that, they doubled every ten years.[8] A significant number remained unregistered and therefore it was hard to know precisely how many there were. Government sources put the figure at 13,000, with total enrolment close to 1.7 million.[9] The vast majority of students were between five and 18 years old. Only those advancing into higher religious studies were older. According to the government's own estimates, ten to 15 per cent of the madrasas had links with sectarian militancy or international terrorism. The trail of international terror often led to the madrasas and mosques.

Madrasas were basically conservative institutions before they were radicalized during the 1980s Afghan jihad. The growing army of extremists fought the anti-Soviet Afghan jihad alongside Arabs and Afghans. They later served the cause of jihad from Kashmir to Chechnya to Bosnia, Egypt and Yemen. At the height of the Afghan jihad – 1982–1988 – more than 1,000 new madrasas were opened in Pakistan, mostly along the borders with Afghanistan in the North West Frontier Province and Balochistan. Almost all belonged to hardline Sunni religious parties like Jamiat-e-Ulema Islam (JUI) and Jamaat-i-Islami (JI), which were Zia's political allies as well as partners in the Afghan jihad.[10] Their location in the two border provinces, which had close cultural, linguistic and sectarian affinities with Afghan Pashtuns, made it easier to motivate the pupils to fight for their brethren in distress.

These madrasas did not conduct military training or provide arms to students, but encouraged them to join the 'holy war'. The purpose was to ensure a continued supply of recruits for the Afghan resistance. The message was simple: all Muslims must perform the duty of jihad in whatever capacity they could. It was the responsibility of the Pakistani military, particularly the ISI, to provide training to the recruits in camps inside Afghanistan and Pakistan's tribal region. As the Afghan jihad progressed, so did the influence of the jihadists coming out of these madrasas. The USA indirectly – and sometimes directly – promoted militancy, the culture of jihad and supported the clergy in its war against communism.

Special textbooks were published in Dari and Pashto by the University of Nebraska-Omaha and funded by USAID with an aim to promote jihadist values and militant training. Millions of such books were distributed at Afghan refugee camps and Pakistani madrasas, where students learnt basic maths by counting dead Russians and Kalashnikov rifles.[11] The same textbooks were later used by the Taliban in their madrasas.

As General Zia attempted to consolidate his authority through Islamization at home and jihad in Afghanistan, the madrasa system was profoundly transformed. The Islamization process nurtured many, often mutually hostile, varieties of fundamentalism. In a society where many sects coexisted, the measures representing the belief of the dominant sect acted as an identity marker, heightening sectarian divisions and promoting sectarian conflicts. As a result, sectarian divisions were militarized. The zealots began to look inwards and fight a new jihad against sectarian rivals, particularly Shias. The madrasa phenomenon drew international attention, particularly following the rise of the conservative Taliban regime in Afghanistan. The movement was largely the product of hundreds of seminaries in the Pashtun belt on the border with Afghanistan.

The link between madrasas and the Afghan jihad is exemplified by the Darul Uloom Haqqania madrasa. Founded in 1947 by Haq's father, Maulana Abdul Haq, a well-respected Islamic scholar belonging to the Deobandi order, Darul Uloom Haqqania developed into a centre for pan-Islamism with the beginning of the Afghan war. It saw a huge expansion with the support of the government and funds from abroad. Like other Deobandi institutions, Darul Uloom was controlled by a faction of JUI, a mainstream religio-political party that was part of a six-party conservative alliance known as Muttehida Majlis Amal (MMA). The party became an important part of the Afghan jihad. The seminary traditionally had a large number of students from Afghanistan, but they increased considerably with the influx of Afghan refugees.

By 1985, about 60 per cent of the students in the seminary were Afghans. It also attracted students from Tajikistan, Uzbekistan and Turkmenistan. From the beginning of the Afghan jihad, the school had relaxed the rules concerning attendance, allowing the students to take time off to participate in the 'holy war'. The seminary, however, drew immense international attention in the 1990s with the emergence of the conservative Taliban movement. Thousands of Afghan, as well as Pakistani students crossed the border into Afghanistan to join the Islamic militia. In 1997 the school was closed for several months to allow the students to participate in the Taliban's war to capture Afghanistan's northern province of Mazar-i-Sharif. Such a large-scale cross-border movement would not have been possible without the collusion of Pakistani intelligence agencies.

Just months before the 11 September terrorist attacks in New York and Washington, the school hosted a conference of Islamic parties and militant groups to express solidarity with bin Laden and the Taliban regime. Masked gunmen in camouflage guerrilla outfits stood guard as Islamic leaders from Pakistan and Afghanistan congregated at the sprawling auditorium on 9 January 2001, vowing to defend bin Laden and to launch a holy war against the West. Besides the 300 leaders representing various radical Islamic groups, the meeting was also attended by a former army chief, General Aslam Beg, and a former

ISI chief, General Hamid Gul. They declared it a religious duty of Muslims all over the world to protect the Saudi dissident whom they described as a 'great Muslim warrior'. One of the objectives of the assembly was to press Islamabad not to comply with UN sanctions against the Taliban. Interestingly, the military government, which had banned political parties holding public rallies, did not try to stop the conference. No action was taken against the militants for the public display of weapons. They obviously had the backing of the intelligence agencies. Islamic seminaries and clerics had never been as numerous and so powerful in Pakistan.

Islamic seminaries also became a transit point for foreign militants aspiring to join al-Qaeda and the Taliban forces in Afghanistan. Very few people had heard about the primitive fundamentalist Madrasa-i-Arabia outside the remote corner of north-west Pakistan until its name sprung on the international scene in connection with the American Taliban, John Walker Lindh. The young American was wounded in battle and captured by US-supported Northern Alliance forces in the Afghan northern province of Kunduz in December 2001.[12]

It was in this isolated and spartan school where there were no amenities that the 19-year-old American learnt his lesson in Islamic sharia and jihad. A new convert to Islam, he spent some six months in this austere madrasa housed in a one-storey building before leaving for Afghanistan in May 2001 to join the Taliban.[13] Lindh, who had grown up in upper-middle-class surroundings in California, chose the school to properly understand Islam. Mufti Mohammed Iltimas, the white-bearded head of the school, remembered him as a hard-working student who was determined to memorize every word of the Qur'an. He slept on a rope bed in a place where there was no hot water and no electricity after 10 pm.[14]

Lindh's introduction to the madrasa came through a Pakistani missionary he met in California in 1998. A Pashtun,[15] Khizar Hayat, who had travelled to America on a preaching mission, was closely linked with the local militant organizations. Even though he was much older than the other boys, Lindh was granted admission to the school. Lindh, who went by the name Suleyman al-Faris, was not in Pakistan to engage solely in scholarly pursuits. During his stay in the madrasa, he frequently met visiting Taliban activists. In May 2001, Hayat took him to the office of a pro-Taliban Islamic militant group, HuM, where he enrolled for guerrilla training.[16]

Lindh was sent to a HuM camp near Islamabad. After learning the use of firearms, he was dispatched to Afghanistan to work with the Taliban. He was not the only American and not the only westerner to have joined al-Qaeda and the Taliban. Many western men, a lot of them Afro-American, were recruited by the Tablighi Jamaat and its front organizations and sent to Afghanistan after receiving basic religious training in Pakistani madrasas and guerrilla training at the camps run by militant groups, closely affiliated with the religious institutions. Some of the madrasas had links with international Islamist organizations like Egypt's Akhwan-ul Muslimeen (Muslim Brotherhood), Indonesia's Jemmah Islamiyah, Algeria's Islamic Salvation Front (FIS) and the Philippines' Abu Sayyaf group, all of whom extended support to al-Qaeda.[17]

Radical madrasas were not restricted to the remote border region in northern Pakistan. In fact, the country's largest city and its main financial centre Karachi, became the hub of militant seminaries. According to one estimate, more than 200,000 students were enrolled in around one thousand madrasas in the city. Not all, but many of them, had links with sectarian or Islamic militant groups. The largest among them was the Jamia Ulumia Islami or Jamia Binoria. The sprawling red-brick campus, with tall minarets right in the heart of the city, served as the backbone of militant Islam and was the breeding ground for 'Islamic warriors'. The country's premier institution for Islamic learning had also become the citadel of Sunni extremist groups. The main campus and eight other affiliated madrasas enrolled more than ten thousand students from Pakistan as well as 30 other countries including China, Central Asia, Chechnya, Malaysia, the Philippines and Britain. Students were taught the concept of jihad as a special subject to prepare them to fight for the cause of Islam. Many of the Taliban leaders were graduates and took guidance from their former teachers for running the fundamentalist Islamic state. The students were sent regularly to Afghanistan for training and orientation during Taliban rule. At the main gate stood a huge banner exhorting Muslims to join Taliban forces in Afghanistan. Over the last two decades, thousands of its students fought in Afghanistan and Kashmir.

Dozens of other smaller and relatively low-profile madrasas spread across Karachi became the base for al-Qaeda 'sleeper' cells in Pakistan. A lean and shy Ahmed Hadi was an ordinary student at Jamia Abu Bakr and the last person one would suspect of being an important cog in the international terrorist network.[18] It was only after Pakistani security forces raided the seminary in Karachi's middle-class neighbourhood of Gulshan-e-Iqbal in September 2003 that his real identity was revealed. Gun Gun Rusman Gunawan was a leading member of Indonesia's Jemmah Islamiyah and the brother of Hambali, the mastermind of the 2002 bombing in the Indonesian holiday resort of Bali in which more than 200 people died. The Indonesian, who was captured along with 11 other Southeast Asian students, had spent four years at the seminary under a fake identity.[19]

Hambali, who was arrested in Thailand in 2003, had contacts with al-Qaeda's top leaders Ramzi bin al-Shibh and Khalid Sheikh Mohammed, both of whom were apprehended in Pakistan.[20] It was the first indicator of a terrorist sleeper cell operating in Pakistan's main commercial hub. Gunawan was granted admission to the Jamia Abu Bakr Islamia in 1999. He was among 15,000 students from Muslim countries who came to Pakistan to study in Pakistani madrasas during the 1990s. Founded in 1978, the seminary had a large number of foreign students mainly from Thailand, Indonesia, Malaysia and African countries.[21]

The arrest of Gunawan provided some indication of the strong links between Islamic seminaries and the international terrorist network. His arrest was followed by a series of raids less than a kilometre away from the Abu Bakr seminary. Another eight Southeast Asian students were arrested from the Jamia Darasitul Islamia, a seminary run by Jamaat-ud Da'awa, the political wing of Lashkar-e-Taiba. This connection compelled investigators to explore Jemmah Islamiyah's links with Pakistan's militant groups. Pakistani intelligence agencies suspected that Gunawan was instrumental in channelling funds provided by al-Qaeda to the Jemmah Islamiyah.[22] Despite the government's crackdown, many madrasas continued to provide safe haven to al-Qaeda sleeper cells.

Over the past several years, there had been a visible rise in the number of madrasa students belonging to families of the expatriate Pakistani community, particularly those living in the USA and Britain. Fired by the desire to become 'true Muslims', hundreds of second-generation expatriates joined Pakistani seminaries each year. Most of them from prosperous middle-class families, they took time off from their schools to learn about their faith. While the majority of the boys confined themselves to Islamic learning, dozens of them got involved in jihadist activities under the influence of militant groups that operated inside some of the madrasas.

It was one such radical madrasa where Shehzad Tanweer, one

of the suicide bombers involved in the 7 July 2005 terror attacks in London, spent time during his last visit to Pakistan. Twenty-two-year-old Shehzad, who blew himself up on a subway train near Aldgate station in East London, was the eldest son of Mohammed Mumtaz Tanweer, who had migrated to England in the 1960s. He grew up in the Beeston area of Leeds, but remained connected with Pakistan through his extended family members who lived in a farming village in Faisalabad district.[23] In December 2004, Shehzad went to Manzoor ul Islamia madrasa in Lahore, which was linked with JeM. He intended to stay there for nine months of religious education, but left just a week later.[24] There are strong suspicions that Shehzad might have met the mastermind of the London bombings during his brief stay there.

The suspected Pakistani connection to the 7/7 attacks brought Musharraf under a renewed pressure to act against militant madrasas. As in the past, he responded this time by ordering a nationwide crackdown on Islamic extremist groups. The police again stormed a number of madrasas and arrested hundreds of suspected extremists. But the entire operation appeared merely superficial; most of them were released after a few weeks.

In his new role as a key ally in the US-led war on terror, Musharraf toned down many policies that had previously fostered militancy and religious extremism. But most of the measures, particularly against the home-grown jihadists, were taken under external pressure and lacked conviction. Very little was done to rein in the militant madrasas, despite their continuing involvement in jihadist politics. While talk about reform went on, fresh batches of volunteers ready to confront what they perceived as enemies of their faith continued to graduate from madrasas.

Even after the ousting of the Taliban regime, many madrasas in parts of Balochistan continued to preach jihad to Afghan students. A major part of Musharraf's anti-extremism drive was to regulate and transform those madrasas whose role in promoting jihad had come under increasing international scrutiny. The move was stalled because of the administration's failure to stop their funding from Pakistanis working abroad, as well as from foreign Muslim charities. The biggest source of financing for madrasas was external – from Muslim countries as well as private donors and Pakistani expatriates. A report by the Brussels-based International Crisis Group (ICG) revealed that Pakistani madrasas and religious centres had received more than 90 billion rupees ($1.5 billion) every year through charitable donations. The amount was almost equal to the government's annual direct income tax revenue.[25] Most of the madrasas, which had in the past received government funding, now relied solely on private charity. Ninety-four per cent of charitable donations made by Pakistani individuals and business corporations went to the religious institutions. Though most donors did not support the politics of religious parties, they felt that Islamic education and the preservation of Islam were the most worthy choice for their donations. Many religious leaders who ran the Islamic seminaries had strong links in Arab countries that went back to the Afghan jihad. For many it had become a 'status symbol' to receive funding from foreign sources.

Muslims in Britain had been one of the largest donors to the Pakistani Islamic institutions and Muslim militant groups, some of whom had been declared terrorists and outlawed by Pakistan's military government. UK-based charities were the main financiers for Islamic groups. Diversion of funds for educational and humanitarian projects to the Islamic militant groups had become a normal practice. 'It is difficult to separate finances for terror from those for charity,' said the ICG report. LeT and JeM, reportedly collected more than £5 million each year in mosques in Britain. Although both the groups were banned in Britain, the Kashmiri diaspora continued to make donations to them.[26]

While Islamabad had repeatedly downplayed the link between extremism and the madrasas, most religious schools continued to preach jihad. After the failed attempts on Musharraf's life in December 2003, the administration launched raids on some extremist madrasas, but such half-hearted and piecemeal measures could hardly help improve the situation. Pakistan's failure to curb extremism owed less to the difficulty of implementing reforms than to the administration's own unwillingness. Musharraf had promised to ban the use of mosques and madrasas for spreading religious and sectarian hatred. However, all those pledges remained largely rhetorical and seemed to have been made under international pressure. The sectarian groups continued to challenge the authority of the state in different ways. Pakistan's failure to strictly enforce laws against the preaching of religious hatred and reining in of the extremist madrasas had largely been responsible for the rise in sectarian-based violence. The failure to deliver to any substantial degree on pledges to reform madrasas and contain the growth of jihadist networks had not only given rise to religious extremism in Pakistan, but also continued to present a threat to domestic, regional and international security.

Several madrasas continued to provide recruits for Taliban insurgents in Afghanistan. Run by JUI, part of the coalition government in the western Balochistan province, the seminaries not only provided the Taliban with ideological training, but also extended material help. Pashtunabad, a congested slum district in the provincial capital, Quetta, had a large concentration of former Taliban activists. A stronghold of radical Islamic groups, it looked more like a Kandahar neighbourhood under the former Taliban regime, and several former Taliban leaders were believed to have taken refuge there. The main madrasa in the neighbourhood was run by Maulana Noor Mohammed, a MMA member of the National Assembly. He appeared convinced that the Taliban would re-establish their control over Afghanistan. 'They will ultimately triumph,' declared the 75-year-old cleric.[27]

But it was Chaman, a dusty border town in Balochistan province, that became the main base for resurgent Taliban fighting against the US and Afghan troops. The rise to power of Islamic groups in the two key border provinces gave a tremendous boost to the Taliban's efforts to regroup. Many provincial ministers and members of Parliament belonging to the ruling alliance became actively involved with the Afghan rebels using the region as their base. Some of the seminaries run by the alliance leaders were used as a conduit for weapon supply to the Afghan rebels. Many Pakistanis belonging to the ruling group also joined the Taliban. The same seminaries from where Taliban forces were initially raised once again became the centre for producing a new generation of Islamic warriors.

Abdul Hadi fled his home in Afghanistan's southern Helmand province soon after the invasion of Afghanistan by the US-led coalition forces. The thickly bearded former Islamic fighter was spending time at a madrasa in Chaman. 'I am waiting for a call to join jihad against the un-Islamic regime,' the black turbaned mullah told me in the summer of 2003. Hadi was among the thousands of Taliban who melted away into Pakistani seminaries. 'They all want to go back and fight to re-establish the Taliban control over Afghanistan,' said Hafiz Allauddin, a Pakistani seminary teacher who had fought alongside the Taliban forces. They were optimistic that Afghanistan would return to puritan Islamic rule once the American forces left the country.

Not only are the madrasssas harbouring and aiding existing Afghan warriors, they are also creating new ones. More than 8,000 new pupils have enrolled in the seminaries in the border areas alone since the fall of the Taliban. 'There is a constant stream of them. It is hard to find accommodation for the newcomers,' said Hafiz Hameedullah, the head of one seminary. Unable to halt the expansion and prolific output of these seminaries, Musharraf faces a new generation of jihadists on the dangerous and unstable border with Afghanistan – one that military force alone can never subdue.

5

THE CONFLICT
WITHIN

Thumping their chests, hundreds of Shia mourners had crammed the narrow lane in the western Pakistani city of Quetta on the afternoon of 2 March 2004. The annual procession commemorating the martyrdom in the sixth century of Imam Hussein, the grandson of the Prophet Mohammed, moved at snail's pace. Suddenly, a huge explosion sent a massive shudder through the crowd. All hell broke loose as gunmen on the rooftop of surrounding buildings opened indiscriminate machine-gun fire and lobbed grenades into the procession. Meanwhile, two suicide bombers detonated themselves in the middle of the procession. Their bodies dangled from the balcony over the electricity wires. The ghastly carnage left at least 44 people dead and scores of others wounded.[1]

It was the third time in six months that the army garrison town bordering Afghanistan had been drenched in blood by Sunni militants. In July 2003 it had witnessed one of the deadliest acts of religious violence in the country's history, when attackers armed with machine guns and grenades stormed a Shia mosque. More than 2,000 worshippers were praying inside. The three gunmen first opened fire with automatic weapons and then two of them removed the pins from the grenades they were carrying, causing terrifying explosions and killing 55 people, including themselves.² It was the first time suicide bombing was used in such an attack, lending a new and dangerous dimension to sectarian terror. An earlier attack in June had killed 13 police trainees from the Shia Hazara community. The violence spread to Karachi and parts of Punjab province, leaving more than 350 people dead in the year 2004.

The 2 March Quetta massacre coincided with the bomb attacks on Shia processions in the Iraqi cities of Baghdad and Karbala, which had left more than 200 people dead. Although no direct link between the two incidents could be established, there appeared to be some familiar pattern among the different theatres of jihad across the globe. The perpetrators were driven by the same ideological world-view and the dynamics of their operation appeared similar. The objectives and the goals of Pakistani sectarian terrorists in the post-9/11 world appeared closer to those transnational jihadists. It was two-track jihad: they simultaneously fought internal sectarian jihads and external jihad against the West in general and, more specifically, against the USA.³

Religious sectarianism, the principal source of terrorist activity in Pakistan, presented the most serious threat to the country's internal security. Sectarian terrorism had been deeply intertwined with the Islamization of the state, as non-Sunni sects felt increasingly threatened by the Sunni orthodoxy propagated by the power of the state.

The spate of killings in Quetta and other parts of the country had sent a grim reminder that the religious terrorist network was not only intact, but had also expanded. The surge in sectarian terrorism raised serious questions about Musharraf's efforts to combat Islamic extremism. It was all the more inexplicable given Pakistan's success in capturing key al-Qaeda leaders.

Heavily armed terrorist groups continued to operate despite the government's claim that it had rooted out Islamic extremism. While the administration silently watched the situation drift into anarchy, the armed marauders carried out their deadly operations with impunity. The pattern and scale of violence had indicated that the sectarian militants were armed and well organized. Pakistan's largest city and commercial capital, Karachi, and Punjab province had long been the main centres of sectarian violence; now the sphere of strife had extended to new areas, with a series of bloody attacks in the western border city of Quetta where such incidents were previously unknown.

The upsurge in Sunni militancy was linked to al-Qaeda and the Taliban insurgents using Pakistan as a base for their activities. The connection had emerged after an investigation showed that Dawood Badani, a close relative of Khalid Sheikh Mohammed and Ramzi Yousuf, was the prime suspect in the Quetta attacks which had been carried out by Lashkar-e-Jhangvi (LeJ), the Sunni group closely linked to al-Qaeda and to former Taliban rulers in Afghanistan.[4] Claiming responsibility, the group said the attacks were a protest against the Musharraf government, Iran and the United States. A videotape distributed by the group showed that the two suicide bombers were madrasa students. LeJ and other Sunni extremist groups had a history of sectarian violence in Pakistan, but those tensions were inflamed by the US military intervention in Afghanistan and Pakistan's support for it.

Sectarian conflict in Pakistan took an organized militant form in the 1980s. It had its roots in the so-called Islamization process initiated by General Zia ul-Haq's military regime. The government's secular disposition gave way to a professed determination to Islamize the society. The Islamization of law, education and culture illustrated the Sunni sectarian bias of the Pakistani state. General Zia's Islamic penal code was derived entirely from classical Sunni-Hanafi orthodox sources. The official dissemination of a particular brand of Islamic ideology not only militated against Pakistan's sectarian diversity, but also bred discrimination against non-Muslim minorities. The political use of Islam by the state strengthened a clerical elite and created sectarian groups that aggressively pushed their militant ideas.[5]

The move towards the establishment of a Sunni-Hanafi state, reflecting the beliefs of the dominant sect, created a sense of insecurity among the Shia minority community. The dynamic of exclusion and minoritization, which had existed since the creation of the country in various forms, was sanctified by General Zia's Islamization.[6] As a result, the more orthodox and militant version of Sunni Islam had grown in strength and public influence. The promotion of Deobandi orthodoxy intensified the sectarian conflict. The spread of jihadist literature from Afghan training camps to Pakistani madrasas in the 1980s fuelled radicalism among the students. Islamization of education created mass sectarian consciousness far beyond the confines of the madrasa, which resulted in a dramatic shift towards extremist Sunni orthodoxy and anti-Shia militancy. More extremist Sunni groups demanded a constitutional amendment to declare Shias a non-Muslim minority and excommunicate them from the realm of Islam.

The Shia community reacted strongly to the enforcement of the

Hanafi laws by the military regime. Until 1979, Pakistani Shias were a politically moderate community and had supported secular political parties. But General Zia's Islamization and the Iranian revolution spurred them into political activism. The Islamic revolution in Iran had inspired Shias everywhere. Tens of thousands of Shias gathered in Islamabad in 1980 to protest their marginalization by the Sunni majority, the biggest show of strength by the Pakistani Shia community.[7] It was also the period when a Shia political party known as Tehrik Nifaz-e-Fiqh Jafaria (TNFJ) (Movement for the Implementation of Shia Jurisprudence) was formed, a move reflecting the community's new-found assertiveness. As the only Shia Islamic state, Iran became the centre for spiritual guidance and political support for most Pakistani Shias. The military government and its Sunni allies perceived it as an Iranian conspiracy to export its revolution to Pakistan.[8]

The divide, deepened by the actions of the state, could never be bridged. The Shia revolutionary idealism was followed by the emergence of militant Sunni sectarian organizations. Sipah-e-Sahaba Pakistan (SSP; Army of the Prophet's Companions) was formed in 1985 by the fiery Deobandi cleric Haq Nawaz Jhangvi with a one-point anti-Shia agenda.[9] A prayer leader at a mosque in the central Punjab city of Jhang, he was reported to have close links with Pakistani intelligence agencies. An offshoot of JUI, SSP represented a state-sponsored and Saudi-backed movement against Pakistan's pro-Iran Shia minority.[10] It sought to turn Pakistan into a Sunni state.

A market district in southern Punjab, Jhang was the birthplace of organized sectarian militancy in Pakistan, and the rise of SSP reflected its socio-economic division in the area. The bazaar and merchants supported the Sunni militant group in order to counter the Shia feudal aristocracy which had traditionally dominated local politics.[11] With funding from Saudi Arabia and some other Arab countries and tacit support from the military regime, SSP extended its organization across the country. It had a student wing, a welfare trust and a vast network of local offices. The outfit also operated as a political party, regularly contesting elections in Punjab province.[12] With almost a million card-holding members, SSP emerged as one of the most well-knit Islamist groups.

Initially the SSP cadres came from Deobandi and Ahle Hadith madrasas,[13] which had proliferated during the anti-Soviet jihad. But later it established its own madrasas mostly in Punjab and Karachi. It also drew support from among the urban poor and middle classes and received funds from expatriates in the Middle East.

External factors contributed hugely to stoking sectarian conflict in Pakistan. The Iranian revolution evoked a strong reaction throughout the Muslim world. The spill-over effect of the Shia revolution worried many Arab rulers, as well as the Pakistani military regime, which was trying to establish an Islamic system of a different kind. The rivalry between Sunni Arab states and Shia Iran was further heightened during the Iran-Iraq war. Money poured in from Arab countries anxious to counter the radical Shia Islam sponsored by Iran's revolutionary regime. In the process, Pakistan became the battlefield in an intra Islam proxy war. Iran and Saudi Arabia supported their respected allies. The Saudi government had consistently backed and funded the Deobandi school of thought in Pakistan which had many similarities to the Wahabi version of Islam.[14] Madrasas funded by Saudi Arabia, Kuwait and other Gulf countries, especially after the Soviet invasion of Afghanistan, became the centre of Sunni militancy, as well the recruiting ground for sectarian organizations.[15]

Deobandi and Ahle Hadith mullahs whipped up anti-Shia sentiments. Some Sunni leaders were on the payroll of Iraq. Pakistani and Iranian intelligence agencies had also been actively involved in the proxy war being fought on Pakistani streets since the 1980s.[16] The rise of foreign-backed sectarian militancy set in motion a seemingly unending cycle of violence. Afghanistan's war-hardened fanatics declared their own jihad at home against the Shia community. Armed with sophisticated weapons they started targeting rival mosques and Shia leaders.[17]

Although the Shia and Sunni conflict in Pakistan pre-dated the emergence of the SSP, there had been a major escalation in sectarian violence since the anti-Shia riots in Lahore in 1986. Two subsequent events were to change the dynamics of the sectarian violence. In 1987, Allama Ehsan Elahi Zaheer, a Saudi-backed Sunni cleric, was killed in a bomb blast in Lahore. The following year, a prominent Shia leader, Arif Hussaini, was murdered in Peshawar. He had spent time in Iran and was believed to have been closely associated with Iran's Islamic regime. The assassin was a serving army officer, Majid Raza Gillani, which raised suspicions of the ISI's involvement in the murder.

The violence spiralled with the murder of SSP founder Haq Nawaz Jhangvi in 1990, believed to have been carried out by Shia militants. Sectarian clashes broke out in Jhang and spread to other parts of the province. With some 5,000 to 6,000 well-trained militants, the SSP unleashed a reign of terror. The SSP supporters blamed Iran-backed

Shia militants for the assassination of Jhangvi. In December that year, Sunni militants gunned down Sadiq Ganji, Iran's consul general in Lahore, in retribution. The incident drew international attention to the conflict, which reached a peak in 1994, one of the worst and the bloodiest years, with at least 74 people killed in sectarian attacks. Most of the deaths occurred in attacks on Shia religious gatherings. Many policemen were also killed in targeted attacks. Iranian interests were particularly targeted by the Sunni extremists. In January 1997, an Iranian cultural centre was set on fire in Lahore. A few days later a similar attack in the southern Punjab town of Multan killed seven people including an Iranian diplomat. In another attack five Iranian air force personnel were killed in Rawalpindi.[18] Shia militants retaliated with a bomb attack at Lahore High Court, which killed the new SSP chief, Ziaur Rehman.

The sectarian conflict took a more violent turn with the formation in 1996 of LeJ. A breakway faction of SSP, the new sectarian outfit led by Riaz Basra, believed in using terror tactics to force the government to accept its demand of declaring the Shia community a non-Muslim minority and establishing an orthodox Sunni Islamic system in the country. Born to a poor farmer in the central Punjab district of Sargodha, Basra received his primary education at a madrasa in Lahore before joining the anti-Soviet jihad in Afghanistan. An injury forced him to return home and he joined SSP in 1986. A fiery orator, Basra quickly rose up in the hierarchy. In 1988, he became the chief of the party's propaganda department; the same year he stood in elections for a Punjab state assembly seat from Lahore.

Basra's notoriety as the most dangerous terrorist grew further after he was arrested for the murder of Sadiq Ganji in 1994. He made a daring escape from an anti-terrorism court in Lahore and later fled to Afghanistan, but he would often return to Pakistan to organize terrorist attacks. LeJ made its mark as the most feared terrorist outfit soon after its inception. Although the number of its hard-core cadres had never been more than five hundred, the group was responsible for most of the sectarian killings over the last decade. By 2001, LeJ had been involved in 350 incidents of terrorism.

Most of the LeJ militants came from among the rural unemployed and Deobandi madrasas, particularly those in southern Punjab, but its highly secretive and mobile organization made it more lethal. Unlike other Islamic militant groups, LeJ avoided media exposure and tried to operate as covertly as possible. Its only contact with the outside world was through occasional fax messages to newspaper offices claiming responsibility for attacks. Its other source of propaganda was its publication *Inteqam-i-Haq*. LeJ activists were divided into small cells that would dissolve after each action, making it more difficult for the police to break the network. The militants were taught to die rather than be captured by the security forces. 'To become a martyr is the dream of every Mujahid. It is a gift from God and will send a message to the enemy that a Mujahid would prefer to die in an interrogation cell rather than disclose any secret that could harm other Mujahids,' a guideline to party activists said.

Every LeJ activist would go through a tough regimen and ideological training before being sent on a terror mission. He was not supposed to maintain any links with family members during training or divulge any information to them about the group: 'Our relation is with God and whatever we are doing is for God. All other relationships are meaningless. Therefore try to avoid making friends and keeping in close touch with your relatives.' Police officials said it was never easy to interrogate people whose dream was to become martyrs.[19]

In Afghanistan, Basra became closely associated with the Taliban militia, which had by then extended its control over a large part of the strife-torn country. The rise of the Taliban in Afghanistan gave the Sunni sectarian groups a new impetus. The rising power of the armed, battle-hardened zealots became alarming and there was already talk about the Talibanization of Pakistan. 'Kabul ke baad Islamabad ... Taliban, Taliban [After Kabul, Islamabad. Taliban, Taliban],' shouted a group of mullahs who had gathered at the Lahore High Court in May 1994 soon after Taliban forces had captured Kandahar. They were there for the hearing of a blasphemy case against two Christians. 'Come forward our Taliban to protect Islam in Pakistan.' The slogans were a manifestation of the heady sense of power generated among the religious zealots in Pakistan by the success of the Afghan Taliban. Some of the local militant groups sought to replicate the Taliban's sharia-based system in the border areas of the North West Frontier Province.

The Taliban also helped reinforce the old jihad ties between Pakistani sectarian groups and drug-smuggling cartels in Afghanistan. This mutually beneficial relationship resulted in the 'Islamization of criminal activities'. Afghanistan became a safe haven for Pakistani jihadist and Islamic extremist groups. Inspired by a Sunni revolution and anti-Shia jihad, hundreds of Islamic zealots joined the Taliban-operated terror training in Afghanistan. SSP and LeJ militants were also reportedly involved in the massacres of Shias and in the battle against the opposition Northern Alliance forces. The conservative Afghan regime gave protection to Basra and to some other terrorists wanted by Islamabad on murder charges. During their stay in Afghanistan, the fugitives developed close links with al-Qaeda. Basra was the chief of the Khalid bin Walid training camp in the Sarobi district near Kabul. Pakistani authorities, who backed the Afghan conservative regime, remained indifferent or sometimes consciously looked the other way to this dangerous nexus.

Most of the LeJ cadres were also involved in Pakistan's proxy war in Kashmir. The continuing state patronage of Islamic militancy in return produced an escalation in domestic sectarian conflict. The two were closely intertwined. Pakistan's elected civilian governments in the 1990s had to bear the brunt of sectarian violence and the resultant insecurity and alienation it generated. Both the Benazir Bhutto and Nawaz Sharif governments took steps to combat sectarianism but, given the military's backing for regional jihad, those efforts failed. The jihad connection made the sectarian militants more strident and with easy access to sophisticated weapons they turned more violent.

By the mid 1990s, sectarian violence had spread from traditional arenas in Punjab and the northern region to urban heartlands. The nature of the attacks also changed. The initial pattern of targeting leaders, diplomats and other public figures extended to mosques and religious processions. Government functionaries, judges, police officers and doctors were assassinated because of their faith. In 1995, more than 250 people were killed in targeted attacks on Shia worshipping places in Karachi and other parts of the country. In 1997, celebrations of the 50th year of Pakistan's creation were accompanied by an unprecedented wave of sectarian killings. More than 100 people, most of them Shias, were killed in ten days in the run up to the celebrations in August that year. Riaz Basra was blamed for the massacre.

The widespread violence forced the government to take tougher action against sectarian organizations. Dozens of LeJ militants were killed by the police on orders of Shahbaz Sharif, the Chief Minister of Punjab, which had become the main centre of sectarian violence. For the government, extrajudicial killings appeared the only way to combat the highly motivated and well trained militants. Because of death threats, the judges of the lower judiciary – and even some of the superior judiciary – were reluctant to hear cases that involved leaders of LeJ and other powerful sectarian groups. In 1997, the then Chief Justice of the Supreme Court of Pakistan, Sajjad Ali Shah, asked the authorities to send him a list of the judges who avoided such cases.[20]

LeJ retaliated by plotting to kill Prime Minister Nawaz Sharif, his brother Shahbaz and other senior members of his government. In January 1999, Nawaz Sharif escaped an attempt on his life when a bomb tied to a bridge close to his house in Lahore exploded just a few minutes before his cavalcade was to pass.[21] Basra, who was at the top of the list of most wanted terrorists, remained elusive. The Taliban authorities ignored several requests from the Pakistani authorities to extradite him saying that he was a great 'mujahid'.

On 14 August 2001, General Musharraf outlawed LeJ and ordered a nationwide crackdown on the sectarian militants. The decision came in the wake of a series of attacks on Shia mosques and Christian churches. In a nationwide speech on the 55th anniversary of Pakistan's independence, the military ruler vowed to root out what he described as the 'most shameful and despicable examples of terrorism'.[22] Five months later, on 12 January 2002, he banned another five militant and sectarian organizations, including the SSP. It was largely pressure from the international community in the aftermath of 9/11 that forced Musharraf to act against the Islamic extremists.

The fall of the Taliban regime came as a huge blow to LeJ and other militant groups, which had used Afghanistan as a base for ideological and military training for years. Basra fled to Pakistan with hundreds of his followers who had fought alongside the Taliban against the US forces. The militants returning home launched a new jihad against 'internal enemies'. In coordination with al-Qaeda and other groups, LeJ unleashed a series of terror attacks targeting western interests and Shia and Christian worshipping places. The footprints of LeJ could be found in the attacks on the US Consulate in Karachi in May 2002 and in a car-bomb attack outside the Sheraton Hotel, which killed some 12 French engineers.[23]

On 30 January 2003, the US State Department added LeJ to its list of terrorist organizations and to those outfits covered under the executive order. Announcing the decision, a State Department spokesman said that LeJ activists had ties with al-Qaeda and the Taliban, in addition to LeJ involvement in the killing of American citizens. Investigations had shown that the group was responsible for the deaths of two American consulate officials who were killed when gunmen ambushed their vehicles on a busy road in Karachi in March 1995. Garry C. Durrell, aged 45, an undercover CIA official who was sitting on the back seat of a Hilux van died on the spot, while Jackie Van Landingham, 33, a consulate secretary, succumbed to her injuries on the way to hospital. A third employee, Mark McCloy, escaped with a shot to his ankle.[24]

The killing of the American officials came amidst a surge in sectarian and factional violence that had led to hundreds of deaths in Karachi, making it one of the most dangerous cities in the world. But it was the first time foreigners were targeted. Investigations indicated that the daring attack on the diplomatic vehicle was LeJ seeking revenge for the extradition to the USA of Ramzi Yousuf. The pattern of the attacks indicated that the same gang of terrorists involved in the attacks on Shia mosques weeks before could also be involved in the killing of American officials.[25]

Pakistani authorities vigorously targeted LeJ following a series of attacks that jolted Pakistan in the aftermath of the US invasion of Afghanistan. During 2002, the security forces met with major success when they killed or captured a significant number of LeJ activists. Those who were killed also included two top LeJ leaders, Basra and Asif Ramzi. Basra and his three associates were killed in May that year in a shoot-out with police near Mailsi in Multan.[26] Ramzi, believed to be the second-in-command to Basra, was killed in December in an explosion at a chemical warehouse on the outskirts of Karachi.[27] One of the most wanted terrorists, he was involved in more than 80 cases of murder and was wanted for the attacks on the US Consulate and Sheraton Hotel. Ramzi was the key link between the local militants and al-Qaeda trying to regroup in Pakistan. Pakistani and US security officials suspected that Ramzi had manufactured the explosives used in the US Consulate attack.

On 17 June 2002, the security forces captured another notorious LeJ leader, Akram Lahori, wanted in more than two dozen murder cases. A deputy to Basra, he was a key planner of various sectarian-based terrorist attacks in Karachi and was believed to have trained many potential suicide bombers. Despite those setbacks, however, the group appeared to retain a substantial capacity to strike, and continued to provide logistical support and personnel to al-Qaeda and Taliban operating from their bases in Pakistan's tribal region. The death of senior LeJ leaders did not bring any respite to the violence. A new breed of well-trained and battle-hardened militants took over the charge.

The increasing use of suicide bombing in terror attacks gave a new and more dangerous dimension to the sectarian war. Both Shias and Sunnis started deploying suicide bombers to inflict maximum casualties. Mosques, religious processions and rallies became the prime targets of suicide attacks in the sectarian war. Unlike suicide bombers elsewhere who simply detonated their explosive-strapped bodies, Pakistani militants hurled grenades and fired on the crowd before blowing themselves up in order to cause maximum damage.[28]

Poverty, unemployment, romantic notions of jihad and the growing influence of radical Islamic groups were the main reasons for a young man to turn into a suicide bomber. Between March 2002 and May 2004 there had been 20 cases of suicide bombing, which had killed more than 200 people. The targets varied from western nationals to Christian and Shia worshipping places. The majority of the attackers were unemployed and came from poor families. The 22-year-old Kamran Mir, who blew himself up inside a Christian church in Taxila in August 2002, killing several worshippers, was an unemployed school drop-out. He was trained by LeJ. The other two suicide bombers involved in the attack on a Shia religious procession in Quetta on 2 March 2004 were jobless former madrasa students. Abdul Nabi and Hidayatullah were made to believe that Shias were infidels and that they should be eliminated.

Despite their proscription, most of the militant groups continued their activities. Some of them resurfaced under new banners. Their leaders were temporarily detained, but none of them were tried in a court of law, even those against whom cases were pending. The example of Azam Tariq exposed the government's lack of sincerity in curbing religious extremism. While many politicians were prevented from fighting elections on patently frivolous grounds, the SSP leader, accused of sectarian killings, was allowed to contest from jail. He was freed after he agreed to join the pro-Musharraf alliance in the National Assembly. To retain Tariq's support the government ignored the non-bailable warrants of arrest issued against him by anti-terrorism courts. He was assassinated in 2003, apparently in a revenge attack by rival Shia militants.[29]

The 42-year-old SSP leader was notorious for his virulent anti-Shia rhetoric. He was charged in several murder cases which had also earned him a two year jail sentence in the mid 1990s. Born to a poor farming family in the small town of Chichawatni in Punjab province, he graduated from a local madrasa before joining SSP. A firebrand cleric, Tariq went from being an ordinary activist to the head of the SSP in less than ten years. As the group's murder index shot up, so did Tariq's popularity among Sunni zealots. He was elected to the National Assembly no less than four times. He formed a new party, Millat-e-Islam, after the government proscribed the SSP. He escaped many attempts on his life before falling to an assassin's bullet outside Islamabad.[30] His death led to a spate of revenge killings across the country. After Tariq's death his followers disintegrated into several splinter groups and many of them joined LeJ.

Though the government cracked down on those new groups which had replaced the outlawed outfits, the measures could not succeed in the absence of a coherent long-term strategy. It was easy enough for the militants to operate under new banners when their leaders moved around freely. Their hate literature was freely distributed across the country and pulpits of mosques were used by the mullahs to preach violence. The infrastructure of the banned sectarian groups and their capacity to carry out terrorist attacks remained unaffected, as was evident in the surge in sectarian violence during 2004. The pattern and scale of the violence demonstrated their extensive support network.

The gruesome killings of 40 people in twin bomb blasts in Multan on 7 October 2004 highlighted the depth of the sectarian violence that continued to plague Pakistan. The attack occurred at a large SSP rally marking the first anniversary of the assassination of their leader.[31] The bombing came a week after a suicide attack inside a crowded Shia mosque in the city of Sialkot in Punjab province, which had killed at least 30 worshippers.[32]

The rising tide of sectarian violence was also linked to the inability of intelligence agencies and the police to pre-empt and investigate sectarian crimes. The inaction could partly be attributed to fear of sectarian retaliation. Terrorists had killed many police officers who were investigating sectarian killings in Punjab and Karachi. In 2002, a police officer, Mohammed Jamil, was killed in Jhang after he had arrested several LeJ activists. In July 2004, a Rawalpindi police inspector was assassinated on his way to court to give evidence against the terrorists involved in an attack on a Shia mosque.[33] The penetration of law enforcing agencies by terrorist organizations was particularly perturbing. A suicide bomber responsible for the attack on a Shia mosque in Karachi in May 2004 turned out to be a police constable who was also a member of SSP. At least two policemen were involved in the attack on a Shia procession in Quetta on 2 March 2004.[34]

Notwithstanding Musharraf's promise to eradicate extremism, the issue had never been on the government's priority list. Without any legal mechanism or a long-term strategy in place, the administration was unable to prevent the flow of funds to unregulated madrasas and other religious groups involved in extremist activities. The government's failure to curb the jihadist madrasas had largely been responsible for fuelling Islamic extremism.

Most religious schools continued to preach hatred and intolerance. As a consequence, the ranks of sectarian extremists swelled. After the failed attempts on Musharraf's life, the administration launched raids on some radical madrasas, but such half-hearted and piecemeal measures could hardly improve the situation. Security agencies had raided sectarian seminaries only to back down under the pressure from Islamic parties. In August 2004, the police raided a mosque and a madrasa in Islamabad to arrest the prayer leader and his brother for their involvement in terrorist activities, including collaboration with al-Qaeda. The two were not only released and charges dropped, but they also retained their government jobs despite a long history of inciting sectarian hatred.

While Musharraf was praised by the international community for his role in the war on terror, the frequency and fierceness of sectarian terrorism continued to rise. The sectarian conflict in Pakistan was also a consequence of the military government's policy of marginalization of secular democratic forces. Despite his close alliance with the USA, Musharraf continued to rely on the religious right to counter the liberal opposition. The politics of expediency was also a major factor in his government's failure to curb religious extremism and sectarian forces.

6

KASHMIR

A GENERAL ON
A TIGHTROPE

The bitterness was palpable among the young fighters squatting on the floor of a dingy, cold room in their hideout outside Muzaffarabad. Some of them had just returned from a guerrilla operation on the other side of the Line of Control, dividing the disputed state. They looked frustrated and exhausted with their dishevelled beards and dirty clothes. Some of them were quiet while others talked about their future plans.

It was the most testing of times for the veterans of the 14-year-long guerrilla war after Musharraf had assured India that Pakistani territory would not be used for cross-border operations. Most of them were visibly frustrated and resigned to the fact that their jihad might well be coming to an end. 'We have no choice but to return to our homes,' said 30-year-old Mohammed Ashfaque, in a voice choked with emotion. A resident of Srinagar in Indian-controlled Kashmir, he had left his home and joined the guerrilla struggle some ten years ago after his brother was killed by Indian forces. However, others sounded more defiant and vowed not to lay down their weapons.

Meeting on the sidelines of the South Asian Regional summit in Islamabad, in January 2004, Musharraf and Indian Prime Minister Atal Bihari Vajpayee, had agreed to start a peace process to resolve all outstanding issues, including the Kashmir dispute, through bilateral negotiations. Musharraf was more categorical this time in his pledge to switch off the tap for Kashmiri militants. He had promised to curb the jihadists before, but in the past he had hedged his bets, ordering only a temporary halt, in the hope that India would reciprocate by sitting down for talks.[1]

With India back to the negotiating table and after two assassination attempts on him involving jihadist groups, Musharraf had more reason than ever to crack down on his home-grown militants. He could not allow the militants to take over the country. His tone became increasingly conciliatory towards India and he hinted that he was willing to drop Pakistan's long-standing demand that a plebiscite be held in Kashmir under the 1948 UN resolution to determine its status as long as India was equally forthcoming.

Musharraf's peace overtures had angered the militants, who accused him of having conceded too much ground to India by reversing Pakistan's long-standing aggressive Kashmir policy. The jihadists saw the war in ideological and civilizational terms. Any concession to the 'enemy' was therefore a very serious matter. Many Islamist leaders described the peace process as the beginning of the end of the Kashmir jihad.

Islamabad's policy shift was also driven by external factors. Musharraf's change of tack had also placed him on the horns of a serious dilemma. Islamabad's new role as a key US ally in the war on terror was no longer compatible with Pakistan's use of those proxies, which underscored its Kashmir policy. Yet, while Musharraf was quick to abandon support for the Taliban, he was reluctant to break ties with the militants waging 'a holy war' in Kashmir.

In fact, Musharraf had sought to use his country's broad cooperation with the United States to gain some leeway for continuing Pakistan's proxy war in the disputed Himalayan state. He tried to draw a fine line between what he described as 'freedom fighters' and terrorists. But America was not interested in such distinctions.

For more than half a century, the Kashmir cause had been almost the *raison d'être* for Pakistan's existence – not to mention for the role of the armed forces in the politics of the state.[2] Musharraf's assumption of power had alarmed India at the time, as he was known for his aggressive stance on Kashmir. Once in power, however, Musharraf displayed the pragmatic tendencies which would later cause him to disappoint fighters like Mohammed Ashfaque so bitterly. The first sign of a thaw came in June 2001, when the two countries agreed to a ceasefire along the 1,000-kilometre Line of Control, dividing the Indian and Pakistani sides of the disputed territory.[3] That helped to ease tensions and cleared the way for the first high level government contact between the two countries. In July 2001, the Indian Prime Minister, Atal Bihari Vajpayee, invited Musharraf for talks after dropping his precondition that Pakistan should first put an end to the infiltration of militants into Kashmir. That put the onus on Musharraf to come up with some offer to defuse tensions.

Musharraf was under tremendous strain when he proceeded to Delhi for talks with the Indian leader. Closely watched by both hardliners and peaceniks, often with contrary agendas, General Musharraf walked a political tightrope. He was under scrutiny, not only by the conservative, militant Islamic groups, but also by the hardline generals. The Jamaat-i-Islami and Islamic militant groups had warned him not to deviate from a single point of the Kashmir agenda.[4] His own future was at stake, and dependent on the outcome of the most crucial diplomatic mission he had ever undertaken. His hardline generals were opposed to any concession on Kashmir. The officers, a number of whom had served in the ISI, argued that it was the 'success of jihad' that had forced India to come to the negotiating table. They wanted Musharraf to continue supporting the Islamic militants fighting the Indian forces.

Although he had appeared stronger with his ascension to the presidency, Musharraf continued to face growing domestic opposition to the perpetuation of military rule. The pressure on Musharraf not to let the talks fail was enormous, as Pakistani leaders had constantly been calling for a negotiated settlement of disputes with India. However, any room to manoeuvre was restricted by the long-standing, thorny Kashmir issue, which was the major cause for the festering conflict in the region.

While the summit was made possible largely because of strong international pressure,[5] it had created its own dynamics. There were strong internal pressures forcing both countries to start a dialogue. For Musharraf, in order to prevent Pakistan from economic collapse, it was important to ease tension with India. A few weeks before his departure to India, in an interview on Pakistan state television, he had declared that Pakistan's economy was not compatible with its defence capability. A de-escalation was necessary, to win the support of the international community and to restart the flow of foreign aid.

On the very first evening of the summit, Musharraf gave a speech which seemed to push all the right buttons: 'The legacy of the past years was not a happy one ... blood has been spilt, precious lives have been lost.we must not allow the past to dictate the future,' he declared in his speech at the Indian President's dinner.[6] Musharraf's call for peace changed the atmosphere and set a positive tone for the summit. The General seemed to have established a good rapport with the ageing Indian Prime Minister. Unlike any other summit, the Agra summit had no prior agreed-upon agenda and most of the meetings were one-on-one.

Inevitably though, the summit ended in a stalemate on 16 July 2001, with the two leaders unable to agree on the wording of the declaration.[7] The deadlock did not come as a surprise. The final breakdown came when India refused to accept the centrality of the Kashmir issue and insisted on including the question of 'cross-border terrorism' in the declaration. Pakistan also showed its reservations over the reference to the Agra process as a continuation of the Simla and Lahore declarations.[8] Both sides blamed each other of intransigence, but the reality was that neither leader was prepared to resist pressure from their respective hardliners.

Musharraf's position certainly didn't leave much room for compromise in negotiations. Never before had a Pakistani leader brought Kashmir to the centre of the summit table as forcefully as he did. His blunt talk with the Indian media editors on 16 July, which was televised by several networks, was also used by the Indian hardliners to obstruct an accord. The mood on the Indian side turned visibly bitter when Musharraf declared there should not be any illusion that the main issue confronting the two countries was Kashmir. 'I will keep saying it whether anyone likes it or not,' he said.

All was not lost, however.[9] Musharraf and Vajpayee bade each other goodbye with a promise to meet again and pick up the threads from there. Despite the acrimony and bitterness that marked its closure, the Agra summit had broken the ice and revived the process of dialogue which had frozen after the Kargil conflict in the summer of 1999. The Indian Prime Minister accepted Pakistan's invitation for a return visit to Islamabad. It was also agreed to hold summit meetings between the Indian and Pakistani leaders once a year, and biannual talks at the foreign ministerial level to discuss issues relating to peace, security, confidence-building measures, Kashmir, narcotics and terrorism.

Not surprisingly, the stalemate at Agra was hailed by extremists in both India and Pakistan, who hoped to thrive in an atmosphere of tension. Islamic militant groups like LeT intensified suicide attacks in Kashmir and vowed to extend attacks inside India. Musharraf had provoked the ire of Islamic fundamentalists when he warned them against religious terrorism and militancy and tried to restrict the activities of militant groups, many of whom were fighting in Kashmir.

Even more disturbing was the resumption of the exchange of artillery fire along the Line of Control, breaking the eight-month-old ceasefire. With the intensification of guerrilla attacks, India stepped up efforts to get Pakistan branded as a terrorist state. But this attempt to isolate Pakistan received a setback, as Musharraf's decision to support the US-led war in Afghanistan, improved Islamabad's international standing.

The 11 September terrorist attacks and their aftermath had changed the entire regional security scenario and triggered a rapid downslide in India-Pakistan relations. Worried with Pakistan's role as a key US strategic ally, India lost no time in urging Washington not to forget its sufferings from 'Pakistani-backed cross-border terrorism'. New Delhi tried to use the 'war on terror' to its advantage. It portrayed the Kashmir problem purely as a matter of combating terrorism and made the case that it also had the right to pursue militants from Pakistani-controlled Kashmir, exactly as the USA hunted down al-Qaeda and the Taliban in Afghanistan.[10]

The tension mounted further in October 2001, following the LeT suicide attack by militants on the Kashmir assembly building in Srinagar which claimed 36 lives. The incident occurred as US forces were in the last stages of preparation to launch an attack on Afghanistan. Indian leaders and military commanders warned of 'hot pursuit', sending troops into Pakistani-controlled Azad Kashmir to destroy militant camps there.[11] Musharraf denounced the attack as an act of terrorism, but that failed to pacify India. Both countries traded accusations, backed by an 'ominous troop build-up' along the border.

The situation raised serious concerns in Washington. Fearing that a fire could break out at any time in the base camp of its anti-terror campaign, the USA rushed its Secretary of State, Colin Powell, to India and Pakistan. The Bush administration, which had initially chosen to distance itself from the Kashmir conflict, showed greater enthusiasm to defuse tensions. Powell succeeded in persuading India and Pakistan to exercise restraint, but it was only a matter of time before the situation flared up again. A terrorist attack on the Indian Parliament on 13 December renewed the threat of war.

India quickly blamed two Pakistani-based Islamic militant groups, JeM and LeT, for the attack. This audacious raid on the symbol of Indian power brought the two newly nuclear-powered nations once again to the brink of war. India retaliated by severing diplomatic relations and cut rail and air communications and put Pakistan on notice to rein in the militant groups or face the consequences of war. The gravity of the terrorist attack and the post-9/11 global security environment provided India the excuse to consider military action, to stop what it described, as cross-border terrorism.[12] Meanwhile, India demanded that Pakistan hand over 20 'most wanted terrorists', including Masood Azhar, Ahmed Omar Saeed Sheikh and five other men involved in the December 1999 hijacking of an Indian Airlines plane. The new Bush doctrine of pre-emptive strikes against the source of terrorism and the changes in the international rules of engagement afforded India the chance to engage Pakistan in brinkmanship.

In the third week of December, India launched 'Operation Parakaram' (Valour), which constituted the heaviest Indian troop mobilization since the 1971 war. It was a deliberate move by New Delhi, amidst the war on terror, to threaten Pakistan with military strikes if Islamabad did not stop sponsoring cross-border terrorism. There was every indication that India would not shy away from going to war. With Pakistan's counter-mobilization, nearly one million troops sat eyeball to eyeball across the India-Pakistan border. Both countries moved ballistic missiles and troops close to their shared border. There was a considerable risk of nuclear escalation.

The threat of war, coupled with US pressure, forced Pakistan to take action against the Islamic militant groups. On 12 January 2002, Musharraf banned LeT and JeM, which were blamed by India for the 13 December attack. He promised not to let Pakistani territory be used for cross-border terrorism.[13] Some two thousand activists of banned extremist groups were detained in a nationwide crackdown.

Musharraf, however, made it very clear that the measures against the Islamic extremist groups did not change his position on Kashmir. 'Kashmir runs in our blood. No Pakistani can afford to severe links with Kashmir. We will continue to give all diplomatic, political and moral support to the Kashmiris,' he declared.[14]

India reacted positively to Musharraf's 12 January speech and subsequent moves to curb the militants. Nevertheless, it kept its military on high alert and in forward positions. The Indian leaders wanted to see whether Musharraf's pledge was translated into practice. They refused to resume negotiations and normalize relations with Pakistan until all their conditions were met, including their extradition demands.

Musharraf's 12 January speech drew domestic as well international, support. But the measures taken by his government were insufficient against the activities of the jihadist groups. The ban was not applied to Pakistani-controlled Kashmir, or the semi-autonomous tribal areas bordering Afghanistan, which enabled militant organizations to shift their infrastructure and cadres to these regions. Hundreds of Islamic militants, returning from Afghanistan after the collapse of the Taliban regime in December 2001, had moved to the Pakistani part of Kashmir and were ready to join the armed struggle on the other side of the border. Most of these militants belonged to the three outlawed Islamic groups.

It became apparent that, while promising to curb Islamic extremism and sectarianism, Musharraf was still not willing to completely de-link Islamabad's connection with the Kashmiri militants. Meanwhile, India's refusal to pull back troops from advance positions and resume negotiations with Pakistan also tied his hands. Cross-border infiltration of militants into Indian-controlled Kashmir slowed down, but never completely stopped. Most of the militants detained following the 12 January declaration, were released. On 20 March 2002, the CIA chief, George Tenet, told the United States Senate Armed Services Committee that the chances of war in the region were the highest since 1971.

In the midst of the military stand-off with India, Musharraf decided to hold a referendum to extend his term in the office of President. In his address to the nation in March 2001, Musharraf declared his intent to enter politics and stay at the helm, a far cry from the 'reluctant coup-maker' of October 1999. With a feeling of déjà vu in the air, Musharraf announced that he was seeking public approval for an extension of his tenure in office, for an additional five years beyond the three-year-period stipulated by the Supreme Court.[15] The General also announced plans to introduce a new political formula, which he claimed was in conformity with the country's requirement for progress and stability. He declared that the military would continue to play a dominant role in the new political system, which was to emerge after the parliamentary elections scheduled for October 2002. Predictably, Musharraf received more than 90 per cent of the votes in a highly rigged referendum held in April 2002. The dubious polls not only dented Musharraf's credibility, but also sharpened the political polarization as the country braced for a possible war.[16]

A series of suicide attacks by militants on a bus and in the residential quarters of an Indian army camp in Kaluchak in Kashmir on 14 May 2002 killed 35 people, mainly women and children, and brought the region closer to the nuclear precipice. Free of Islamabad's control, the militants had tried to push the two countries towards a military conflict. India quickly moved its forces to forward positions on war alert. It also expelled Pakistan's ambassador, closing the last line of direct communication with Islamabad. With missiles and heavy weapons in place, an Indian attack appeared imminent between 29 and 31 May.[17] Nuclear signalling from both sides reminded the world of the gravity of the situation. Some Pakistani leaders openly warned of using nuclear weapons to counter India's overwhelming conventional military superiority.[18] In the third week of May, Pakistan tested a series of nuclear-capable ballistic missiles and stepped up its nuclear weapons programme.[19]

As the world faced perhaps its tensest nuclear stand-off since the Cuban missile crisis in 1962, the USA and Britain launched frantic diplomatic efforts to defuse the situation. President Bush and Colin Powell called the Indian and Pakistani leaders several times, urging them to pull back. On 28 May, the British Foreign Secretary, Jack Straw, visited Islamabad and asked Musharraf to take tougher measures to counter cross-border terrorism. He reminded Pakistan that as a UN member it had the responsibility to bear down 'effectively and consistently on all forms of terrorism, including cross-border terrorism'.[20] In Delhi the next day, Straw called on the Indian leaders to exercise restraint. He also told them that Musharraf had promised to close down 'terrorist camps' operating in Pakistani-administered Kashmir and curb infiltration into India.

Serious strains had emerged in relations between Washington and Islamabad after reports that the ISI was still linked with the militant groups. On 31 May, Colin Powell publicly accused Pakistan of continuing infiltration across the Line of Control, despite Musharraf's assurance that it would be halted.[21] The following day, Musharraf told the BBC that he had issued instructions to end the crossing and stop all militant activities. But the statement did not satisfy the Bush administration which had demanded that Pakistan shut down cross-border infiltration permanently. 'When and if, it does stop, it must also stop permanently,' Colin Powell retorted. International patience was clearly running out with Musharraf's game of deception.

Musharraf was firmly wedged between a rock and a hard place. He sincerely wanted to prevent a war, but at the same time did not want to be seen as the leader who gave up his country's 'sacred' cause: Kashmir. He badly needed a face-saving device if he was to take further steps backward to meet the expectations of the international community. Musharraf tried desperately to maintain his balancing act. His 'blow hot, blow cold' posture accurately reflected the difficulties he faced at home, where he was, once again, taking a controversial position on a sensitive issue.

On 1 June, the USA, Britain, France, Canada, Japan, Australia and some other countries, issued travel advisories asking their citizens to leave India immediately and warning others against travelling to the country.[22] Pakistan was already on the 'travel advisory' list after 9/11. The warning led to the exodus of thousands of businessmen, visitors, tourists and diplomatic personnel from India. This threatened the closure of foreign and multinational companies and caused much annoyance in Delhi, which perceived the advisory as an attempt to pressure it against launching an attack on Pakistan.

Once again, intensive US intervention was the key to walking both sides back from the brink. On 6 June, the US Deputy Secretary of State, Richard Armitage, arrived in Islamabad to build on Straw's visit and hammer out a deal between India and Pakistan. A former wrestler and a veteran diplomat, Armitage was known for his blunt talking. He had met Musharraf several times in the past and appeared to have developed a good rapport with the Pakistani military leader.

Armitage had one critical objective when he arrived for talks at the sprawling presidential secretariat at the Margala foothills on the afternoon of 6 June: to extract an assurance from Musharraf that would satisfy India and remove the threat of a potential nuclear war.[23] Musharraf had previously pledged to stop the infiltration of Islamic militants into Kashmir, but Armitage wanted him to go one step further. The talks between the two men had stretched to two hours, when Armitage put the critical question: 'What can I tell the Indians?' he asked. He wanted to know whether Musharraf would agree to a 'permanent end' to the cross-border terrorist activity long accepted by Pakistan. 'Yes,' Musharraf replied. An elated Armitage flew to Delhi the next morning to brief the Indian leaders on his talks with Musharraf.[24]

Musharraf's agreement to the word 'permanent', backed by US assurances to India that he would keep his word, immediately led to the easing of tension. It was a hugely significant foreign policy victory for India, which, for more than a decade, had sought an end to the cross-border terrorist attacks. Indeed, Musharraf had no other option, as his refusal to concede would have had disastrous consequences. 'If Pakistan had not agreed to end infiltration, and America had not conveyed that guarantee to India, then war could not have been averted,' Vajpayee told an Indian newspaper a week later.

The Musharraf-Armitage agreement was a turning point in Pakistan's long-standing policy of using militancy as an instrument for its proxy war in Kashmir and paved the way for a new relationship between two nations long divided by a bloody, tense history. In return for his concession, Musharraf received private assurances from US officials that they would stay involved. On 5 June, President Bush had called Musharraf and gave his firm commitment that his administration would remain engaged to resolve the Kashmir conflict. Musharraf told Armitage that he expected an early and substantial response from the Indian side to make his action sustainable.[25]

Within days of Armitage's departure, a thaw was evident. India responded to Musharraf's steps to curb cross-border terrorism by moving its naval fleet back to its base and allowed commercial over-flights. It also announced the revival of diplomatic relations with Pakistan. That effectively ended the longest military stand-off between the two countries.

Pakistan's military and the ISI had always kept a fairly tight control on their militant clients and the restrictions resulted in an immediate drop in the infiltration of militants into Kashmir. But it never completely stopped. Some militant groups were not prepared to toe the new Pakistani line and continued to send their men into Kashmir. Pakistani officials argued that it was impossible to completely seal the LoC.[26] For Musharraf, the major challenge was how to rein in the powerful militant groups. Predictably, his decision to stop cross-border infiltration, evoked angry reactions from the militant groups who, for more than a decade, had fought Pakistan's proxy war.

The atmosphere in the room was grim. A sense of unease gripped the two dozen guerrilla commanders, who had come to meet with a senior ISI officer at an army base in Muzaffarabad in the last week of May. The capital of Pakistani-controlled Azad Kashmir had long been the headquarters of more than a dozen Kashmiri militant groups. Some two hundred kilometres from Islamabad, the city was at an equal distance from Srinagar, the capital of Indian-administered Kashmir.

'We don't have a choice given the tremendous pressure on Pakistan,' Major-General-Khalid Mahmood told them. 'So, you have to stop all cross-border operations.' Several of the guerrilla commanders leapt to their feet, shouting that Pakistan should not surrender to Indian and American pressure. 'After ditching the Taliban, Musharraf has now betrayed the Kashmiri cause,' said a senior commander belonging to HuM, one of the largest Islamic militant groups involved in the separatist war in Kashmir. 'How can we accept this?' The commanders were bitter and vengeful, and left the meeting declining the officer's invitation to join him for lunch.

This outburst of anger towards Musharraf and his policies appeared logical. Thousands of militants had perished fighting Pakistan's war in Kashmir. Islamic militant leaders, who had depended for over a decade on the active support of Pakistan's army for their cross-border guerrilla actions, viewed Islamabad's move as a betrayal of the Kashmiri freedom struggle. 'We have lost so many friends, brothers and relatives in the Kashmir struggle. What was that for?' asked Amiruddin, a veteran Kashmiri guerrilla fighter. He reflected the sentiments of thousands of jihadist cadres trained and armed by the Pakistani military establishment. 'We are not going to sit quietly.'

The orders came as hundreds of fresh guerrillas were waiting at their base camps in Azad Kashmir to cross the border. It was generally at that time of the year that infiltration took place. 'The volunteers are becoming increasingly upset over the delay. They have not been informed about Pakistan's ban,' said the commander. He complained that the communication link between the guerrilla fighters inside Indian Kashmir and their base on the Pakistani side had been cut off and that training centres inside Azad Kashmir had been closed down. 'Many of our colleagues are stuck across the border without reinforcements and supplies,' he said.

Pakistan's decision to withdraw support had caused a setback to the militancy, but did not bring it to an end. The militant infrastructure remained intact and outlawed groups continued working, either under new banners, or merged into others. Hundreds of Pakistani fighters who were inside Kashmir at that point had continued their jihad, ignoring Pakistan's policy shift. Most militant leaders hoped that the restrictions were temporary and still had faith in the army. 'The army will always be our ally,' a senior militant commander told me.

Facing down the jihadists was not going to be an easy task for Musharraf. Since an indigenous insurrection against Indian domination broke out in Kashmir in 1989, some 10,000 fighters had crossed the border to help their Kashmiri brethren. They were not prepared to give up the cause on Islamabad's orders. As an inevitable consequence of Pakistan's policy of using jihad as an instrument of covert war, some elements within the intelligence agencies had been radicalized by the Islamists. The handlers had become coloured by the ideology of the militants. They were unhappy with Musharraf's decision to support America's war on Afghanistan's Islamic regime, which they had helped install. But even deeper was the resentment on the reversal in Kashmir. There was a strong anti-American feeling in the military ranks. Many officers believed that western countries, particularly the USA, had not come to Pakistan's support when it faced the threat of war from its nuclear rival.

Once again Musharraf was walking a tightrope. His position had become even more tenuous after he ordered his troops to stop the infiltration. He had come to the conclusion that there was now a conflict of interest between the militants and the military. But it was not clear whether other army officers agreed with him. There was a strong feeling in the army that India was trying to humiliate them by dictating terms for peace. Some hardline retired generals, who had been responsible for organizing the Kashmiri 'jihad', warned Musharraf that there was a limit to how far the army would go along with a policy of using force against those who were seen as fighting for Pakistan's interest in Kashmir. Lt.-General Hamid Gul, a former ISI chief and a fiercely anti-American former commander, accused Musharraf of 'going too far in appeasing the west' and taking a 'step back' on the Kashmir issue. 'By calling those attacking the Indian forces, terrorists, General Musharraf is only echoing the Indian position,' he declared.[27]

Despite military de-escalation, there was a wide gap between what the Indian leaders demanded and what Musharraf could deliver. India's mistrust of the Pakistani military leadership had thwarted all moves by the international community to bring the two sides to the negotiating table. It was only after the relatively peaceful polls for the Kashmir state assembly in October 2002, that Delhi and Islamabad opened secret back-channel diplomacy. Beginning in April 2003, Vajpayee's Principal Secretary, Brajesh Mishra, and Musharraf's top aide, Tariq Aziz, held several meetings in London, Dubai and Bangkok exploring avenues to begin a peace process.[28]

A seasoned bureaucrat, Tariq Aziz was a college-mate of Musharraf's and had worked as his principal secretary after the military takeover.

A former income tax officer, he was more into political wheeling and dealing and had no experience of diplomacy. However, being Musharraf's closest aide, he was considered the best man for this secret and extremely delicate job. Even the foreign ministry was kept out of the loop. Facilitated by the USA, this was the first senior official contact between the two countries for nearly two years. Tariq Aziz was later appointed secretary of the National Security Council.

In April 2003, the Indian Prime Minister extended a 'hand of friendship' to Pakistan during a public address in Srinagar. Pakistan's Prime Minister, Zafarullah Khan Jamali, responded by speaking to Vajpayee and invited him to visit Islamabad.In yet another highly symbolic gesture, India announced the resumption of bus links with Pakistan. The twice-weekly coach service between Delhi and Lahore had been abruptly suspended 18 months earlier, after Islamic militants had attacked the Indian Parliament in Delhi. The bus service, which started in February 1999, had significant symbolic value. Vajpayee had travelled to Lahore by the inaugural coach for his historic meeting with Pakistan's then Prime Minister, Nawaz Sharif.

Given their deep-rooted mistrust of each other, the process remained a slow diplomatic dance, with the two governments circling one another warily, each making tentative offers. The efforts at that stage were largely aimed at de-escalation and the restoration of the situation that existed prior to the military stand-off, rather than any great leap forward.

Pakistan moved very cautiously, given its traditional suspicion of its much bigger, and militarily powerful, neighbour. It was reluctant to open its airspace to Indian planes and remove all trade barriers. Pakistan feared that lifting the overflight ban could provide India with an opportunity to establish close trade links with, and consolidate its influence in, Afghanistan. There were strong apprehensions in Islamabad that the emerging process could prove to be another false start if India raised the size of the table, rather than picking up the thread from previous talks.

Kashmir remained the thorniest issue as the two countries moved towards a rapprochement. The events of May and June a year before had indicated how quickly the situation could escalate into a fully fledged conflagration, with both countries appearing all too willing to engage in nuclear sabre-rattling. There was no sign of flexibility yet on the Kashmir issue on either side. While India was eager to demonstrate that the Kashmir violence was totally Pakistani sponsored, Pakistan appeared equally adamant to keep up the pressure on Delhi.

Although Musharraf had agreed to clamp down on militant groups, the situation on the ground did not change much. Pakistan's promise of a complete halt to support for the Islamic militants did not seem credible at that stage. Pakistani military officials contend that a total turnaround in Pakistan's policy could not be possible without some reciprocity from India, for example, reduction of troops and an end to human rights violations in the state. 'We will lose all leverage if we just pull out our support to the Kashmiris without any show of flexibility by India,' said a senior Pakistani official. 'In the absence of any light at the end of the Kashmiri tunnel, it would be hard for the government to sell any proposal for peace with India to its own people.' It was quite apparent that the military-backed administration was not ready to put the Kashmir issue on the backburner. The military officers, who stood by Musharraf when he moved away from Pakistan's long-standing policy of supporting the conservative Taliban regime in Afghanistan and joined the US-led coalition against terrorism, were not likely to maintain their loyalty towards him if he had decided to make a radical shift on the Kashmir issue.

With India agreeing to resume peace talks, Pakistan faced increasing pressure to come down hard on Islamic guerrilla groups and destroy militant infrastructure. A serious international concern was that Pakistan's inability to contain militancy could continue to be a significant obstacle to the normalization of relations between the two countries. While acknowledging that there had been a decrease in infiltration and that the level of violence in Kashmir had declined, Washington was not fully satisfied with the situation.

The situation then took a most dramatic turn in January 2004, when Vajpayee came to Islamabad to attend the seven-nation South Asian regional summit. Few had expected any breakthrough when the aged Indian Prime Minister went to pay a 'courtesy call' on Musharraf at the imposing presidential palace on 5 January. Although there had been hints of a possible meeting, nobody was sure until it actually happened. The outcome of the 65-minute parley between the two leaders went beyond anybody's expectations. Not only were some significant decisions taken to move the process of normalization forward, but a road map for further interaction was also clearly stated.

Most importantly, Musharraf pledged to prevent the use of the territory under Pakistan's control 'to support terrorism in any manner'. It was the first direct commitment of this nature since the Pakistani-backed armed insurgency in Kashmir began in 1989. The joint statement also declared that both leaders were 'confident' of reaching a peaceful settlement of all bilateral issues, including Kashmir. It was a great leap forward in the relations between the two countries, which had been on the brink of nuclear war just a year before.

The outcome of the Islamabad meeting was not the result of a sudden surge of goodwill. The script was prepared after intensive back-channel diplomacy between Brajesh Mishra and Tariq Aziz. From 1 to 4 January, the two officials were in regular contact. Mishra also met with the ISI chief, Lt.-General Ehsan ul-Haq. Those interactions remained secret, even from Pakistani foreign ministry officials. Only the President's Chief of Army Staff, General Hamid, and Tariq Aziz were involved in the preparation of the joint communiqué. Foreign Secretary, Riaz Khokar, was handed a copy just a few hours before the summit meeting.[29] Musharraf's change of course on the Kashmir policy indicated that the Pakistani military establishment had finally acknowledged that support for militancy could not dislodge India from the disputed land. But there had also been concern that, in the absence of such pressure, India would not agree to a negotiated settlement of the Kashmir dispute. Vajpayee's agreement on a composite dialogue on all bilateral issues, including Kashmir, gave Musharraf some leeway to convince his generals of the need for peace with India.

Musharraf went one step further when he declared his readiness to consider all possible alternatives for the Kashmir solution. In November 2004, he outlined a step-by-step approach towards resolving the decades-old dispute, which involved making some parts of the disputed territory independent or placing them under joint Indian-Pakistani control. Indeed, the suggestion to identify the region, demilitarize it and change its status, signified a radical shift in Pakistan's Kashmir policy.[30]

Though premature, the proposal indicated a significant come-down from Pakistan's traditional hardline position of holding a plebiscite, under the 1948 UN resolution that required Kashmiris alone to decide their political future. For the first time, a Pakistani leader had suggested making the territory a joint protectorate.

Finding a solution acceptable to both sides had always been a difficult task, even in the best of circumstances, as Kashmir has been so deeply intertwined with India and Pakistan's perceptions of national security and identity. Domestic political compulsions had made the issue more complex. What had made securing peace even more difficult was the past baggage of mistrust and suspicion the two nations continued to carry. It had been such an accident-prone relationship that any incident could derail the whole process.

Musharraf's turnaround divided the separatist movement in Indian-administered Kashmir. The moderate elements supported his peace initiatives. For them, militancy could not provide the solution to the festering problem and it was time for the political parties to play their roles for a negotiated settlement of the issue. Once dismissed by the Pakistani military establishment as 'weak links', the moderate Kashmiri leaders became Musharraf's new allies.

Mirwaiz Umar Farooq, a charismatic young Kashmiri leader, remembered his first meeting with Musharraf in New York in September 2001, when the Pakistani military leader accused him of being 'cowardly' for suggesting a non-militant course towards the solution of the Kashmir problem. 'The meeting ended on a bitter note,' Mirwaiz recalled when I met him in his heavily guarded house in Srinagar in April 2005.

The mood had completely changed when the two met again in Holland three years later, following the Indo-Pak rapprochement. 'It was I this time asking him to go slow on the peace process. Musharraf sounded too enthusiastic about the prospect of reaching a settlement,' Mirwaiz said. The Kashmiri leader was thrown into separatist politics as a teenager after the death of his father, Mirwaiz Maulvi Farooq, in 1989. As a prayer leader at Srinagar's Jamia Masjid, he wielded considerable spiritual and political influence in the disputed state. He led the moderate faction of the All Parties Hurriyat (Freedom) Conference (APHC), a loose coalition of more than 32 organizations, that wanted militancy to give way to political struggle. 'Militancy has played an important role in drawing international attention to the Kashmir issue, but now we should concentrate on a political struggle,' he declared.[31] The moderates were also concerned about the struggle falling into the hands of the extremists.

The resumption of the Indo-Pak talks was fully backed by the moderates, though Musharraf's change of tack shocked the hardliners who had been fighting for the annexation of the entire disputed state with Pakistan. Their bitterness was palpable when the bus service between Srinagar and Muzaffarabad was restored on 7 April 2005, after a 57-year hiatus. It was a momentous occasion when the new Indian Prime Minister, Manmohan Singh, waved off the first bus with its 19 passengers. Described as the mother of all confidence-building measures between India and Pakistan, the bus link reunited divided Kashmiri families. But for the militants it was a betrayal of their cause.[32] In an attempt to derail the peace process, the militants attacked the Tourist Reception Centre in Srinagar, where the passengers of the inaugural bus were kept under strict security.

'This is not what we have sacrificed thousands of lives for,' Syed Ali Shah Geelani, the head of his own faction of APHC, told me when we met at his Srinagar residence, a day after the bus had left for Muzaffarabad.[33] The 70-year-old, white-bearded Geelani was the chief of Jamaat-i-Islami in Kashmir, and had close links with the Islamic militants fighting Pakistan's proxy war. For his ardent support for Pakistan, he was often described as an ISI agent until Musharraf's turnaround. With Pakistan now betting on the moderates, Geelani felt isolated. But his loyalty to Pakistan was unquestionable. 'Musharraf is destroying Pakistan. Things will change once he is gone,' he said.

7

THE WAR
COMES HOME

AL-QAEDA
IN PAKISTAN

On the edge of a busy highway, near the northern city of Kohat, hundreds of people would gather every day at a makeshift shrine to pay homage and pray for four al-Qaeda fighters killed in a gunfight with the Pakistani security forces. Colourful streamers tied to a pole raised over a pile of rocks marked the spot where the 'martyrs' had died. 'It is a sacred place where the blood of the soldiers of God was spilt,' Noor Mohammed, a local trader, said as he knelt to kiss a stone, still stained with blood.

The traffic slowed as a mark of respect as buses approached the memorial and the faithful alighted to pray and collect sand from the mound. 'It is holy earth,' said Abdul Ghani who, like many villagers, believed that it would bring God's blessings to his home. The shooting had occurred in the first week of July 2002, when police stopped a van carrying four Chechens at a security checkpoint in the village of Jarma.[1] Fleeing from Afghanistan, they were in search of a safe haven. The al-Qaeda militants, who were armed with machine guns and rocket launchers, fought for over an hour, but were outnumbered by the security forces and killed. Villagers thronged to the spot after the fighting, many of them embracing the dead, while others even took body parts to bury them inside the compounds of their houses.

They believed that martyrs would never die and their presence would bless their homes.

Hundreds of villagers took part in the funeral prayers of the four al-Qaeda fighters, whom they described as 'holy warriors'. Many policemen on duty had also joined the faithful. They had erected a sign naming the site 'martyrs of Islam square', and lit candles in memory of the dead. The shrine soon became the focus of anti-government agitation. Thousands of angry protesters blocked the highway for several hours shouting slogans in support of Osama bin Laden and against the USA. Clashes between the police and the protesters had continued for several days. Jarma was the second place in the North West Frontier Province with a shrine commemorating al-Qaeda fighters. Arwali Fort, in the Kurram tribal area bordering Afghanistan, had also been turned into a shrine earlier that year when several al-Qaeda fugitives were killed.

The war had come to Pakistan after the fall of the Taliban rule in Afghanistan. Thousands of al-Qaeda fighters fleeing the US bombardment of the Tora Bora[2] caves in eastern Afghanistan, crossed over unguarded mountain trails and disappeared into the lawless tribal areas. By mid December 2001, more than 1,000 al-Qaeda operatives, including most of the chief planners and, presumably, bin Laden himself, had managed to escape bombardment by American B-52s and attack helicopters that were plastering the mountainous terrain. Another wave of fugitives had entered Pakistan in March 2002, during the allied force's Operation Anaconda against al-Qaeda positions in the eastern Shahi Kot mountains. Many others followed in the next several weeks.[3]

There were not enough US troops to cover all possible escape routes and Pakistani forces had serious problems sealing the border. In early December there were only 1,300 US troops in Afghanistan, spread over 17 areas, and hardly one-third were acclimatized to the altitude.[4] Pakistani troops had entered the autonomous tribal areas only once before – in 1973 – to put down a revolt. It was a bloody 18-month fight and the officers hoped never to repeat it. Musharraf had spent two weeks negotiating with the tribal chieftains before they finally agreed to the deployment. Troops had just started moving into positions along the western border, when armed gunmen stormed the Indian Parliament on 13 December. India immediately went on a war footing, blaming Pakistani-based Islamic militants linked with al-Qaeda for the attack. Musharraf halted troop deployment to the Afghan border; he had to protect his eastern borders. Tora Bora fell three days later on 16 December. By that time, hundreds of al-Qaeda fighters had escaped into Pakistan, including many senior leaders. Many of them made their escape bribing Afghan warlords.[5] They journeyed through twisting mountainous passes – trails with a long history of smuggling – that linked eastern Afghanistan with Pakistan's lawless tribal region and melted in among sympathetic locals. At some places, particularly in the Tirah valley, the daunting mountains rose up to 10,000 feet, making the job of the Pakistani security forces extremely difficult.

In many cases, the soldiers looked the other way as foreign fighters crossed over to the Pakistani side and many in the ISI arranged safe passage for the fugitives. Then there was the question of legality. The lawless tribal regions were beyond Islamabad's rule. The government's writ only ran along the main roads, therefore security forces could not set up checkpoints on unfrequented routes. Pakistani intelligence agencies did not have any effective network there to check the movement of foreign fighters. Fearing an internal political backlash, Musharraf was also reluctant to go the whole hog to pursue the militants. He was not willing to launch large-scale military operations against al-Qaeda, while most of his troops were massed along the Indian border due to tensions over Kashmir.

The expansion of the war into Pakistan carried the risk of increasing political unrest, particularly when Musharraf's support for the United States had sparked considerable opposition from Islamic political parties. Anti-American and pro-bin Laden sentiments had run high in the North West Frontier Province in the immediate aftermath of the routing of Taliban rule. The increasing hostility of the local population had made the situation even more difficult for the security forces searching for al-Qaeda fugitives. Reports of the presence of US personnel in the border areas gave the situation an explosive twist. Covert US military units had been conducting reconnaissance operations inside Pakistan and had participated in raids on suspected al-Qaeda hideouts in the border region.[6] American forces had not only been active in Paktia and Paktika provinces in Afghanistan, but also in adjacent tribal areas in Pakistan where the government in Islamabad had only a limited writ. US operations on its territory had made the Pakistani government nervous and it wanted Washington to keep a low profile on the issue, which had also involved the presence of American warplanes, special operation troops and regular forces at four Pakistani bases. Islamic radical leaders threatened to intensify agitation if the troops did not stop the hunt for the al-Qaeda men sheltered by the locals. Heavily armed fugitives would fiercely resist Pakistani efforts to arrest them and scores were killed in clashes with the security forces. When cornered they would fight to the death.

bin Laden had around 3,000 Arab fighters with him when the US-led coalition forces invaded Afghanistan. There were many militants of other nationalities – Chechens, Uzbeks and East Asians. According to some estimates, only a few hundred of them were killed by US bombing or taken prisoner. Among the top leadership, only Mohammed Atef, the chief of al-Qaeda's political wing, had been killed; almost the entire leadership of the group was intact. Where did they go?

Fifteen hundred miles of a porous border with Pakistan was the major exit point for the fleeing militants. Many of them used Pakistan as a transit to the Gulf and other Arab countries. In many cases, they were helped by sympathetic Pakistani security officials and Arab diplomats, who provided the fugitives with money and transport to get out of the country. A Saudi-owned vessel was reported to have smuggled 150 al-Qaeda and Taliban to the Bangladeshi port of Chittagong.[7]

Most had stayed in Pakistan. The non-Arab Uzbeks, Chechens and Sudanese took shelter in the tribal region. It was, however, in Pakistan's crowded cities that most al-Qaeda operatives found refuge, as opposed to the country's network of fundamentalist Islamic schools or its isolated tribal villages. With the help of their allies among Pakistani militant organizations and supporters within the intelligence agencies, many al-Qaeda leaders moved to big urban centres from where they could regroup and revive contacts with operatives, within the country and abroad. Al-Qaeda had mutated into a form that was no less deadly and even more difficult to combat. Pakistani and American investigators were confronted with cells that were all over the place, developing a horizontal structure, without any apparent large centre of coordination.

Pakistani militant groups provided al-Qaeda with logistical support, safe houses, false documentation and, occasionally, manpower. The Pakistani intelligence community received sound evidence suggesting that bin Laden's deputy, Ayman al-Zawahiri, was al-Qaeda's principal contact with the Pakistani jihadist community. This nexus had been strengthened when hundreds of Pakistani militants who had received ideological and military training at al-Qaeda camps returned to Pakistan following the fall of the Taliban.

Al-Qaeda's connection with the local Islamic militant groups was fully revealed during the investigation of the kidnapping and murder of Daniel Pearl, a *Wall Street Journal* reporter. The *Journal's* South Asia bureau chief, who was 38 years old, vanished in January 2002 while researching a story on terrorism. In May, police found his body buried in a nursery on the outskirts of Karachi. Pakistani and US investigators determined that the reporter lost his life in a joint operation of Pakistani militants and al-Qaeda.[8]

Pearl's kidnapping was the first violent response of the al-Qaeda-linked Pakistani militant groups to the American attack on Afghanistan. It came just ten days after President Musharraf's 12 January speech in what appeared to be a retaliatory action by defiant Islamic militants. The murder was not only a retaliation for Musharraf's action against Islamic activists, but it was also meant to signal to the United States that its war against al-Qaeda was far from over and that its treatment of al Qaeda prisoners could have serious repercussions for US citizens. The kidnapping was planned to embarrass General Musharraf, particularly in light of the fact that it came at a crucial time. Musharraf was due to meet with President Bush at the White House in the first week of February, as a reward for his response to the crisis in Afghanistan.[9]

The kidnapping was conceived and organized by Ahmed Omar Saeed Sheikh.[10] The plot included two separate cells, one that trapped Pearl and publicized the abduction, and another that actually kidnapped and held him captive. It was mid January 2002 when Sheikh first met Pearl under the false name of 'Bashir'. A very articulate man, he convinced the journalist that he was an acolyte of an Islamic cleric with whom the reporter was seeking an interview. Following Sheikh's directive, Pearl proceeded to Karachi.[11]

Pearl was visibly excited about his 'scoop' when he left the office of the Associated Press in Karachi's posh Clifton district on the afternoon of 25 January 2002. He had pursued a story on the al-Qaeda network in Pakistan for several weeks and had been promised an interview that evening with a Muslim cleric, believed to have close links with Richard Reid, the 'shoe bomber', who was facing trial in the USA for attempting to blow up a passenger airliner. Reid, a British national who visited Pakistan shortly before the incident, was said by US officials to have trained with al-Qaeda. The man Pearl thought he was going to meet was Sheikh Mubarak Ali Shah Gilani, leader of a shadowy militant group called Tanzimul Fuqra, which had long been on the US State Department's list of terrorist organizations.[12] There was nothing amiss when Pearl called his wife Mariane, a freelance journalist, a few minutes before his scheduled meeting. 'He just told me he was heading for the restaurant,' said Mariane.[13]

Mariane had worked on various stories with her husband, but could not join him on his last project because of her advanced pregnancy. At seven in the evening, Pearl alighted from a taxi in front of the restaurant, Village, located in a busy downtown commercial district. He did not realize that he had walked into a trap. His zeal in following up the story was too strong for him to realize the dangers inherent in the situation. Instead of taking Pearl to the meeting he expected, a driver, arranged by Sheikh, drove him to a secluded nursery, where he was held for about a week before being killed.

In an e-mail message that also carried pictures of Pearl in chains, the captors put forward a list of demands, including the better treatment and release of Taliban prisoners held by Americans at Guantanamo, and the release of US F-16 fighter planes that Pakistan had already paid for; the planes hadn't been delivered because of US sanctions related to Islamabad's nuclear weapons programme. A second message gave a 24-hour deadline for their demands to be met or they would kill Pearl: 'We are weaker than some countries, but we are not shameless. We have investigated Daniel Pearl and we came to know that he is not a CIA official, but a Mossad agent. Therefore, we warn that if the United States does not meet our demands within 24 hours, then we will kill Daniel Pearl.'[14] By this time, Pearl was probably already dead. The investigators believed he was killed around 30 January, after two attempts to escape.[15]

Sheikh handed himself over to the ISI in Lahore on 5 February 2002, after security agencies detained some of his relatives. Sheikh told ISI agents that he had lost contact with the people holding Pearl and suspected that he might have been killed.[16] It was about this time that President Musharraf, visiting President Bush in Washington, told reporters that he was 'reasonably certain' that Pearl was alive and would be rescued. He did not give any indication that Sheikh was already in ISI custody. Instead, Sheikh's capture was announced a day after Musharraf left Washington. Pakistani authorities asserted that he was arrested on 12 February. The missing week raised questions about the ISI's motives.[17] It was still a mystery whether the President was informed by the spy agency of the actual situation when he was with President Bush. But, according to highly placed sources, ISI agents were confident they could cut a deal for Pearl's release by offering to release Sheikh in return. The plan probably would not have worked, however, as the people holding Pearl had different intentions.[18] Sheikh definitely lost control once Khalid Sheikh Mohammed arrived on the scene.

Sheikh refused to defend himself in his trial before an anti-terrorism court, saying, 'it was a waste of time,' and warned of a 'decisive war between Islam and the infidels'. He appeared defiant as the judge pronounced him guilty of conspiring in Pearl's kidnapping and sentenced him to death. 'We will see whether those who want to see me dead succeed or get killed first,' he declared as he was shifted to a death cell in Hyderabad prison.[19] His reference was clearly to Musharraf, whom he had already been plotting to assassinate.

Pakistani intelligence agencies were the least equipped to deal with the new situation that had developed after the fall of the Taliban regime. Hundreds of foreign operatives fleeing from Afghanistan were looking to turn Pakistan into a new base for their terror operations. A more sophisticated intelligence network was required to counter the new threat. Developments since 9/11 had led to radical changes in the ISI, but it still took several months for the agency to develop a sound counter-terrorism infrastructure to track the network, whose tentacles had spread from the inhospitable mountains in the lawless tribal region, to bustling city neigbourhoods.

Pakistani authorities set up a new Counter Terrorism Cell (CTC) within the ISI to hunt down al-Qaeda fugitives. Headed by a Brigadier, the cell worked closely with the FBI and CIA. It had set up a swift-acting internal anti-terrorism department with specially trained personnel. The spy agency had vast experience in intelligence and counter-intelligence activities, but fighting terrorism was an entirely new experience. Pakistan had also established a National Crisis Management Cell, within the Interior Ministry to meet the new terrorism challenge. Headed by an active-duty brigadier, the cell worked closely with the FBI.

With new high-tech equipment and better human intelligence in place, al-Qaeda operatives lurking in Pakistani cities became more vulnerable to capture. The CIA had developed extensive intelligence assets that had helped track important al-Qaeda leaders hiding in Pakistan. The agency had also used huge amounts of money to buy information. All of that had helped in netting top al-Qaeda operatives. It was in a crowded town, rather than the lawless tribal area, that the US and the Pakistani intelligence agents bagged their first big catch.

Just before dawn on 28 March 2002, scores of FBI agents and

members of Pakistani security forces stormed a two-storey modest house in Faisal colony, a middle-class neighbourhood in Faisalabad, one of Pakistan's largest industrial towns. Before the half-asleep inhabitants could realize what was happening, soldiers had swept in, breaking the main door and smashing the windows. Some of the men inside tried to reach for their weapons, but it was too late for any resistance. Those who tried to escape through the broken windows were shot by FBI agents. One died on the spot, another was hit in the groin and chest. The operation had been organized and conducted by the FBI and the CIA, which had been given a free hand by the Pakistani military government.

The lightning raid was conducted after electronic surveillance by American agents detected satellite phone calls from Afghanistan which pinpointed the location of one of al-Qaeda's two top operatives.[20] The Americans kept the information top secret and only President Musharraf and ISI chief, Lt.-General Ehsan ul-Haq, were kept in the picture.[21] After a thorough check, the agents finally established the identity of the wounded man lying on the floor in a pool of blood. He was the man they wanted to catch: Abu Zubaydah.

His face covered with a towel, Abu Zubaydah was placed in an armoured vehicle and driven immediately to a waiting plane. Once his condition stabilized, he was flown to US military headquarters at Bagram in Afghanistan for interrogation.[22] That night, the operation in Faisalabad and subsequent raids in the central Punjab city of Lahore netted more than 60 suspected terrorists, including 29 foreigners, mostly Arabs and Afghans. Among them were 13 Yemenis, three Palestinians, three Libyans and two Saudis.[23] That was the first major success in the hunt for al-Qaeda operatives who had fled from Afghanistan.

Abu Zubaydah, also known as Zayn al-Abidin Mohammed Husyan, had long been considered a key member of al-Qaeda's inner circle. Since the death of the al-Qaeda commander of military operations, Mohammed Atef, in a bomb attack in Afghanistan, he had moved up the organization's hierarchy. Abu Zubaydah had been an elusive suspect. Few photographs of him existed, he had used at least 37 aliases and was considered a master of disguise. Born to Palestinian parents in Saudi Arabia in 1971, Abu Zubaydah grew up in a Palestinian refugee camp in the Gaza strip, where he was active in Hamas, before he was recruited by al-Zawahiri's Islamic Jihad. He had a long history of involvement with the al-Qaeda. In 1999, a Jordanian military court sentenced him to death in absentia, for plotting to attack tourist sites in Jordan.[24]

A key recruiter for al-Qaeda, Abu Zubaydah was appointed as chief of operations by bin Laden in 1996.[25] He was responsible for training thousands of Islamic militants in al-Qaeda training camps in eastern Afghanistan. When bin Laden and his inner circle planned an attack, it was Abu Zubaydah who would contact the cells in the field to conduct them. Bin Laden put him in charge of the millennium plot to bomb the Radisson Hotel in Jordan and the Los Angeles International Airport on New Year's Day, 2000. He had also been in operational control of the attack on the USS *Cole* in October 2000. US investigators believed Abu Zubaydah knew names, faces and locations of al-Qaeda operatives the world over. His arrest came as a gold mine of information to the investigators and led to the arrest of Jose Padilla, the Hispanic American arrested in Chicago in May 2002, who was believed to be coming to the United States to let off a 'dirty', or radiological, bomb.

The al-Qaeda leader had developed strong connections with Pakistani Islamic militants groups during his stay in Peshawar, where he recruited and vetted al-Qaeda volunteers before sending them for training in Afghanistan. The house he was occupying in Faisalabad, was arranged by a member of Lashkar-e-Taiba. The central Punjab city had been a stronghold of the group and it was quite apparent that the al-Qaeda leader chose the city to set up his operational headquarters. Several members of the outlawed outfit were among those captured during the raid.[26] The fact that LeT had strong connections with Wahabi Saudi clerics may also be one of the reasons for the strengthening of its bond with al-Qaeda. The capture of Abu Zubaydah came as a serious blow to al-Qaeda, but the network nevertheless continued to operate in Pakistan.[27] The terrorist group was battered but not beaten. A motley collection of old hands and new recruits from among Pakistani militants had managed to form a nucleus that pushed forward with plans to attacks targets, both inside and outside Pakistan. The country's largest city and its commercial capital, Karachi, had turned into al-Qaeda's new operational headquarters. Even before 9/11, the city had been used by the militants as a transit point to Afghanistan. Several hijackers involved in the attacks in New York and Washington had passed through the city.

Scores of al-Qaeda operatives took shelter in the sprawling metropolis. Mainly rich Arab nationals, better at blending in, vanished into the mega-city of 12 million on the Arabian Sea. According to a senior police official, they were in lower-class and middle-class neighbourhoods –

they were everywhere. Endless clusters of apartments, teeming slums and a porous coastline, from which fugitives could slip away to the Persian Gulf countries, made the city an ideal place to hide. Hundreds of madrasas in slum areas run by radical mullahs also provided a safe haven for the Islamic radicals. Some of the al-Qaeda fugitives moved to more affluent districts in big apartment complexes, or even bought high-walled privacy.

Al-Qaeda decentralized its activities, as American and Pakistani intelligence agencies attacked its nerve centres. Many scattered again, travelling back and forth. The masterminds of the 11 September terrorist attacks, Khalid Sheikh Mohammed – known in intelligence circles as KSM – and Ramzi bin al-Shibh, made their base in the city with the help of a vast network of home-grown jihadists. Raids on militants' hideouts and homes had uncovered huge stashes of sophisticated weapons and electronic equipment that indicated their strong local links. In some cases, they also appeared to have received help from their sympathizers in the intelligence agencies and the police.

During 2002 and 2003, Karachi had virtually turned into a terror capital. Islamic militants carried out more than half a dozen terrorist attacks in the city, targeting western nationals and US assets. All of them carried al-Qaeda imprints. In March, a suicide bomb attack outside the Sheraton Hotel had killed 11 French engineers working on a submarine project.[28] They were mistaken for Americans. A few weeks later, the same al-Qaeda-linked Harkat-ul-Mujahideen-al-Alami struck again, targeting the American Consulate building on a busy Karachi street, killing several Pakistanis, including some policemen. The group also plotted to assassinate President Musharraf while he was on a visit to Karachi in May 2001. Karachi reflected the trial and tribulation of a nation, which had increasingly become hostage to the forces of terror. The city was, however, more accessible to the law-enforcement agencies.

One newly constructed, half-empty, five-storey apartment building, in a commercial neighbourhood of Karachi's Defense Housing Society, had been under surveillance as a possible al-Qaeda safe house for weeks after a lead from the CIA. Interception of a satellite phone conversation between al-Qaeda leaders reinforced suspicions about some important operative residing in one of the apartments. But Pakistani security officials had no idea who it could be.

It was just after dawn, on 11 September 2002, when Pakistani intelligence operatives, aided by a team of police commandos, quietly entered the building. As they moved up the stairs to the fourth floor, a hand grenade exploded, blocking their way. The hail of bullets that followed forced them to retreat. 'We never expected that kind of resistance,' recalled a police officer. The area was turned into a veritable battleground with the militants firing from the top-floor apartment. After an intense shoot-out lasting three hours, the commandos succeeded in breaking down the apartment doors. Two of the militants were mowed down while five others were captured.[29]

A young woman clutching a child ran out bare-footed. She was the wife of one of the slain men. The security personnel were horrified when they saw one of the fatally wounded inscribing in his blood on the wall as he died, 'Laillaha illallah' (There is no God, but one). Some of them later repented their participation in what they described as an 'unholy exercise'.[30] From a short distance away, FBI agents monitored the operation.

The Pakistani intelligence officials, who emerged from the building dragging a blindfolded young bearded man, did not have the slightest idea that they were holding one of the world's most notorious terrorists: Ramzi bin al-Shibh. The defiant al-Qaeda leader shouted, 'Allah-ho-Akbar' (God is great), as he was put into a police van.[31] The capture, on the first anniversary of 9/11, of one of the planners of the attacks, was certainly the biggest success in the war against al-Qaeda since the arrest of Abu Zubaydah.

A roommate in Hamburg, Germany, of Mohammed Atta, the ringleader of the 11 September plot, bin al-Shibh had played a vital role in organizing 9/11.[32] From his base in Germany, he handled the logistic and financial arrangements for the hijack team. Bin al-Shibh, who worked closely with KSM, had spent much of the spring of 2001 in Afghanistan and Pakistan, helping to move the hijackers as they passed through Karachi. He also reported directly to bin Laden about the preparations for the attack in an al-Qaeda facility, known as 'Compound Six', near Kandahar.[33]

Bin al-Shibh had moved to Karachi from Afghanistan soon after the fall of the Taliban regime and tried to regroup al-Qaeda. Just a week before his capture, the Arab television station Al-Jazeera had broadcast an interview in which bin al-Shibh and KSM claimed to have masterminded the 9/11 attacks. Bin al-Shibh called himself the head of the al-Qaeda's military wing. Pakistani investigators believed that the American intelligence might have tracked down Bin al-Shibh by intercepting his conversation with Al-Jazeera's London's bureau chief,

Yosri Fouda, who interviewed the al-Qaeda leader in Karachi.[34]

Pakistani security forces had arrested several other al-Qaeda operatives in subsequent raids on suspected terrorist hideouts in different parts of the city, but missed the man they wanted to capture most: KSM. They had to wait another five months before they could get hold of him.

In the first week of February 2003, Pakistani police and intelligence personnel finally nabbed KSM from a house in a middle-class neighbourhood in Pakistan's western border city, Quetta.[35] But his detention was kept secret for a month to buy time to track down other terrorists. On 3 March, Pakistani authorities announced that they had arrested KSM from a house in Rawalpindi's Westridge district. The delay and deliberate concealing of the actual place of arrest had borne fruit: the subsequent capture of a dozen other al-Qaeda militants.

The pre-dawn raid on the Westridge house of a woman leader of Pakistan's largest mainstream Islamic political party, Jamaat-i-Islami, produced another important catch: Mustafa Ahmed Hawsawi, a Saudi Arabian national, who was accused of bankrolling the 11 September attacks. Hawsawi, who initially identified himself as a Somali, allegedly funded the hijackers through bank accounts in the United Arab Emirates. He was also believed to be al-Zawahiri's financier, as well as being indicted in the United States on two counts of terrorism. In Quetta, the police also nabbed Mohammed Abdur Rehman, the son of the blind Egyptian cleric convicted in New York in 1995.[36]

KSM was apparently tracked by intelligence agencies for four weeks before his capture. Pakistani security forces had earlier captured his two young sons, Yousuf al-Khalid and Abed al-Khalid. They were detained in September 2003, after a raid on an apartment in Karachi's Defence Housing Society, which was used by KSM as a hideout. The al-Qaeda operational chief narrowly escaped arrest, while his sons were found hiding in a third-floor, two-bedroom apartment. Pakistani authorities believed that the arrest of his young sons would force KSM to surrender. It didn't happen. The boys were reportedly flown to the USA after their father's arrest. Among the items found in his possession was a photograph of a smiling KSM with his arms around his sons.[37]

KSM's capture was the biggest coup in the US war on terror. Ranking number three in the al-Qaeda leadership, he was also the head of the military operations wing of the terrorist network. His central role in al-Qaeda planning began to unfurl after his arrest and interrogation. Many of the past decade's major terrorist incidents – and some recently interrupted plots – were linked to a single, clannish al-Qaeda branch set up by the architect of 9/11. The group includes one of KSM's nephews, Ramzi Yousuf, who was convicted for the 1993 World Trade Center bombing, and another, Musaad Aruchi, who had masterminded attacks in Pakistan.[38] KSM's capture revealed astonishing insights about the network's penetration into local groups. His interrogation by American intelligence officials provided the most definitive information yet on al-Qaeda's ties to Pakistani militant groups.

Previously, KSM had always been thought to be a senior deputy to bin Laden, but his role, and that of his allies, now appeared to be far more significant. His relatives and associates from Pakistan had been linked to other attacks and plots in Africa, Southeast Asia, the UK and the USA. His nephew, Ammar al-Baluchi, had helped facilitate travel and financing for the senior al-Qaeda operative, Riduan Isamuddin, to carry out terrorist attacks in Southeast Asia. Riduan's agents were behind the October 2002 Bali bombing in Indonesia, that killed more than 200 people.[39] According to terrorism experts, KSM's arrest and the closing down of his web of relatives and associates – who were believed to be working out of Pakistan's lawless tribal areas and the port city of Karachi – was crucial to combating Islamic militancy globally.

The authorities discovered that KSM had received huge support from his extended family members living in Balochistan and Karachi. Many of them had been active in Pakistani Islamic militant groups and Pakistani authorities said his nephew, Musaad Aruchi, also known as Abdul Karim Mehboob, had knowledge about the al-Qaeda's fresh plan to hit financial centres in New York and Washington. Aruchi's arrest from an apartment in Karachi's slum district of Lyari, was described by Pakistani officials as a major breakthrough, because of his connection with other al-Qaeda operatives, particularly those planning to target the United States.[40]

KSM had frequently stayed in the house of the JI woman activist in the Westridge locality of the Rawalpindi cantonment area, from where security forces had also captured Hawsawi. The house belonged Dr Abdul Quddus, a microbiologist who had worked with the World Health Organization for many years. His wife had been a leader of the party's women's wing, while his nephew, a major in Pakistan's army, had also sheltered KSM in his house in the Kohat army garrison.[41] This underscored the support network that al-Qaeda enjoyed among mainstream Pakistani Islamic parties. There were several other incidents in which JI members were found to have provided refuge to al-Qaeda activists. In January 2003, two al-Qaeda operatives were arrested after a shoot-out in the house of another leader of the party's women's wing in Karachi. Dr Khawaja Javed, a leading physician, and his brother were arrested for harbouring senior al-Qaeda operatives and their families in their sprawling residential compound outside Lahore. Both had close links with the party.[42]

Pakistan's most powerful Islamic political party, JI, was the original face of jihad in Afghanistan in the 1980s and saw its rise under the patronage of General Zia's military rule. The group was the second-largest component of the six-party right-wing Islamic alliance, Muttehida Majlis Amal (MMA), that had swept the polls in two key provinces bordering Afghanistan in October 2002. In terms of organizational capability, media skills, political experience and influence within state institutions, the JI was the most powerful religious lobby in the country. It traditionally had close ties with the military and had played a major role in the Islamization of the state and society.

In many ways, JI had been the main architect of official Islam in Pakistan. Founded in 1941, the party has wide international contacts. It had very close ties with the Muslim Brotherhood in Egypt. The party's founder, Abul Aala Mawdudi, is the best-known South Asian Islamic scholar, whose influence was visible in revivalist movements across the Muslim world. JI's politics are pegged around an extended structure of subsidiary organizations. Mawdudi had forbidden women participating in public life, but the party boasts the most active women's wing of any political party. They had been at the forefront of the protests against the arrest of al-Qaeda leaders, and many al-Qaeda operatives were arrested from the houses of JI women activists.

Those incidents brought the party under close scrutiny for its links with terrorist networks. Security officials maintained that JI activists, who had actively participated in the Afghan war against Soviet occupation, developed close contacts with the Arab fighters and the links continued after the war was over. While senior JI leaders disassociated themselves from al-Qaeda, others defended the Arab fighters, describing them as 'Islamic heroes'.[43]

On 24 June 2003, President Bush and President Musharraf jointly announced at Camp David that the al-Qaeda network had been dismantled and many of its chief operators captured. But the claim appeared to be premature. Despite these successes, the terrorist network was still very active in Pakistan. Three months later, Al-

Jazeera aired a new videotape tape of bin Laden walking through mountainous terrain with al-Zawahiri. In an audiotape accompanying the video footage, the men warned of the real battle to come. The terrain where the video was filmed led to fresh speculation about his whereabouts. Intelligence agencies believed it could be between Pakistani Chitral and Kunar, across the border in Afghanistan.

In July 2004, Pakistani intelligence services received yet another indication about bin Laden's whereabouts. The information extracted from some newly captured al-Qaeda operatives, including its communication chief, Naeem Noor Mohammed Khan, had provided the clearest idea about bin Laden's possible presence in the tribal area. The dragnet closed along the border with Afghanistan, but soon the hunt went cold as the Saudi militant moved away from his suspected hideout. Pakistani authorities believed it was the closest they had come to capturing bin Laden.[44]

Meanwhile, Pakistani intelligence agents did not have the vaguest idea just how big a catch they had made when, on 12 July 2004, they arrested a young computer wizard from Lahore. They first heard about Naeem Noor Mohammed Khan after the arrest of Gun Gun Rusman Gunawan, the brother of Hambali, the mastermind of the 2002 Bali bombing.[45] The Indonesian, who was captured along with 11 other Southeast Asian students, had spent four years at a seminary in Karachi under a fake identity. Their interrogation led them to Naeem. Initially, intelligence agents only knew that the computer engineer was doing communication work for al-Qaeda.

When investigators examined his home computer, however, they realized that Naeem was the key connection between bin Laden's inner circle, holed up in the mountainous terrain in Pakistan lawless tribal region, and al-Qaeda operatives around the world.[46] The information gleaned from his computer provided an unprecedented insight into al-Qaeda's inner workings. The trove of data recovered from Naeem's computer revealed al-Qaeda's plan for fresh terrorist attacks against the USA and Britain; specific targets included Heathrow airport in London and top financial institutions in America.[47]

A well-educated young man from a middle-class background, 28-year-old Naeem hardly fitted the profile of a hardened terrorist. A computer whizz-kid who had abandoned a promising career for the call to jihad, he became a crucial cog in al-Qaeda operations in Pakistan. Naeem was lured into jihad when he was still a teenager and had just got into Karachi's top engineering university.[48] He came into contact with al-Qaeda through an Arab operative, whom he met in Dubai in 1997, during a family wedding. The bright, soft-spoken youngster made a splendid prospect for recruitment. Although his family background could hardly be called Islamist, Naeem was greatly influenced by radical causes from Palestine to Bosnia and Chechnya. His father worked as a senior purser for Pakistan International Airlines and his mother was a Botany lecturer at St Joseph's College for Women in Karachi, run by the Roman Catholic Church. The impressionable teenager soon met with other al-Qaeda members, who welcomed him into their midst. In 1998, he was dispatched to Afghanistan to attend a three-month commando training course at bin Laden's Al-Farooq camp in Khost.[49]

Returning to Pakistan, Naeem, who was also known as Abu Talha, set up a small communications centre in Lahore, which turned into a major al-Qaeda network after the collapse of the Taliban regime in Afghanistan. Naeem became the bridge between al-Qaeda leaders and their operatives. From his communications centre, he relayed coded messages on the Internet from the al-Qaeda leadership, hiding in caves in tribal areas, to their operatives abroad. He would also send emails directly to the cells, not only in the USA and Britain, but also in terrorist crossroads like Malaysia and Indonesia. Naeem, a close ally of the KSM clan, also worked in conjunction with Aruchi in cultivating al-Qaeda cells in Europe and elsewhere.[50]

Naeem had other important tasks as well. He handled operative reports and recommendations and, together with his own observations, sent them via courier to the terrorist leadership sheltering in Waziristan's mountainous region. He had made at least five trips to Britain over the previous six years, including a brief stint at City University in London. He also collected intelligence to plan terrorist attacks on important installations in Britain. Investigators recovered maps and detailed plans for an attack on Heathrow airport. One of Naeem's cousins, Ahmed Babar, had been working on the terrorist plan in close association with Dhiron Bharot, alias Essa al-Hindi, the head of al-Qaeda's cell in London. The information recovered from Naeem's computer led to the arrest of al-Hindi and some other operatives by the British police.[51]

The capture of the man who worked as bin Laden's back channel exposed an intricate web of al-Qaeda contacts in Pakistan, Britain and the USA. Information received during his interrogation helped not only to break al-Qaeda's cell in Britain, but also in tracking down Ahmed Khalfan Ghailani, a Tanzanian national indicted for murder in connection with the 1998 bombings of US embassies in East Africa. Pakistani security forces captured the man, who had a $25 million prize on his head, from a hideout in Gujrat on 25 July, after a fierce gun battle which lasted for several hours.[52] Two South African men, who were being trained for suicide bombing, were also apprehended in the raid. Ghailani was considered the most important catch by Pakistani security forces, second only to KSM. 'We have done nothing against you and Pakistan. Why are you doing this to us?' Ghailani shouted as he was taken out of the house.[53]

Ghailani, who had moved to a sprawling house in an up-market neigbourhood in the central Punjab town almost a year earlier, was a master forger and would prepare travel documents and passports for al-Qaeda operatives. Also an explosives expert, he would seldom leave the house where he lived with his Uzbek wife, staying inside for months at a stretch. His wife had also been associated with the international jihadist network, and her sister was involved in a suicide bombing in Russia. Ghailani was a key member of the al-Qaeda network operating from Pakistan, which included Naeem Khan, Abu Hamza Rabia, an Egyptian, and Abu Faraj al-Libbi. The house worked as al-Qaeda's regional headquarters, manned with a sophisticated communications system. The information gleaned from the computers and other written material found in the house provided the most substantive insight yet into al-Qaeda's worldwide network and its terror plans. During the interrogation, Ghailani and his companions revealed plans for terrorist attacks, not only in the USA and Britain, but also in Africa. There was also a scheme to target the top Pakistani leadership, and a detailed map of Islamabad airport was recovered.[54] Ghailani's capture led to the arrests of some two dozen more al-Qaeda operatives across Pakistan. It was the single largest haul in Pakistan's war on terror.

Long accused of not doing enough to stamp out terrorism on its soil, Pakistan, at least, made a significant breakthrough with the subsequent high-profile arrests. The wave of arrests and intelligence discoveries in Pakistan in mid 2004 caught many US officials and outside experts by surprise. It had revealed a network of operatives connected to past al-Qaeda operations and aligned with the imprisoned masterminds of the 11 September 2001 attacks. More importantly, the material gleaned from the two computers seized during the raids and the information received from the captured men had provided intelligence agencies with a rare insight into al-Qaeda's modus operandi. That proved to be the biggest breakthrough in the efforts to dismantle the terrorist network, whose tentacles spread from the mountains of Waziristan to Europe, Africa, East Asia and America.

The capture of Ghailani and Naeem caused a huge dent in al-Qaeda's network, but the group had shown its great capacity to organize into new cells. It was difficult to completely dismantle the loosely connected and highly mobile groups and it took almost ten months for Pakistani security forces to capture another key al-Qaeda operative. Abu Faraj al-Libbi, a Libyan national, had been working as the head of al-Qaeda's external operations after the capture of KSM, and was the key link with the Pakistani militants. Al-Libbi's name came to the surface after he was identified as the mastermind behind the failed assassination attempts on Musharraf in December 2003. He had been on the list of the six 'most wanted' men in a Pakistani poster campaign for his involvement in a series of terrorist actions.[55]

Al-Libbi was captured in a dramatic raid, while he was being driven on a motorbike in Mardan, a town in the North West Frontier Province. Intelligence agents tracked down this most wanted fugitive after arresting a messenger. After the series of arrests of high-profile operatives a year earlier, al-Qaeda had to minimize the use of electronic communications and largely relied on manual messaging. However, that also made them more vulnerable. Al-Libbi and Rabia had taken over al-Qaeda's operations after Ghailani's capture. Al-Libbi's arrest led to some startling revelations about his contacts across eight countries. The al-Qaeda hierarchy had always been fluid and complex, so speculation about al-Libbi being the third in command in the organization is hard to confirm, but he was certainly a very important man in the global terrorist network. He was a major facilitator and chief planner for al-Qaeda.[56] It is, however, not clear whether al-Libbi and Rabia were in direct contact with bin Laden or al-Zawahiri, who were still believed to be operating from the mountainous border between Pakistan and Afghanistan.

Rabia was killed in December 2005 by a missile fired by a US predator aircraft on his hideout in a village in North Waziristan.[57] He had figured on the CIA's wanted list with a bounty of $5 million for his capture. Rabia had inherited the job of chief of al-Qaeda's operations in Pakistan, after al-Libbi's arrest. Reputed to be one of the organization's top five officials, he oversaw relations with international al-Qaeda cells and other foreign terrorist groups. In al-Qaeda's structure, the operational commander was the most active of all senior leaders.[58] In his late thirties, Rabia was reportedly sent to Iraq after the American invasion in 2003, but was deemed too valuable to al-Qaeda central command in Afghanistan.

Rabia was the target of another predator attack on 5 November, 2005. He escaped, but eight people, including his wife and children, died in the strike. His death, a month later, weakened the organization's ability to coordinate terrorist attacks from the border region of Pakistan and Afghanistan. Rabia was believed to be a key link between bin Laden and other al-Qaeda operatives and his death could mean that Pakistani and American security forces were closing in on the top al-Qaeda leader.

The presence of al-Qaeda in Pakistan had thinned as a result of this series of high-profile captures, and also because many others had shifted to new venues of jihad, particularly to Iraq following its occupation by the US forces. Besides, Pakistan was no longer a safe haven for the terrorist network.

Musharraf's growing crackdown on al-Qaeda's command structure forced the terrorist organization to adapt, breeding new militant Islamic threats in Pakistan that the security forces found harder to uproot. Several new terrorist cells emerged out of the outlawed militant outfits. Most of them comprised a new breed of young militants coming from educated middle-class backgrounds, rather than the religious school students who were associated with Islamic militancy in the past.

Thousands of Islamic guerrillas, trained by the ISI to fight against Indian forces in Kashmir, were now frustrated by Musharraf's policies and provided ready recruits to these new terrorist cells. As external avenues for waging jihad were being closed, the militant Muslim youth increasingly turned inwards and targeted the military or the state. This new cadre boasted highly qualified professionals and university graduates. Children of opportunity rather than deprivation, they were the masterminds behind many of the terrorist attacks in the country.

The creation of the Karachi-based Jundullah (Army of God) was a prime example of al-Qaeda's changing face in Pakistan. The group was founded by Attar Rehman, a university graduate, who was arrested in June 2004 on the charge of masterminding a series of terrorist attacks in Karachi, targeting security forces and government installations.[59] The eldest son of a businessman, he grew up in a middle-class neighbourhood in Karachi. His family house was the biggest in the area and was known by the neighbours as the 'White House'. Many of his close relatives, including one uncle, were settled in the USA.

His classmates at university remembered him as a very quiet person. He didn't give any indication of his potential involvement with the terrorist network.

Rehman's journey to jihad began after he graduated from the University of Karachi with a master's degree in Statistics in 1991. Like thousands of Pakistanis, he went to Afghanistan to receive military training at a jihadist camp. A tall and heavily built man in his early thirties, Rehman was initially associated with Islami Jamiat-Talba, the student wing of Pakistan's most powerful mainstream Islamist Party, Jamaat-i-Islami. He later broke away from the party to form his own militant group. Rehman told his interrogators that he formed Jundullah after the arrest of top al-Qaeda operatives in March 2003, including that of Khalid Sheikh Mohammed. The group was closely associated with al-Qaeda's network in Pakistan, which had grown in strength despite the capture of hundreds of its operatives.[60] It drew its cadres mainly from the educated and professional classes.

A well-knit cell comprising some 20 militants, most of them in their twenties and thirties, Jundullah was the most fierce of the militant groups behind a spate of violent attacks in Karachi in 2004. The group hit the headlines after a daring attack in June 2004 on the motorcade of the army's top commander in Karachi, General Ahsan Saleem Hayat, who a few months later was appointed by Musharraf as his second-in-command in Pakistan's army. General Hayat narrowly escaped, but 11 people, including eight soldiers, were killed in the attack right in the centre of a busy city street. It was the most serious terrorist attack against Pakistan's military since the two failed assassination attempts on Musharraf in December 2003. Rehman did not show any sign of remorse when he was presented before a high security anti-terrorism court in Karachi. 'I have not done anything wrong,' he shouted as he emerged from the courtroom.

Jundullah was also involved in attacks on army rangers, police stations and a car bombing outside the US-Pakistan cultural centre in Karachi. Among others who were arrested for their association with Jundullah was Akmal Waheed, a cardiologist, and his brother Arshad Waheed, an orthopedic surgeon. They were accused of sheltering al-Qaeda fugitives. Both men were in their mid thirties and were senior officials of the Pakistan Islamic Medical association and active members of Jamaat-i-Islami. Many JI cadres had fought in Kashmir and Afghanistan, and the more militant ones turned to terrorist groups like Jundullah after Musharraf's policy turnaround.

Jundullah's existence showed how the new jihadist cells quickly emerged after others were wound up. The rise of splinter cells made the task of Pakistani security forces increasingly difficult. According to a senior police official, terrorist groups multiplied with the intensification in the crackdown against Islamic militants. Some of these groups were involved in sectarian attacks, but others targeted western assets and security forces. Most of these cells had just four or five members, making them much more effective.

The militants responded to the arrest of key Pakistani and al-Qaeda activists with a suicide bomb attack targeting the Prime Minister-designate, Shaukat Aziz, during his election campaign in the city of Attock. A former Citibank executive, who served as Musharraf's finance minister since the military takeover, Aziz was accused of being an American agent by radical Islamic groups. He escaped unhurt, but his driver and eight others were killed. An obscure group, the Islamboli Brigade – a group that officials allege is linked to al-Qaeda (it took its name from Anwar Sadat's killer) – claimed responsibility for the attack. In a message posted on an Arabic news website, the group warned of a series of retaliatory strikes if the government handed over detained al-Qaeda operatives to the USA. 'One of our blessed battalions tried to hunt down the head of one of America's infidels in Pakistan, but God wanted him to survive,' said the message, which also warned of a series of violent strikes if Musharraf did not change his pro-US policy.[61]

Since 9/11, Pakistan had delivered hundreds of al-Qaeda fugitives, but there was still no trace of the most wanted man. American and Afghan leaders had appeared convinced about bin Laden's presence in Pakistan and that possibility generated shudders in Pakistan's military establishment. In June 2005, Porter J. Goss, the Director of the CIA, said he had 'an excellent idea' where bin Laden was hiding, but lamented that the al-Qaeda leader had taken advantage of 'sanctuaries in sovereign states' beyond American reach. Although Goss did not name Pakistan, it was very much implicit. The capture of the man who was regarded by hardline Islamists, and even by the majority of common Pakistanis, as a hero, would completely destabilize the government. Was Musharraf, America's most trusted ally, prepared to risk his life and power by capturing the world's most dangerous man?

The possibility of seizing bin Laden presented a serious dilemma for Musharraf. While his capture would further boost US support for the Pakistani President, it could also cause a serious public backlash. The Islamists could use the issue to whip up anti-government and anti-American sentiments in the country and this might have been one of the reasons behind the insistence by Musharraf and other senior Pakistani government officials that bin Laden was not in the country, and their attempts to keep Pakistan's participation in the manhunt as low-key as possible. In an interview with *Time* magazine in October 2005, Musharraf acknowledged that he was not eager for bin Laden to be caught in his country. 'One would prefer that he is captured somewhere outside Pakistan, by some other people,' he said.

Faced with mounting US pressure, Musharraf took another critical decision in February 2004, ordering his forces to launch the biggest offensive yet against al-Qaeda fugitives in Waziristan tribal region. The US authorities had warned that they would cross the border and bomb al-Qaeda and Taliban sanctuaries if Pakistan did not take action. Musharraf's war on terror was about to move from a security operation to a full-scale military conflict.

8

THE TRIBAL
WARRIORS

Pakistani soldiers had dug into stone bunkers on a strategic mountaintop, close to the Afghan border, while gunship helicopters hovered over a village down in the valley. The boom of artillery fire echoed in the distance as troops tried to flush out suspected al-Qaeda fighters holed up in a mud compound. Pointing his baton towards the arid hill on the horizon where his soldiers had advanced, Major-General Niaz Khattak boasted: 'It is only a matter of time before the entire South Waziristan region will be cleared of terrorists.' A short man with a greying thick moustache, the commanding officer, a Pashtun from the North West Frontier Province, was visibly pleased with the performance of his men as he stood on the windy escarpment of Karwana Manzai, shortly after it was captured from rebel control.

One of the villages captured by General Khattak's troops was Nano, the home of former Guantanamo Bay prisoner, Abdullah Mehsud. The one-legged, 29-year-old rebel commander had risen to prominence after masterminding some spectacular guerrilla attacks on Pakistani troops. Abdullah, whose real name was Noor Alam, had fought for the Taliban before he was captured by the US coalition forces in Afghanistan in December 2001. A member of the Mehsud tribe that inhabited South Waziristan, he had joined the rebels after he was freed from US custody in March 2004. His long hair and daredevil exploits had earned him notoriety, and he had become a hero for anti-US fighters active in both Afghanistan and Pakistan.

Abdullah had turned to militancy after failing to obtain a commission in Pakistan's army in the early 1990s. Many of his relatives and an uncle were army officers and it was his life-long passion to follow in their footsteps. A dejected man, he went to join the Taliban forces in Afghanistan. The two and a half years he had spent at Guantanamo prison further radicalized him, and he became one of the most hunted guerrillas of the military operation.

Abdullah had fled just before the troops arrived in a village on a mountaintop some ten miles from the Afghan border.[1] The stout-walled mud-brick compound where he once lived looked much the same as any dwelling in Pakistan's mountainous hinterland, with firewood stacked neatly outside in preparation for the approaching winter. The fort-like sprawling structure also served as his operation headquarters. Inside, there was a stockpile of heavy machine guns, rocket-propelled grenades and bomb-making equipment. A visibly frustrated General Khattak blamed the US authorities for not carrying out a thorough investigation before freeing Abdullah. 'In hindsight it was a major blunder,' declared the General. The literature and material recovered from the compound showed that al-Qaeda leaders had been operating from the area, but had probably escaped to some other part of the country.

Despite some military success, the bloody war in this treacherous mountainous terrain was far from over. Guerrilla forces had scattered and continued to ambush government forces. 'It is a deadly war where we are fighting an invisible enemy,' said an officer who had been involved in the fighting for the previous six months. 'We never know where the next bullet is coming from.' But the greatest cause for frustration for General Khattak and his officers was that there was no sign of the man that Pakistan's American allies in the war on terror really wanted him to catch: Osama bin Laden. 'I have had no indications, no intelligence of bin Laden's whereabouts,' Khattak declared.

This was November 2004, almost eight months since General Khattak, along with more than 7,000 troops, had started the hunt operation against al-Qaeda fugitives in the lawless tribal region. It was the largest operation since Pakistan had thrown its support behind the US campaign in Afghanistan after 9/11. Known as Pakistan's wild west, Waziristan had long been regarded as one of the most likely hiding places for bin Laden and his deputy, Ayman al-Zawahiri. It was the first time that Pakistani forces had set foot on the fiercely autonomous territory. The 5,000-square-kilometre swathe was the largest of seven tribal agencies on Pakistan's western border with Afghanistan. Inhabited by one million fiercely independent Pashtun tribesmen, Waziristan was a land of high, difficult mountains and deep, rugged defiles. With its long porous border with Afghanistan's Paktia and Khost provinces, Waziristan had become a major trouble spot for US and Afghan forces, particularly as Taliban insurgents escaped to the Pakistani side after attacking coalition posts.

The treacherous, inhospitable mountainous region, which had been used by the American CIA and the Pakistani ISI in the 1980s as a base for their covert operation against the Soviet occupation forces in Afghanistan, had been turned by al-Qaeda-linked militants into a base for the battle against their erstwhile patrons. The strategically located border region was used as a launching pad for the mujahidin into Afghanistan during the Afghan jihad. For the hundreds of anti-Soviet fighters, trained and funded by Pakistani and American intelligence agencies, the terrain was not unfamiliar. Many of the Arab fighters had stayed back in the area after the end of the anti-Soviet war in 1990. Some of them had also married into local tribes and so were not seen as aliens by the residents. But it was only after the ousting of the Taliban regime by US forces that the ideological bond between the locals and the foreign fighters turned into a real relationship. When bin Laden and several top associates escaped US bombing raids and an Afghan-led ground assault on the mountain complex at Tora Bora[2] in December 2001, up to 2,000 al-Qaeda fighters crossed into the Pakistani tribal area through difficult mountain passes, many of them ending up in Waziristan. It was widely suspected that bin Laden and al-Zawahiri were also among them. Hundreds of militants fleeing the US bombing were captured or killed by Pakistani security forces while trying to move to other parts of Pakistan or to other countries. Many others were captured by the tribesmen and sold to the CIA for a hefty bounty ranging from $3000 to $25,000. Most of these detainees later landed in the American prison at Guantanamo Bay.[3]

For more than two years al-Qaeda fugitives had moved freely, turning the border areas into a new base for their operations. Clusters of towering mud compounds in a valley surrounded by rugged mountains close to the Afghan border served as the world's largest al-Qaeda command and control centre, as well as a guerrilla training facility for foreign and Pakistani militants. Several hundred Uzbek, Chechen and Arab militants lurked inside, training, recruiting and plotting attacks in Pakistan and the West and operating a sophisticated propaganda factory, complete with video-editing machines and CD burners. At least 15 camps had operated under the protection of sympathetic tribesmen, mostly around Wana and Shakai.[4] In early spring 2004, just a week before the start of General Khattak's military campaign, senior al-Qaeda leaders had gathered there for a 'terror summit'. Among those who attended was Abu Faraj al-Libbi,[5] who would become bin Laden's top operational planner. Many al-Qaeda operatives from other countries had travelled to this remote region to participate in the meeting. At the top of the agenda that day were plans to carry out attacks on the USA and Britain.[6]

Musharraf had faced mounting American pressure to capture bin Laden and move against the terrorist network operating from the border region. US jets had frequently bombed al-Qaeda and Taliban sanctuaries inside Waziristan as America's frustration with Pakistan's inaction grew. Musharraf told tribal leaders that American forces could enter the region if the militant sanctuaries were not dismantled. In March 2004, George Tenet, the CIA Director, made a secret trip to Islamabad to discuss a new strategy with senior Pakistani military and intelligence officials to rout al-Qaeda and Taliban operatives from the tribal areas. American troops had already stepped up activities across the border in the Afghan provinces. US military officials had hoped that efforts by Pakistan, combined with a change in American counter-insurgency tactics in Afghanistan, would create a 'hammer-and-anvil' effect to trap al-Qaeda fighters between US and Pakistani forces. Some 20,000 US troops had been involved in the military campaign against al-Qaeda and Taliban rebels in Afghanistan and, as part of the new anti-terrorist strategy, the Pakistani army was to work as 'the anvil'.[7]

The military campaign in Waziristan coincided with a visit to Pakistan in March by the US Secretary of State, Colin Powell. The Bush administration had offered a carrot by asking Congress for a five-year, $3 billion assistance package and designating Pakistan as a significant non-Nato ally, clearing the way for its military to acquire new weapons systems from the USA.[8] The operation was being paid for with millions of dollars from the CIA, supported with equipment from the National Security Agency and carried out by Pakistani soldiers and intelligence units. There were also a limited number of US military personnel assisting Pakistani forces involved in the hunt for al-Qaeda fugitives. As the operation proceeded, Pakistani officials said that the number of American personnel involved in the search operations was not more than a dozen and that they were just helping Pakistani troops with communication and intelligence. But the involvement of even a limited number of American personnel in the raids became a politically sensitive issue.

The price for treading on an uncharted path was high. The military operation provoked intense anger among the local tribesmen who saw the move as a threat to their fiercely guarded autonomy. In July 2002, Pakistani troops had, for the first time in 55 years, entered the Tirah Valley in the Khyber tribal agency. Soon they were in the Shawal Valley of North Waziristan, and later in South Waziristan. The deployment was made possible after long negotiations with various tribes, who reluctantly agreed to allow the military's presence on the assurance that it would bring in funds and promote development work in the area. However, the situation changed once the military operation started in South Waziristan. The tribesmen considered the military action as an attack on their autonomy and an attempt to subjugate them.[9] Attempts to persuade them into handing over foreign militants failed and, with apparent mishandling, the military offensive against suspected al-Qaeda militants turned into an undeclared war between the Pakistani military and the rebel tribesmen. Anger grew as government forces demolished the houses of members of the defiant tribes as collective punishment and seized their properties, even in other parts of the province. Wana, the administrative headquarters of South Waziristan, looked like a besieged town with thousands of government troops taking up positions in the surrounding hills. The conflict had threatened to spill over into other tribal areas.

Waziristan, which was divided into north and south regions, had largely been inhabited by two main Pashtun tribes, the Waziris and the Mehsud, likened by Sir Olaf Caroe, a British scholar and administrator, to panthers and wolves respectively. 'Both are splendid creatures, the panther is slyer, sleeker, and has more grace, the wolf pack is more purposeful, more united and more dangerous.'[10] These two tribes and their numerous sub-groups co-existed in what could be defined as 'a state of chronic feud', but they would unite against outside invaders.[11] No foreign invaders, from Alexander the Great and Genghis Khan to the British Empires, had ever been able to control Waziristan. A stretch of arid land, the region had served as a buffer between rival empires since the eleventh century. Protected by mountain fastness, the Mehsud and the Waziris had historically resisted British authority. When the Durand Line was established as the border between Afghanistan and British India in 1893, Waziristan became an independent territory, outside the bounds of effective British rule.[12] Since it became part of Pakistan in 1947, the government had continued the British practice of pacification through payment of subsidies to tribal chieftains. Normal Pakistani laws did not apply. Waziristan was administered exactly as it had been under the British colonists. All powers had rested with a centrally appointed political agent who exercised absolute judicial authority in the area. He could jail any tribesman without trial and could impose collective punishments on entire villages. The ungovernable borderland separated Pakistan and Afghanistan and people on both sides were ethnic Pashtuns who had long despised and ignored the dividing Durand Line. The frontier had further blurred during the Taliban rule in Afghanistan, with thousands of Pakistani tribesmen joining conservative Islamic forces with the active encouragement of the military and the ISI.

Its mountainous terrain had made Waziristan an ideal place for guerrilla warfare. The landscape was dotted by forts built by the British in the early part of the last century, in their largely unsuccessful colonial bid to control the region and crush the resistance of the native tribes. In 1937, the tribesmen rose in rebellion against the British forces in response to a call for jihad by the Faqir of Ipi, a tribal leader who exercised both religious and temporal powers. The tribal insurrection started after the British forces engineered the escape of a Hindu girl kidnapped by a young Pashtun and taken to Waziristan. The girl had reportedly converted to Islam and taken the name of Islam Bibi before marrying the boy. The event was celebrated according to the tribal rituals. The British authorities somehow managed to whisk away the girl and the incident was taken as an unforgivable insult to the tribal elders. Fiercely hostile towards British rule, the Faqir of Ipi whose real name was Mirza Ali Khan, made an impassioned call for holy war.[13]

Thousands of armed tribesmen battled the British army with heavy casualties on both sides. The hit and run tactics by the rebels proved very successful. Even air strikes failed to break the resistance. The guerrilla warfare stretched to over two decades. After independence in 1947, the Faqir of Ipi continued his armed struggle against the new Pakistani state, which he condemned as un-Islamic. He never surrendered, but his support progressively petered out over the years.

He died in 1960, but his legend had survived. Many in Waziristan likened bin Laden to the Faqir of Ipi. 'Both men fought against invaders and for the cause of Islam,' said Mohabat Wazir a trader in Wana. 'Like Faqir Ipi, they would never be able to get bin Laden.'

The Waziris lived on both sides of the Durand Line between Pakistan and Afghanistan. Many of their men had taken part in the Afghan jihad in the 1980s and fought alongside the Taliban against the US forces and their Afghan allies. The men were born fighters and learnt the use of guns at a very early age in keeping with local traditions, acquiring more sophisticated fighting skills during the long years of the Afghan war. They used that skill to put up fierce resistance to the Pakistani army.

Though the tribesmen were religious, the rise of militant Islam in Waziristan was a recent phenomenon. In 1947, people were deeply unhappy to be part of Pakistan and supported the Pashtun nationalist struggle for the establishment of an independent 'Pashtunistan'.[14] The movement, which had gained popular support in the North West Frontier Province in the 1950s and 1960s, was basically secular; it was in the 1980s that radical Islam took root. Pakistani military rulers not only used Islam to mobilize support for the Afghan jihad against Soviet forces, but also to undermine Pashtun nationalism. Pakistani intelligence agencies, in collaboration with the CIA, funnelled millions of dollars and weapons through the tribal area. The region became a conservatory which fomented the growth of radical Islam, sustained by a network of Saudi-funded madrasas. In the late 1980s, after the end of the Soviet occupation of Afghanistan, the supply of money and weapons had stopped, but foreign-funded madrasas continue to flourish. Less than 30 per cent of the tribesmen attended school, while 90 per cent would drop out before completing their education. With little economic activity, most people lived on smuggling, gun-running or drug-trafficking. The rise of the Taliban in Afghanistan had given further impetus to the spread of militancy. Thousand of tribesmen had joined the conservative Islamic militia.

Until 1997, the tribal areas did not have adult franchise and only a small number of *maliks* (tribal elders), had voting rights. Political parties were banned, and the vacuum was filled by the mullahs. Hence it did not come as a surprise when, in the 2002 parliamentary elections, the hardline Islamic alliance, Muttehida Majlis Amal,[15] not only swept the polls in Waziristan, but also formed the government in the North West Frontier Province for the first time in 58 years. That had provided a conducive environment to the Taliban and al-Qaeda remnants to turn the tribal region into their sanctuaries.

It was not only ideological bonds and sympathy that helped al-Qaeda fugitives buy the support of the tribesmen, but also money – the people were poor and easily lured by it. In an area where there was no other employment, the influx of al-Qaeda money was just one more way by which tribesmen gained influence.[16] bin Laden's men distributed millions of dollars among the tribal elders in return for shelter. Local fighters, enlisted by al-Qaeda, received up to $250 each as monthly wages, many times more than the monthly wages of a government soldier.[17] The militant commanders used to get advances for their services running into millions. The residents also received huge monetary benefits by renting out their compounds for shelter and training camps. Most of the al-Qaeda funds came through illegal and informal channels from Arab countries. While the tribesmen were familiar with the art of resistance, they had also learnt the art of extortion from outsiders who tried to buy them.[18]

The Pakistani security forces launched an offensive against the militants in the second week of March 2004, once the deadline for the tribesmen to hand over foreign fighters had expired. The military authorities had boasted that the operation would be over in a couple of days, but the intensity of the fighting shocked the Pakistani army commanders. The army suffered heavy casualties in the 12 days of bloody fighting. On 16 March, at least 50 soldiers were killed and many others captured by the tribesmen and their foreign guests when they raided militant hideouts.[19] The fiercest battles took place in Kaloosha and Shin Warsak, where scores of suspected al-Qaeda fighters had lived under the protection of local militants. Finding themselves surrounded, scores of paramilitary troops threw away their weapons and fled for their lives. 'Many soldiers took shelter inside a mosque when they came under fire,' Ehsan Wazir, a local resident, told me when I went to Kaloosha a few weeks later. 'Among them was a colonel who came out with the Qur'an on his head begging for his life. He was let go after the tribesmen stripped off his uniform.'

It was a no-win situation for the government forces They could not abandon the operation halfway and had to use bombers and gunship helicopters against what was earlier described as a 'handful of foreign militants and some local miscreants'. Among the foreign militants, mostly from Uzbekistan and Chechnya who had taken shelter in the area, was Tahir Yaldashev. The militant leader had become the head of the Islamic Movement of Uzbekistan (IMU) after its founder, Juma Namangani, was killed in the US bombing campaign in Afghanistan in November 2001. Yaldashev had since worked with al-Qaeda and the Taliban leadership, carrying out raids on US and allied forces in Afghanistan. He was very popular among the militants because of his leadership qualities and fiery speeches. He was badly wounded during the raid on his compound, but managed to escape the dragnet.[20]

The militants struck again a few days later when they ambushed an army caravan near Sarwakai village, massacring some two dozen soldiers and capturing several others. Not a single soldier in the convoy escaped. Government forces also lost a number of military vehicles and equipment. The charred, twisted steel scattered over the winding roads illustrated the ferocity of the rebel attack. In the first couple of weeks the military had lost more than 120 soldiers. Pashtun paramilitary soldiers deserted the government forces in droves as the offensive against al-Qaeda and their tribal supporters, descended into chaos.[21] Those who belonged to the local tribes had refused to fire on their brethren. Some of them, perhaps, had also been inspired by a videotape recorded by al-Zawahiri in which he had called Musharraf a traitor and urged Pakistani troops to disobey the order. 'Fight the supporters of the devil,' he exhorted.

The tape also reinforced the suspicion that the al-Qaeda's number two had been hiding in the border areas protected by sympathetic tribesmen. The videotape caused serious embarrassment to Musharraf who, just a few days before, had claimed that his forces had encircled 'a high-value target'. He tried to play down al-Zawahiri's ranting. 'Zawahiri is on the run. For heaven's sake, it is just one tape. Let's not get excited,' he told an American TV network.[22]. But he was certainly a worried man.

Ayman al-Zawahiri, a bespectacled, 52-year-old eye surgeon, had emerged from a privileged upbringing in Egypt to become one of the world's most wanted terrorists. As a teenager, al-Zawahiri worked his way through various Islamic movements to overthrow the secular Egyptian government. In 1960 he joined an Islamic revolutionary group the Muslim Brotherhood, which had been founded in the 1920s.[23] He later ended up with an Islamist jihad group, which had masterminded the assassination of Egyptian President, Anwar Sadat, in 1981. Al-Zawahiri was arrested in the crackdown on Islamic militants that followed Sadat's murder. Although he could not be directly linked with the assassination plot, he was handed down a three-year prison sentence. The jail experience further radicalized him. In the 1980s, al-Zawahiri relocated himself to the Pakistani city, Peshawar, and joined the Afghan mujahidin in the jihad against the Soviet forces.[24] There he also befriended bin Laden.

The two worked closely for many years. After the withdrawal of Soviet forces from Afghanistan in 1989, the war-hardened and more radical al-Zawahiri returned to Egypt to wage a new struggle for Islamic revolution in his home country. He tried to reorganize his Islamic jihad group, bringing into its fold the Afghan war veterans. Increasing government pressure, however, forced him to leave Egypt again. In 1992, he joined bin Laden in Sudan and later, in 1996, followed the Saudi militant to Afghanistan. In 1999, an Egyptian court sentenced al-Zawahiri to death in absentia, for his alleged involvement in a series of terrorist attacks, including the 1997 massacre of more than 58 mostly western tourists in the Egyptian town of Luxor.[25]

In Afghanistan, al-Zawahiri had developed the idea of an international terrorist network. In June 2001, he formally merged his Islamic jihad group with al-Qaeda and became second-in-command in the organization. The Egyptian fugitive has often been described as a terrorist ideologue. Many analysts have described al-Zawahiri as the primary intellectual force behind al-Qaeda. He played a key role in consolidating al-Qaeda's alliances with other terror groups and was believed to be a master of operational planning for terrorist attacks.

In 1998, al-Zawahiri was indicted, along with bin Laden, for his alleged role as mastermind of the 1998 bombings of US embassies in Kenya and Tanzania that killed 224 people.[26] He is believed to have played a significant role in the September 2001 attacks in Washington and New York. After the 9/11, the US State Department offered a $25 million reward for information leading to his apprehension. Al-Zawahiri's influence on bin Laden has been profound; he helped him become more radical, more anti-American and more violent.

Pakistani army commandos came very close to seizing al-Zawahiri in mid 2004, when they raided an al-Qaeda safe house in South Waziristan. The vast mud compound was used as the group's hidden command centre. Buried was a huge cache of weapons, radios and sophisticated electronic equipment, including a video-editing machine. Pakistani intelligence officials believed the place had been used by al-Zawahiri, but he had apparently fled days before the raid.

In April 2004, the catastrophic failure of the Pakistani army's operation in Waziristan forced the authorities to make a truce with the militants who were led by a young Waziri tribesman. The 27-year-old Nek Mohammed, with his flowing, long hair and beard and piercing eyes, had emerged as a hero among the tribesmen, after his blistering guerrilla attack had forced government troops to retreat. His pro-al-Qaeda fighters had eluded capture for six weeks and had killed 120 government soldiers.

For Nek Mohammed, the journey of 'holy war' had started at the young age of 14 when, as a madrasa student, he fought alongside the Afghan mujahidin in the anti-Soviet war. He moved to Kandahar in 1994 to join the emerging Taliban militia. He fought against the US coalition forces in Afghanistan and returned home after the Taliban were routed. Back in Waziristan he organized his tribesmen to defend al-Qaeda against attacks by the Pakistani army.

Lt.-General Safdar Hussein, the top army commander responsible for anti-terrorism operations in north-western Pakistan, helicoptered into Shakai on 26 April to sign a truce with Nek Mohammed. Amid much fanfare, the General hugged and garlanded the rebel commander.[27].He agreed to halt the army operation against Nek Mohammed's militants, compensate the Wazir tribesmen for war damages and free most of the 160 suspected al-Qaeda militants captured by his forces. Under the deal, Nek Mohammed and other militant leaders were granted amnesties and also allowed to keep their weapons. In return, the militants promised not to attack government troops, but they were not bound to hand over foreign fighters. The militants had also refused to give any commitment to stop raids on the American and Afghan government forces across the border. 'We cannot stop our jihad until Afghanistan is free from foreign invaders,' declared Nek Mohammed after signing the accord.[28]

The deal marked a temporary halt in the hunt for foreign militants in the tribal areas. Pakistani authorities justified what they described as a 'reconciliation', saying it was aimed at weaning the tribesmen away from foreign militants or al-Qaeda. But Nek Mohammed and his supporters celebrated the truce as a victory for jihad. By giving in to militant tribesmen backing al-Qaeda, Islamabad risked the wrath of its allies. The truce exposed the difficulty the government forces faced in confronting the fiercely independent and heavily armed tribesmen.

Within days the agreement was in tatters, as militants launched a series of attacks on military posts. Fierce fighting broke out with the army raiding militant hideouts with helicopter gunships. It was the first time military authorities had used airpower against the militants.

The army's deadly response made things worse. Mounting civilian casualties fuelled anger, even among those tribesmen who did not support the militants. The biggest success for the military came in June 2004, when Nek Mohammed was killed by a precision-guided missile.[29] The death of the top militant commander brought a brief respite in the battle, but the war was far from over. Nek Mohammed's mud grave in Shakai had turned into a shrine, visited by scores of tribesmen every day.[30] A soldier of jihad who turned his gun against Pakistan's army had now become a legend. He was remembered by his fellow tribesmen as a 'martyr of the faith'. 'He lived and died like a true Pashtun,' reads a banner on his grave.

His supporters, led by Abdullah Mehsud, had continued to engage Pakistani security forces in a drawn-out guerrilla war. Their targets included those tribal chiefs who had collaborated with the Pakistani military. One by one, all those who had backed military operations against the militants in South and North Waziristan were killed. Faridullah Khan, a Waziri tribal elder and former senator, virtually signed his own death warrant when, in March 2004, he facilitated the entry of army troops to his home village, Shakai in South Waziristan. His men helped soldiers to demolish the houses of the tribesmen linked with the al-Qaeda. He even permitted soldiers to use his fort-like house.

I saw Faridullah at an army sponsored tribal jirga in Shakai in April 2005. Escorted by armed guards, Faridullah, who sported a huge turban and a bushy moustache, declared, 'Al-Qaeda were all over the valley. But this year they are on the run. Peace has been restored.' Twenty-four hours later, Faridullah was dead. The killers had waited at a diversion of the main road, when his jeep passed on the way from a meeting with the army commander. The militants had blasted the vehicle with rocket-propelled grenades. Ironically, Faridullah was killed a day after General Khattak had declared that South Waziristan had been cleared of foreign terrorists.

The list of victims, which included government intelligence operatives and tribesmen accused of spying for the US and Pakistani governments, continued to rise as the Pakistani security engaged in a never-ending war. Often, the killers would leave a charge sheet on their victims, warning others of a similar fate. Malik Sana Pir had been a marked man since he organized a *jirga* (assembly) of his Malikshahi Waziri sub-tribe in North Waziristan's forested Shawal Valley and announced his support for the military campaign. A week later, unknown men with masked faces gunned him down. Targeted killings haunted every village and revenge became the name of the game. Abdullah Mehsud, still defiant and at large, had been blamed for the cycle of revenge killings.

General Khattak had lost hundreds of soldiers in battles with al-Qaeda and its tribal supporters before he could establish partial control over this extremely hostile land. But peace had remained elusive. The militants had continued to hold sway, despite the military's claim of having cleaned up the region. In many cases, the government had bribed the militants to buy peace. Pakistani military authorities had confirmed having paid more than half a million dollars to top militant leaders, in the wake of the botched military operations, to repay their debts to al-Qaeda. The money was given to four Taliban commanders who had earlier been on Pakistan's list of most wanted terrorists.[31] The authorities had often paid tribal leaders to maintain peace in their areas, but it was the first time money went to finance an al-Qaeda operation. This policy of appeasement did not work as the militants continued to use the territory as an effective base of operations.

9

ROGUE IN
THE RANKS

THE NUCLEAR
BLACK MARKET

A senior member of the Bush administration, who visited Islamabad soon after 11 September, raised, during a meeting with Musharraf, the US concern about some Pakistani nuclear scientists having contacts with al-Qaeda and the Taliban regime in Afghanistan. There was a growing anxiety in Washington about the possibility of nuclear weapons falling into the hands of Islamic fundamentalists and making their way to al-Qaeda-linked terrorist groups. The apprehension had grown after intelligence reports that the scientists might have been helping al-Qaeda to acquire weapons of mass destruction (WMD).[1]

On 23 October 2001, acting on an American request, Pakistani authorities detained for interrogation Bashiruddin Mahmood and Abdul Majeed, two retired senior officials at the Pakistan Atomic Energy Commission (PAEC).[2] The British-trained scientists had had a long career in Pakistan's nuclear programme and had held a variety of senior positions until they retired in summer 1999. They had strong Islamic fundamentalist leanings and had devoted themselves to relief and reconstruction work in Taliban-ruled Afghanistan since then. They had set up a non-governmental organization known as Ummah Tameer-e-Nau (UTN), which worked on various development projects in Kabul and Kandahar.

The long-bearded Bashiruddin Mahmood had worked as head of the Khoshab nuclear facility until he resigned in protest against the government's willingness to sign the Comprehensive Test Ban Treaty (CTBT). Even during his service he was suspected of having links with Islamic militant groups and he publicly supported the Taliban, describing them as a model for Pakistan. He advocated extensive production of weapons-grade plutonium and uranium to help equip other Islamic nations with these materials. He termed Pakistan's nuclear capability 'the property of the entire *Ummah* [Muslim community]'. Pakistani security authorities had long viewed his continuation in the sensitive post at the PAEC as dangerous and, in 1999, he was tranferred to a less important position. He was greatly upset by the decision.

Suspicion about the activities of UTN increased after the fall of the Taliban government. In November 2001, the coalition forces and media found several documents in the UTN office, which demonstrated that the organization was interested in developing biological weapons. They recovered designs for a crude system of delivering anthrax.[3] The premises in Kabul's wealthy neighbourhood was also used as a residence for Bashiruddin Mahmood during his stay in the Afghan capital. Hundreds of copies of a document called 'Biological warfare: an imminent danger' were also found there. Pakistani security agencies arrested all seven members of the UTN's board of directors, most of them retired officers of the armed forces or nuclear scientists. In December 2001, President Bush placed the UTN on the list of the organizations supporting terrorism.

Under interrogation, Bashiruddin Mahmood and Abdul Majeed told Pakistani investigators that they had had a series of meetings with bin Laden, the last of which took place in August 2001. They reportedly discussed with the al-Qaeda leader the development of chemical, biological and nuclear weapons.[4] Bashiruddin Mahmood also provided information about the infrastructure needed for a nuclear weapons programme and the effects of nuclear weapons. Pakistani officials, however, dismissed the possibility of nuclear technology being passed on to al-Qaeda by the two detained scientists. Pakistani security officials contended that both the scientists were not weapon experts, and therefore of little value to al-Qaeda. The two men were released and then rearrested and detained for several months. They were finally freed without any charge in mid 2002, despite the conclusion that they had violated a secrecy oath during their visits to Afghanistan. The main reason cited by Pakistani authorities for not putting them on trial was that it would have caused further international embarrassment and risked disclosure of nuclear secrets.

The US also wanted the Pakistani authorities to detain two other nuclear experts for questioning on their possible connection with Islamic militant groups. Suleiman Asad and Mohammed Ali Mukhtar were believed to have been associated with Pakistan's most secret nuclear installations. But they were never detained. The detention and interrogation of Bashiruddin Mahmood and Abdul Majeed, however, sent a strong signal that Pakistan was determined to stop any illicit exports that could advance others' nuclear weapons programmes.[5]

American concern over nuclear proliferation highlighted what later became a growing source of tension between Washington and Islamabad. Some two years later, Pakistan was at the centre of a serious nuclear proliferation scandal when, in February 2004, the country's top scientist, Dr Abdul Qadeer Khan, who was credited with fathering the 'first Islamic atom bomb', confessed to selling nuclear weapons technology to other countries.

For almost three decades, the country's most revered scientist had supervised a vast clandestine nuclear black-market network with tentacles spread over three continents. With the help of middlemen belonging to various countries, it supplied nuclear materials to Libya, Iran and North Korea. He claimed it was all due to ideological reasons and not for money, as he wanted to strengthen the defence capabilities of Islamic countries.

Dr Khan was seen as Pakistan's national hero. Ever since the successful nuclear tests in May 1998 that established Pakistan as the world's seventh nuclear power, he has been an iconic figure. He headed Pakistan's main nuclear facility, Khan Research Laboratories (KRL), named after him, for more than 26 years. Dr Khan had turned the facility into an unaccountable state. With unlimited government resources, which were free of auditing restrictions, he managed to purchase restricted materials from European and American companies that helped Pakistan develop nuclear capability. The network he built up during that period was later passed on to other countries.

Having fallen from grace, Dr Khan went on to spend his days in the solitude of his well-protected villa in Islamabad. The only visitors he is allowed to meet are the intelligence officials who continue to quiz him for more information about his network, which has still not been completely broken, and secrets of his nuclear black market continue to uncoil, revealing a vast global enterprise.

Born into a modest family in Bhopal, India in 1936, Dr Khan migrated to Pakistan in 1952, five years after the creation of the new Muslim state.[6] Memories of the bloodbath in the aftermath of the partition of India in 1947 left a profound impact on him, and his deep anti-Indian sentiments stem from that experience. After graduating from Karachi University, he moved to Europe in 1961 for further studies. He first went to Germany, where he attended the Technical University in West Berlin, then to Holland, where he received a degree in Metallurgical Engineering in 1967. Dr Khan eventually received a Ph.D. in Metallurgy from the Catholic University of Leuven in Belgium in 1972. He took up a job in the 1970s at a uranium-enrichment plant run by a British-Dutch-German consortium, URENCO, at Almelo in the Netherlands.[7] There he also met his Dutch wife, Hendrina. Dr Khan worked with two early centrifuge designs, then, in 1974, he was assigned to translate design documents for two advanced German machines, the G1 and G2. Those were considered the most sophisticated industrial enrichment technology in the world at that time. He had unrestricted access to the plant. During this period he is believed to have made extensive notes, which were useful in his future work in Pakistan. That was also the period when Pakistan decided to develop a nuclear weapon.

In 1972, just months after the humiliating defeat in the war with India that resulted in the December 1971 dismemberment of the country, Pakistan's President, Zulfikar Ali Bhutto, announced his plans to develop an atom bomb at a secret meeting of scientists and civil and military officials in the southern Punjab city of Multan. Pakistan's decision to acquire a nuclear device was driven both by fear of Indian domination and the desire for prominence in the Islamic world. India's nuclear test explosion in May 1974 gave further impetus to Pakistan's obsession with nuclearization. India's demonstration of nuclear capability reinforced the sense of insecurity in a defeated nation. The two countries had fought three wars since their independence and India's military superiority was fully illustrated in the 1971 war. Against this backdrop, Pakistan's nuclear programme appeared to counter India's conventional superiority and its newly acquired nuclear capability.[8]

Even before this development, Zulfikar Ali Bhutto, then Foreign Minister, had declared in 1966 that if India made a nuclear bomb Pakistan would follow suit. 'Even if Pakistanis have to eat grass, we will make the bomb,' Bhutto asserted in an often-quoted statement.[9]

His ascendancy to the presidency in 1971 and the realization of the country's military vulnerability transformed Pakistan's nuclear programme, which had hitherto focused on civilian energy production, into one with a substantial military component. Bhutto seized the opportunity presented by India's nuclear test in 1974 to press ahead with his own nuclear weapons programme. Security concerns were the primary but not the sole factor in Pakistan's decision to develop the atom bomb. Bhutto's vision of 'an Islamic bomb' also fuelled Islamabad's ambition. 'We know that Israel and South Africa have full nuclear capability. The Christian, Jewish and Hindu civilizations have this capability. The Islamic civilization was without it, but that situation was about to change,' Bhutto wrote from his death row prison cell in 1978, a few months before his execution.[10] The Pakistani leader believed that nuclear capability would secure his country a leading role in the Islamic world.

In September 1974, Dr Khan wrote a letter to Bhutto offering his services to the government. His experience at the Almelo plant was very valuable to the country's nascent nuclear programme. Bhutto accepted his offer and invited him to join PAEC. 'Beg, borrow or steal. We must make a nuclear device to counter the threat posed by India. Money should be no problem,' Bhutto told him.

Dr Khan stayed back at Almelo for more than a year, smuggling out the centrifuge designs and other classified documents. In January 1976, he suddenly left Europe with his family before his espionage was detected. In March, he sent his letter of resignation from Pakistan to his employer in Holland. Dr Khan initially worked at a small centrifuge pilot project run by the PAEC at Sihala near Islamabad. Bhutto later separated the uranium enrichment project from the PAEC and made Dr Khan its head. In July 1976, Dr Khan founded the Engineering Research Laboratories – later renamed Khan Research Laboratories – outside Kahuta, not far from Islamabad.[11] The project, which was placed under direct military control, ultimately led to Pakistan's first nuclear test explosion in May 1998. The procurement of the secret centrifuge design from URENCO by Dr Khan was critical to Pakistan's successful nuclearization. He was charged with stealing trade secrets and sentenced, in absentia, to a four-year prison term by a court in the Netherlands in 1983. The sentence was later quashed on appeal.

Pakistan largely concentrated on the uranium enrichment path to nuclear weapons. As early as 1975, Pakistan had begun to clandestinely acquire hardware and technology for ultra-high-speed centrifuges.

Through smuggling and black-market channels, Islamabad obtained hardware for building an enrichment plant in Kahuta. Dr Khan had built up an elaborate network in the West for the procurement of centrifuge enrichment information. Most of the equipment was acquired from Western European countries. From 1977 to 1980, Pakistan smuggled an entire plant for converting uranium powder into hex fluoride, the gas-fired material used as feed for the Kahuta plant.[12] The classified information, smuggled out by Dr Khan during his employment in Europe, helped develop those contacts. In a later interview with Pakistan's *Defence Journal*, Dr Khan proudly recounted how his team openly procured key components from western companies. 'Many suppliers approached us with the details of the machinery and with figures and numbers of instruments and materials,' he said. 'They begged us to purchase their goods.'

The 1978 communist revolution and subsequent invasion of Afghanistan by the Soviet forces brought about a profound geo-strategic change in the region. Pakistan became a crucial frontline state for the West. To win Islamabad's support against the perceived Soviet expansionism, the USA lifted the sanctions against it. The USA needed Pakistan more than Pakistan needed the USA. The Reagan administration decided to shut its eyes to Pakistan's nuclear weapons programme, which had earlier caused serious strains in Pak-US relations. General Zia's military regime fully exploited Pakistan's emerging geo-strategic importance to the West and accelerated the country's nuclear programme. According to a former senior Pakistani official who was associated with the country's nuclear programme from its inception, by 1983 Pakistan had achieved full nuclear capability and could have conducted a test explosion.[13] In an interview after the 28 May nuclear tests, Dr Khan told me that his organization had conducted several cold tests in 1983 and 1984. He said that he informed General Zia in December 1984 that, if he wanted to test the device, a weeks' notice would be more than enough. But General Zia was not willing to take the risk.

There is strong evidence to suggest that, by 1984, Pakistan had crossed 'the red line' in uranium enrichment to more than five per cent. That was the period when Pakistan feared an imminent attack by India for allegedly supporting the Sikh insurgency in Indian Punjab. Pakistan accelerated its nuclear weapons programme as the threat of war loomed large. In an interview with *Nawai Waqt*, a respected Urdu-language national daily, in February 1984, Dr Khan declared that Pakistan was on the verge of achieving nuclear capability.[14] That was the first time that the head of Pakistan's nuclear weapons programme revealed the country's nuclear status. Apparently the interview was meant to warn India that Pakistan could use a nuclear weapon in the event of a war. The statement was later confirmed by General Zia himself in another interview. The development raised serious international concerns. The US Congress passed the Pressler Amendment in 1985, requiring sanctions against Pakistan, unless the President certified that Islamabad was not developing nuclear weapons. The Reagan administration warned Islamabad of dire consequences if it crossed the threshold of 'five per cent' enrichment.[15] But, because of Pakistan's crucial role in the covert operation in Afghanistan, the USA continued to ignore Pakistan's progress towards nuclear capability.

Most nuclear experts agree that 1985 was the watershed in Pakistan's nuclear weapons programme. That was the year when Pakistan developed nuclear-grade enrichment. The US intelligence agencies concluded in 1986 that Pakistan had acquired nominal capability sufficient to produce enough weapons-grade uranium material to build six to seven nuclear bombs each year.[16]. Yet President Reagan continued to certify that Islamabad did not possess nuclear weapons, thus allowing the flow of aid to Pakistan, which had become the linchpin in the West's war against the Soviet communist bloc.

The death of General Zia in August 1988, in a mysterious air crash, and the restoration of democracy did not bring about any significant change in Pakistan's nuclear policy. Under the new civilian government, the country's nuclear programme continued to be run by the military and the President. Benazir Bhutto, who was elected Prime Minister in December 1988, was kept out of the loop. She was not even allowed to visit the Kahuta facility during her first term as chief executive from December 1988 to August 1990. During her state visit to Washington in 1989, Benazir Bhutto assured the US Congress that Pakistan neither possessed a nuclear bomb nor did it intend to build one. But she was shocked when the US intelligence officials told her about the actual status of Pakistan's nuclear programme. After the ousting of her government, Benazir Bhutto maintained in an interview with ABC television that she was kept in the dark about the programme.[17] That the elected Prime Minister had no control or even knowledge of the nuclear weapons programme was a sad commentary on the state of the civil and military relationship and Pakistani democracy.[18]

Following the withdrawal of Soviet forces from Afghanistan in

1990, Pakistan's usefulness for the USA as a frontline state also came to an end. US nuclear sanctions were re-imposed in August 1990, when President Bush invoked the Pressler Amendment and refused to certify that Pakistan did not possess a nuclear weapon. But the action did not deter Islamabad from continuing its efforts. Many observers believe the US sanctions may have been one of the factors in Pakistan's nuclear proliferation. It is not surprising that most of the cases of transfer of nuclear technology occurred during that period.

May 1998 saw the dawn of a new and frightening nuclear era, with India conducting a series of nuclear tests followed by Pakistani test explosions. The 28 May underground nuclear tests in the Chaghai mountains in Balochistan province signalled the emergence of Pakistan as the seventh overt nuclear power. Pakistan's decision to match India's test explosion brought an end to two decades of nuclear ambiguity between the two estranged South Asian neighbours. The development brought their nuclear prowess out into the open, triggered a dangerous arms race and added an alarming dimension to an already volatile situation, turning the region into a nuclear flashpoint.

India's nuclear tests on 11 May 1998 caught Pakistan by surprise. New Delhi's move posed a serious dilemma for Islamabad. For the previous two decades, Pakistan had linked its nuclear policy with that of India. Its deliberate adoption of nuclear ambiguity had worked well as an effective deterrent, but the situation was drastically altered by the Indian action. Pakistani policy-makers argued that they had no choice but to go for their own nuclear test as the credibility of Pakistan's deterrent had been called into question.

The successful test explosions made Dr Khan's dream of making the country a nuclear power come true. A day after the second test, an overly jubilant Dr Khan boasted in an interview that Pakistani devices were more consistent, reliable and advanced than those of the Indians. Talking to a small group of journalists at the KRL camp office near Islamabad, he claimed the credit of putting Pakistan ahead of India's nuclear programme. 'The fact that we used high tech enriched uranium makes our system more efficient. Very few countries have done that,' he declared.[19]

Pakistan's emergence as an overt nuclear power raised a new concern about the safety of its nuclear weapons. There were also questions about the effectiveness and reliability of the command and control structure. The major international concern was the consequence of an accidental detonation of a nuclear device and the risk of its unauthorized use. These were genuine apprehensions given the hostile relations between newly nuclearized India and Pakistan. There has also been concern of the Pakistani nuclear device falling into the hands of Islamic extremists and passed on to other countries. The worry was not without basis.

For almost three decades, the US and western intelligence had been investigating Dr Khan's suspected ties with the international nuclear black-market network, since he began assembling components for Pakistan's bomb. The first indication that Dr Khan's network traded in bomb designs and nuclear technology emerged in 1995, after United Nations inspectors in Iraq discovered some documents describing an offer made to Baghdad before the 1990–1991 Gulf War. According to an internal Iraqi memorandum, dated 10 June 1990, an unidentified middleman claiming to represent Dr Khan had offered Saddam Hussein help to 'establish a project to enrich uranium and manufacture a nuclear weapon'.[20] There were also some reports that Dr Khan himself had made several clandestine trips to Iraq.

In 1998, Pakistani government investigated the middleman's letter at the request of the International Atomic Energy Agency (IAEA) and declared the offer a fraud. The nuclear agency listed the memo as a key unresolved issue in a 1999 UN report on Iraq's arms programmes. Meanwhile, American authorities had gathered some evidence on Pakistan's nuclear cooperation with North Korea. In the summer of 2001, American spy satellites spotted missile parts being loaded into a Pakistani cargo plane near the North Korean capital, Pyongyang. The parts were delivered in return for Pakistan's nuclear technology.[21] The report led to some US sanctions against KRL, but Washington was still hesitant to impose sanctions against Pakistan for nuclear transfer because of insufficient evidence.

Musharraf had a strong dislike for Dr Khan. 'He is bad news,' he often said privately of Khan. The increasing American pressure offered a good opportunity to sideline the scientist. In March 2001, he removed Dr Khan as head of KRL and appointed him presidential adviser on science, with the rank of federal minister, a post he held until January 2004. Dr Khan was stunned when he heard the news on national television. At first he refused to accept the move, but had little choice. The action did not satisfy the American administration. The US officials suspected that the exchanges with North Korea had continued even after Dr Khan's removal. In July 2002, US spy satellites again spotted Pakistani military cargo planes picking up missile parts in North Korea. Meanwhile, in June 2001, the US Deputy Secretary of State, Richard Armitage, all but named Dr Khan, when he expressed concerns that 'people who were employed by the nuclear agency and have retired' might be spreading nuclear technology to North Korea.[22]

During his visit to Islamabad in the summer of 2002, the US Secretary of State, Colin Powell, was said to have asked President Musharraf to arrest Dr Khan for questioning over the alleged secret trading of Pakistan's nuclear technology to North Korea. He also offered US assistance in investigating into the matter.[23] Musharraf had already sidelined Dr Khan, but he was not prepared to take that extreme step against the country's most revered personality, largely because of fear of a public backlash. Musharraf later told the *New York Times* that he had suspected for at least three years that Dr Khan was sharing nuclear technology with other countries, but argued that the USA had not given him convincing proof.

Pakistan's link with the North Korean nuclear programme, however, ran much deeper and was much more complicated. The defence cooperation between the two nations started in 1994, when Prime Minister Benazir Bhutto visited Pyongyang to negotiate a missile deal with the North Korean leaders. Benazir Bhutto's father, Pakistan's former Prime Minister, Zulfikar Ali Bhutto, had had a lasting friendship with the founder of the North Korean communist regime, Kim Il Sung. There was huge respect for the daughter of Pakistan's first elected leader. She was persuaded by the military leadership to go and see the North Korean leader, Kim Jong. Pakistan desperately needed a nuclear missile system at that point to counter India's threat; US sanctions on military hardware sales had also fuelled the urgency of this need. Benazir Bhutto denied that Pakistan had traded nuclear technology for the missiles. But there was huge scepticism over whether Pakistan, with its economy in a slump, would have enough money to pay the North Koreans. Benazir Bhutto has often said that the USA conspired in the ousting of her second government because of the missile deal with North Korea.[24]

Nonetheless, the deal provided Dr Khan with an opportunity to make a breakthrough with the North Koreans. He visited North Korea 13 times over the next seven years. During those visits, Pyongyang offered to exchange centrifuge equipment for its missile technology, enabling Pakistan to extend the reach of its nuclear weapon deep inside India. North Korean scientists received nuclear briefings at KRL, although even top Pakistani civilian leaders were not allowed to visit the highly guarded secret facility.[25] Pakistani officials insist that they received the first indication about nuclear technology being transferred in 2000, when the ISI conducted a raid on an air force aircraft that was allegedly carrying nuclear material to North Korea. Dr Khan was reprimanded, but no action was taken against him at that point.[26] This is quite intriguing. How could he use an air force plane without the knowledge and consent of the military leadership? Pakistan later developed its own medium- and long-distance missile system based on North Korean technology, which is now the mainstay of the country's nuclear weapons delivery system.

A few years earlier, before international attention began focusing on the dangers of proliferation, some Pakistani scientists had handed out brochures at trade shows in Germany and elsewhere 'that implied that they were willing to sell sensitive centrifuge know-how or items of equipment'. The Pakistani leaders, who had denied for years that the scientists at the country's secret nuclear facility were peddling advanced nuclear technology, had ignored the most conspicuous piece of evidence. The brochure was quietly circulated to aspiring nuclear states, and a network of middlemen bore the official seal 'Government of Pakistan' and a photograph of Dr Khan. It offered for sale components that were spin-offs from Pakistan's three-decade project to build nuclear stockpiles of enriched uranium.[27]

It was in October 2003 that international investigators stumbled upon the most substantive evidence about his role in spreading nuclear technology. The information, pieced together from limited inspections and the documents turned over to the IAEA, showed that a centrifuge of Pakistani design was used at the Iranian nuclear facility.[28] Although Iranian documents submitted to the IAEA made no reference to Pakistan itself, the suspicion about the origin of the centrifuge inevitably fell on Pakistan's main nuclear facility, KRL, which had mastered the requisite technology and where Pakistan's atom bomb was developed. For more than 18 years, Pakistan's role had been well hidden from American intelligence agencies.

Musharraf was stunned when, during a meeting on the sidelines of the Organization of Islamic Countries (OIC) summit conference in Kuala Lumpur in September 2003, Iran's President Khatami cautioned him about an IAEA investigation into a possible Pakistan link with the Iranian nuclear programme.[29] For many years, Pakistan had rejected allegations of the involvement of its top scientists in nuclear proliferation. At about the same time, the US Deputy Secretary of State, Richard Armitage, provided new evidence to Pakistani officials of Dr Khan's involvement in the sale of nuclear technology. They included detailed records of his travels to Libya, Iran and North Korea and other nations, along with intercepted phone conversations, records of financial transactions and accounts of meetings with foreign businessmen involved in an illicit nuclear trade.[30] Musharraf was shocked by the detailed evidence presented to him. The Americans knew much more than the Pakistani authorities about Dr Khan's wealth spread across the globe.

The CIA chief, George Tenet, disclosed that the intelligence agency had successfully penetrated Dr Khan's network long before the IAEA began investigating the illicit nuclear technology sale to Iran. 'We were inside his residence, inside his facilities, inside his room,' Tenet said in a speech at the end of 2004. 'We were everywhere these people were.'[31] He said that CIA agents, working with British spies, had pieced together a picture of the network revealing, scientists, subsidiaries, companies, agencies and manufacturing plants on three continents.[32] As evidence grew, President Bush sent Tenet to New York to meet with Musharraf in September 2003, as the US feared that Dr Khan's operation was entering a new, more dangerous phase.

When confronted with a highly credible investigation report and 'mind-boggling' details about Dr Khan's activities, Musharraf was left with no choice but to cooperate with the IAEA and the USA. It was, perhaps, the most testing time for the military ruler since he had joined the US war on terror some two years earlier. The Bush administration warned him that failure to act on the information could lead to sanctions by the United States and the United Nations. Pressure mounted as Washington threatened to go public with the information on Dr Khan. 'You need to deal with this before you have to deal with it publicly,' Powell told Musharraf.[33] What caused most concern in Islamabad was that an international investigation might open a Pandora's box involving even the military, which had always been the custodian of the country's nuclear programme. It was largely external pressure that forced Musharraf to confront the problem head on. He assured the Bush administration not only of full cooperation in their Iran-related inquiries, but also of further tightening of export controls.

The Iran case presented the most damning evidence yet about

Pakistan's connection to nuclear proliferation. Evidence uncovered by the IAEA showed that the Pakistani link with the Iranian nuclear programme went back to 1987, when General Zia's military government approved a long-standing request from the Iranian government for unpublicized cooperation in its 'peaceful' nuclear programme. But the cooperation was limited to non-military spheres. The transfer of technology is believed to have occurred in 1989. This was the period when General Aslam Beg propounded his doctrine of 'strategic defiance', which envisaged an anti-American alliance of Pakistan, Iran and Afghanistan. The nuclear-related sanctions imposed on Pakistan by the US administration in August 1990 provoked intense anti-American sentiments among the Pakistani generals, who felt betrayed by the American actions.

General Beg, who was the Chief of Army Staff from 1988 to 1991, may not have been a doctrinaire Islamist like General Zia, but he followed many of his policies. He was a highly controversial figure, both in the army and outside. A migrant from the Indian state of Uttar Pradesh, he provoked intense controversy by publicly criticizing Prime Minister Nawaz Sharif's decision to join the US-led coalition forces in the 1990–1991 Gulf War. On a visit to Tehran during the same period, he promised the Iranian leadership that the Pakistani leadership would be willing to provide nuclear technology. Ishaq Dar, a senior member of the Sharif cabinet, confirmed that Beg came back with an offer from Tehran of $5 billion in return for nuclear know-how, but Sharif rejected the offer.[34]

In his confession to Pakistani investigators, Dr Khan had implicated General Beg, among others, in the deal. The allegation was rejected by the former army chief as malicious but, in the same breath, he defended Dr Khan, saying there was nothing wrong with passing on nuclear technology to other countries.[35] General Beg retired in August 1991 and was replaced by a moderate pro-West officer, General Asif Nawaz, who stopped the deal with Iran. Consequently, Pakistan-Iran relations were adversely affected and any cooperation in the nuclear field would have been completely ruled out.

Dr Khan was believed to have travelled to Iran several times in the late 1980s and early 1990s. He claimed that centrifugal uranium enrichment plants were exported to Iran through a middleman and that Pakistan air force planes were used to ferry the goods to Dubai, from where they were taken to their final destination. Drawings and other nuclear materials were also transferred abroad secretly.[36] Most of the transactions took place through a Dubai-based Sri Lankan middleman, Buhary Syed Abu Tahir, who was arrested by Malaysian police in February 2004. Tahir, who also lived in Malaysia, told the investigators that he transported two containers of used centrifuge parts from Pakistan to Iran in 1994 or 1995. The containers were ferried from Dubai to Iran on an Iranian merchant ship. According to Abu Tahir, the payment for the consignment was paid for by an unnamed Iranian. The cash, amounting to about $3 million, was brought in two briefcases and kept in an apartment that was used as a guesthouse by Dr Khan each time he visited Dubai.[37]

Shortly after the IAEA delivered its findings on Iran in a two-page letter in November 2003, Musharraf ordered the ISI and the Strategic Planning and Development cell, which controls the country's nuclear programme, to investigate allegations of proliferation. ISI officials travelled to Malaysia, Dubai, Iran and Libya looking for clues of Dr Khan's involvement in the transfer of nuclear technology. Three senior scientists at KRL were arrested after the investigators found the allegations were correct. But the most difficult part was to confront Dr Khan. The responsibility for interrogating the man at the centre of the proliferation scandal was given to the Director General of the ISI, Lt.-General Ehsan ul-Haq, and the chief of SPD, Lt.-General-Khalid Ahmed Qidwai. They first met Dr Khan in December at his villa in the Margala foothills. Initially Dr Khan denied any wrongdoing. He told the generals that his activities were known to the army chiefs. To cover his tracks, Dr Khan wrote to Iranian officials in November 2003 urging them to destroy some of their facilities and to tell the investigators that the Pakistanis who had aided them had died.[38] The noose around Dr Khan's neck was tightened further with the discovery of new evidence about his link with the Libyan nuclear programme.

In 2003, US agents intercepted a German ship named BBC *China*, carrying parts for a Libyan nuclear facility that led to its renouncing its nuclear ambitions. Evidence uncovered following Libya's decision to give up its nuclear programme in December 2003 revealed how extensive Dr Khan's nuclear smuggling network was. A joint British-American inspection team that visited Libya's nuclear, chemical and biological weapons sites over that period were taken aback when they found that nuclear scientists working on the project had a 'full bomb dossier' from the Pakistanis. The export of nuclear materials to Libya was much greater than to Iran or to North Korea. It included not only complete centrifuges and enriched uranium for weapons, but also the design of the atomic bomb. Pakistanis had also provided information to Libya on how and where to acquire additional components for their nuclear programme.[39]

Ties between Libya and Pakistan went back to 1973, when Pakistan had just started its nuclear weapons programme. Libyan leader Muammar Qaddafi agreed to finance Pakistan's nuclear efforts in exchange for knowledge about how to make nuclear fuel. Libya is reported to have supplied Pakistan with uranium from 1978 to 1980. But Tripoli did not receive any significant help from Pakistan during that period. The transfer of nuclear materials started much later. Libya contacted Dr Khan in 1997 for help in building centrifuges. He held a series of meetings with Libyan officials starting that year and lasting until 2002. The deals were made in Dubai, Istanbul and Casablanca between 1988 and 2001.[40] In exchange for cash transfers to his bank account in the Gulf, Dr Khan helped Libya establish contact with black-market networks. The network Dr Khan had built involved a Malaysian engineering firm and middlemen from Germany. Abu Tahir who was the controlling shareholder in Gulf Technical Industries, a Dubai-based enterprise, would receive the centrifuge shipment from Malaysia, then load them onto a German ship to send to Libya. Until 2003, Libya had received network centrifuge equipment used for the enrichment of uranium and blueprints for making a nuclear bomb, together with a shipment of 1.5 tonnes of hexafluoride gas from Dr Khan's network.

Libya had reportedly paid $100 million to acquire nuclear components from Pakistan and a variety of black-market dealers in The Netherlands, South Africa and Sri Lanka. The enriched uranium was sent from Pakistan to Libya on a Pakistani airliner around 2001, and 'a certain number of centrifuge units' were sent in 2001–2002. By that time, Musharraf was already in power. Documents handed over by Libya to the IAEA revealed that the country had received old Chinese designs for a workable nuclear bomb that had been passed to Pakistan in the late 1970s. The blueprints for a ten-kiloton atomic bomb discovered in Libya were wrapped in plastic bags from the tailoring shop in Islamabad that had stitched Dr Khan's suits.[41] The discovery brought to the focus the audacity of Dr Khan's rogue nuclear network.

The documents from Libya and Iran showed that the Khan network had offered to sell instructions on such complex manufacturing steps as purifying uranium, casting it into a nuclear core and making the explosives that compress the core and set off a chain reaction. Unlike the bomb designs themselves, these manufacturing secrets can take years or even decades for a country to learn on its own. The critical technical information helped these countries to put their nuclear weapon programmes on a fast track.

The problem became more complicated with reports that Dr Khan had smuggled out some sensitive information about his activities. He sent his daughter to London, allegedly with material showing that senior military officials approved of his activities. Pakistani commandos were flown overnight to get the material, which was locked in Khan's apartment in Dubai.[42] Meanwhile, Dr Khan, who was placed under house arrest, finally gave in when he was shown evidence of his activities and bank accounts in Dubai holding several million dollars that a surrogate allegedly opened for him under a false name. The investigators also produced statements from Dr Khan's aides implicating him in the proliferation. On 2 February 2004, Dr Khan signed a confession detailing his illicit network.[43] He then asked to meet with President Musharraf to request clemency. The next day the President and the scientist met for 45 minutes. The meeting started with a tense atmosphere, but a deal was eventually made. There would be no more talk of Pakistani miltiary cooperation with the proliferation network. Musharraf assured Dr Khan that he would be pardoned if he apologized to the nation.[44] The deal made, the scientist was handed a two-page typewritten statement and told to read it on national television.[45]

It was a far cry from his glory days when a distraught Dr Khan, with greying, wavy hair and salt-and-pepper moustache, appeared on state television on 4 February 2004, reading from a well-scripted text, accepting sole responsibility for illicit nuclear trafficking. 'I take full responsibility for my actions and seek your pardon,' he appealed almost in a choking voice. The three-minute dramatic confession turned the national hero into a figure of shame.[46] The idol had fallen from grace for betraying the national trust. The drop scene came in a nationally televised address the next day, when Musharraf announced a state pardon for Dr Khan, citing his services to Pakistan. 'He is my hero and the nation's hero and would remain so as he made Pakistan a nuclear power,' declared the General.

The matter did not rest there; many unanswered questions remained. Could Dr Khan and his cohorts have moved large pieces of equipment without the knowledge of the military, the custodian of Pakistan's nuclear programme? Given the massive security in place for nuclear installations and the personal security of the scientists, could any of them have engaged in clandestine activities without being noticed?

The sheer scale of Pakistan's secret nuclear exports indicates that it could not have been a rogue operation and points to a deeper level of complicity. Musharraf had his own reasons for granting Dr Khan amnesty. The trial of a national hero could have serious political repercussions and provoke opposition within the military. The risk of putting the father of Pakistan's nuclear bomb in the dock was too high. Dr Khan knew too much and his trial could have opened a Pandora's box and placed Musharraf and his military in a highly embarrassing position. Musharraf had protected himself and the military by putting all the blame on one individual.

A major reason cited by the Pakistani leader for not broadening the investigation to the military, or the government, was that it could have serious implications for the country. Musharraf cautioned that Pakistan could face UN sanctions, if official complicity in the transfer of nuclear technology was established. He warned Pakistani journalists not to speculate further on the military's role in peddling nuclear secrets, saying it would not be in the national interest.

A few days later, in an interview with the *Financial Times*, President Musharraf talked about the predicament he had faced dealing with Dr Khan's case. 'It was psychologically a very difficult moment that I had to deal with, that of a person who has done wrong and that person happens to be my hero or the nation's hero for having done something so great for the nation,' said General Musharraf. 'But then, when you saw reality, I put it that a person who has given birth to a child of national significance has done things which actually were trying to kill the child that he gave birth to.'

Apparently, the pardon defused the situation at home and was accepted by Washington at face value. But the delicate balancing act did not bring an end to Musharraf's problems on both domestic and international fronts. He continued to face a separate confrontation with the international nuclear watchdog, the IAEA, demanding full access to Pakistan's nuclear programme in order to ensure that no more nuclear secrets were sold to other countries. The US and other western countries not only wanted to know what had happened in the past, they also sought reassurance that no nuclear proliferation would take place in the future.

The stigma of suspected involvement in an international nuclear black market continues to dog Pakistan. The notion of sharing the 'bomb' for ideological reasons, rather than profit, rang particular alarm bells for the USA. Musharraf's impressive effort at damage control notwithstanding, the proliferation issue is not over yet and, as the US's confrontation with Iran intensifes, there is a looming danger that Khan and his network will be dragged back into the spotlight, testing Musharraf's balancing skills to their limit.

10

THE SIEGE
WITHIN

THE RETURN
OF THE MULLAHS

The House responded with a resounding 'Amen', as a black-turbaned member prayed for the destruction of America. 'Oh God, punish those responsible for the killings of Muslims,' he implored. The newly elected legislative assembly of the North West Frontier Province interrupted its opening session to pay homage to Aimal Kansi, the Pakistani national who had been executed a week earlier in America for killing two CIA officials.[1] For the Islamists he was a martyr. Thousands of people attended his funeral in his home town, Quetta.

Pakistani parliamentary elections in October 2002 had swept radical Islamists into power in the key border province. The success of the MMA, the six-party conservative Islamic coalition,[2] came on the wave of strong anti-American sentiments following US military action in neighbouring Afghanistan. 'It is a war between Islam and the American infidel.' This slogan instantly hit a chord with Pashtuns who believed their ethnic brethren on the other side of the border were being victimized by US forces and the US-supported administration in Kabul. The Islamists also capitalized on anti-Musharraf feelings stemming from his pro-US policies. They charged him with betraying 'Afghan Muslims and siding with the infidels'. The Islamists openly expressed solidarity with bin Laden and Mullah Omar.[3] The campaign also helped the MMA to win votes in the western Balochistan province, where it shared power with a pro-military coalition.

The resurgence of radical Islamists portended ill for a nation in the midst of a war against Islamic militancy, threatening its political, cultural and social stability. The installation of a conservative Islamic government in the two border provinces, which had turned into sanctuaries for the Taliban and al-Qaeda remnants fleeing from Afghanistan, caused great concern to the United States. The MMA was closely linked with the Taliban and its rise to power fuelled insurgency in Afghanistan. There was a marked increase in attacks on US forces and their Afghan allies by the Taliban, who then fled back to the Pakistani Pashtun tribal areas. US military officials had repeatedly threatened hot pursuit of the Taliban into Pakistan.

Pakistan's Pashtun populated areas in the North West Frontier Province and Balochistan are contiguous with the Pashto-speaking region of Southern Afghanistan. That proximity has historically shaped the region and resulted in cross-border kin and group ties. This cross-border ethnic bond had played a significant role in Pakistan's involvement, first in running covert operations against the Soviet forces and, later, helping the predominant Pashtun Taliban movement. The entire top leadership of the MMA was Pashtun and hence had strong cross-border associations. The MMA's electoral success also carried long-term political implications at home as the battle for the very soul of Pakistan intensified.

It was the first time in Pakistan's political history that the mainstream Islamic parties, representing different Islamic sects, had come together. The MMA had grown out of an alliance of religious and jihadist groups that took shape following the events of 11 September and the subsequent US military campaign in Afghanistan. Initially, some three dozen Islamic groups were united under the banner of the Defence of Afghanistan Council to show solidarity with the Taliban regime and Osama bin Laden. It was later renamed the Defence of Afghanistan and Pakistan Council to oppose the US military action in Afghanistan. The council could not do much more than organize anti-US and anti-Musharraf demonstrations. The routing of the Taliban regime came as a serious blow to the Pakistani Islamic movement. Demoralization set in when a US-supported government was installed in Kabul, forcing bin Laden and his men to flee for their lives. As the elections approached, six of Pakistan's most powerful parties, including Jamaat-i-Islami, Jamiat Ulema Islam and Jamiat Ulema Pakistan, regrouped themselves in the form of the MMA. Their shared perception of the post-9/11 world and their anti-US position impelled them to unite on one platform. One common objective was to resist Musharraf's policy turnaround.

Musharraf was bound by the Supreme Court ruling to hold parliamentary elections and transfer power to an elected government by October 2002. He, however, made his intentions very clear: there was going to be no complete transfer to an elected Parliament or to a civilian government. On the eve of the elections, he made sweeping changes in the constitution ensuring that he would continue to hold ·sway in the new order. The controversial redrafting of the constitution exposed Musharraf's plan to establish a 'controlled democracy' in which the military would continue to cast its heavy shadow. It removed all illusions about the country's return to democracy.[4]

The changes gave the President extensive powers, including the right to dismiss an elected Parliament. A military-dominated National Security Council, with overriding powers over Parliament, was to monitor the future civilian government. It was an entirely new constitution in which the source of power was outside the Parliament. Musharraf described the new order as the transition from 'democratic dictatorship to an elected essence of democracy'.

And it was not enough that the military government tried to micro-manage the outcome of the elections and manipulate a 'favourable result'. For several weeks before the nomination papers were filed, Tariq Aziz, the President's powerful principal secretary, had camped out in Lahore, wheeling and dealing with politicians. The country's most influential bureaucrat had an important task assigned to him by his military leader. His job was to knock together a pro-military alliance. Aided by Major-General Ehtesham Zamir, the head of the the ISI's internal wing, Tariq Aziz manoeuvred a list of 'loyal' candidates. Most of them belonged to the Pakistan Muslim League (Quaid) faction, but there were several others who the military government believed were willing to cooperate.[5] They included some of Pakistan's most corrupt politicians, raising questions about Musharraf's pledge to fight corruption. State machinery was blatantly used to get a 'favourable result'.

Tariq Aziz, a close pal of Musharraf's from his student days, has been his key political strategist and had earlier engineered a split in the Pakistan Muslim League. However, it was not just Tariq Aziz's dexterity, but also heavy arm-twisting by the ISI, as well as the administration, which forced many to switch their loyalties. Never before had the spy agency, despite its notoriety, been used in such rampant political manipulation. Many opposition candidates were often summoned by ISI operatives and urged to join the pro-military alliance. Others had even worse experiences. After successfully disqualifying Benazir Bhutto and Nawaz Sharif, the former Prime Ministers, Musharraf had removed his two main rivals from the election field. With the leaders of the largest parties in exile, Pakistan for the first time witnessed an election campaign through remote control.

Musharraf thought he had the elections all sewn up. The ISI had assured him that the race would produce what he wanted: a friendly Parliament full of 'new faces'. And he had no reason to doubt his spooks. The MMA would be a counterbalance to the liberal opposition parties, he was told. The mullahs had won only two seats in the previous elections, so they would not be a threat this time either, only a menace to the opposition. But that assessment went awry, despite the micro management of the elections.

The MMA took full advantage of the fragmentation of the liberal parties generated by the military establishment. Despite their conflict over Musharraf's turnaround on Pakistan's Afghan policy, the traditional link between the military and the Islamists had not been fully severed. Both considered the liberal Pakistan People's Party and the Pakistan Muslim League to be their main adversaries. The two sides mended fences on the eve of the polls after a three-hour meeting between Musharraf and Qazi Hussein Ahmed, chief of Jamaat-i-Islami, the most vocal critic among the Islamists. He reminded Musharraf that his party had always stood by the military, despite their differences over the regime's support of the USA.

There was also a marked softening in the government's rhetoric against religious extremism. Islamic activists rounded up during the anti-American protests were freed. While many anti-military politicians were barred on corruption charges, or disqualified by the clause that required a candidate to have a university degree, the Islamic candidates were given a free hand. Mullahs with madrasa education were allowed to run. The military government even allowed Azam Tariq, the leader of the outlawed sectarian-based party, the SSP, to stand for a National Assembly seat.[6] Azam Tariq, who was alleged to have been involved in scores of murder cases, was freed on bail. The Musharraf government, which had vowed to eliminate extremism, had apparently given its blessing to a known terrorist. The politics of expediency cost both Musharraf and the country dearly.

Musharraf misjudged the rising support for the Islamists. A couple of weeks before the polls he had assured senior American officials that the religious parties would not get more than five per cent of the vote. MMA leaders had started campaigning long before the other parties entered the field. They fully exploited the anti-American feelings among the Pashtuns who were incensed by the US attack on Afghanistan. The absence of Benazir Bhutto and Nawaz Sharif,[7] the crowd-pullers for the Pakistan People's Party and the Pakistan Muslim League, also helped the MMA.

It was a virtual revolution through the ballot box when the Islamic alliance swept the polls in the North West Frontier Province, deposing the traditional power elite. The landslide victory took even the MMA leaders by surprise.[8] The Islamists also consolidated their position in Balochistan. Success was, however, restricted to these two provinces. In Punjab and Sindh, the alliance's influence was marginal. In these, the most populous provinces, the voters did not respond to the anti-US rhetoric and Islamic fervour. Because of the heavy concentration of the vote in one ethnic belt, it translated into a higher number of seats for the alliance in the National Assembly where it emerged as the third largest block. The election result was, however, not an indicator of the rising influence of Islamic fundamentalism. There were several anomalies that helped to amplify the actual strength and popular base of the religious parties. While the MMA was third in the popular vote (11.6 per cent of votes cast), it won 63 national assembly seats, including ten reserved for women, out of 342.

The MMA might not have been directly involved in the militancy, but its components like the JI and the two factions of the JUI had long been associated with jihadist politics.[9] Their activists overlapped with those of militant and sectarian organizations. Former Taliban and jihadist commanders were among MMA candidates for the National and provincial assemblies. The banned jihadist organizations openly campaigned for the alliance. They saw the success of the MMA as a triumph for their cause. There was a visible stridency among the radical elements after the MMA formed the government in the North West Frontier Province and became a coalition partner in Balochistan. Although their success was confined to the Pashtun ethnic belt, the Islamists, for the first time in Pakistan's history, took the political centre stage. They emerged as a major power player, holding the balance in the divided National Assembly.

Despite the military's best efforts, the election results reflected a no-confidence vote against Musharraf's military government. More than 60 per cent of the votes went to the parties opposed to the military regime. For all its pre-poll manipulation, the military failed to contain the liberal forces. The Pakistan People's Party received 25.8 per cent of the total votes cast, with the pro-military Pakistan Muslim League (Q) trailing behind with 25.7 per cent. The Pakistan Muslim League (N) bagged 9.4 per cent, less than the MMA's share of 11.6 per cent. The situation would have been worse for the General, had the elections been conducted in a free and fair manner.

European Union observers called the elections 'flawed'. In a scathing criticism of the election process, their report said that the secrecy of the vote was compromised and the count showed serious shortcomings. They reported that the Election Commission of Pakistan had failed to curb the abuse of state resources, particularly, in favour of pro-military political parties.[10]

The polls had created a horizontal polarization, with all four provinces going in different directions. While the North West Frontier Province went to the MMA, Punjab sided with the pro-military PML (Q). In Sindh, the PPP maintained its stronghold in the rural areas, while the Muttehida Qaumi Movement (MQM), an ethnic-based party representing Urdu-speaking migrants, swept the urban areas. The MMA broadened its support base in Balochistan.

Musharraf faced a very tricky situation with his loyalists failing to get a majority in the National Assembly, which was required to form the federal government. He tried to strike a deal with the MMA, but the negotiations apparently collapsed after the MMA demanded the post of Prime Minister and stuck to its crucial demand that Musharraf give a firm date to step down as Chief of Army Staff. The Islamists also called for the reversal of Pakistan's support for the USA and the withdrawal of American troops from the country.[11] These conditions were obviously unacceptable to Musharraf. It was difficult for the MMA leaders as well to give up their crucial demands because of pressure from the hardliners in their ranks. The MMA was believed to have had the backing of some of the generals, who had been sidelined because of their opposition to Musharraf's pro-American policy. The right-wing generals, who had close links with the Islamists, looked for an opportune moment to embarrass the President.

Despite its divergence on important policy issues, like support for the US war on terror in Afghanistan and the crackdown on jihadist organizations, the Islamists had not completely severed their ties with the military. The MMA leaders had targeted Musharraf personally, but their loyalty to the military had remained unchanged. That was one reason for the military's continuing conciliatory approach towards the Islamists, whom it regarded as its logical ally. The MMA was more than willing to play by the military's rules. The mullahs and the military had worked together against common foes during the cold war and the Afghan jihad and had shared the military's national security perspective and its views on regional issues. The MMA leadership had also been engaged in secret negotiations with ISI officials involved in political fixing. However, because of political considerations, they stopped short of entering into an alliance with the federal government, despite the alliance in Balochistan.

The military, however, pulled out the required number of votes by manipulating a split in the PPP. It was made possible after Musharraf, in a highly controversial move, suspended the ban on floor-crossing which allowed opposition members to switch sides. Most of these turncoats had faced corruption charges and could easily be blackmailed. Almost all of them were given important positions in the cabinet. Faisal Saleh Hayat, a prominent PPP leader, had been charged for defaulting on the repayment of loans from state-owned banks and had spent months in prison, making him extremely vulnerable politically. He was made Interior Minister after the defection. A senior general walked up to him during the oath-taking ceremony to congratulate him for what he described as a 'courageous move in the national interest'!

With all the manipulation and horse-trading engineered by intelligence agencies, Zafarullah Jamali, the pro-military candidate for Prime Minister, barely scraped through. His controversial one-vote majority came as a relief to Musharraf who wanted a pliable prime minister in place. A tribal leader from Pakistan's western Balochistan province, Jamali had a reputation of being an establishment person who was unlikely to take a stand against a powerful military president. An easy going, stoutly built, soft-spoken politician, he had served as Chief Minister for three brief terms in his native province, most recently in 1996. He had also been a federal minister in the military regime of late General Zia ul-Haq in the mid 1990s. His friends called him 'Jabal' (mountain) – a nickname as a young man for not crying after a bad injury during a hockey match.

Musharraf was also sworn in for another five-year term as President, the same day that the new Parliament met. He had extended his term through a controversial referendum in April. The newly elected Prime Minister was just a figurehead as the President continued to call the shots on most matters, particularly on foreign and economic issues. His government, meanwhile, faced a tough challenge from a formidable and vocal opposition in Parliament, especially from the religious right who refused to accept the changes in the constitution made by the President, giving himself sweeping powers.

The installation of an elected Parliament and a civilian administration changed the country's political dynamics. Musharraf came under immense pressure to quit his job as army chief. The conflict between Parliament and the military president over the changes in the constitution had remained unresolved raising serious questions about the sustainability of the new set-up.

The American attack on Iraq in 2003 gave a new impetus to the Islamists to whip up anti-American and anti-Musharraf sentiments and broaden their support base. 'We can topple the government any time,' boasted a senior MMA leader after a huge anti-war rally in Peshawar. Bold and daring words inspired by what was, perhaps, the biggest of the marches organized by the Islamic alliance across the country to protest against the American aggression in Iraq. In a sight rarely seen in Pakistan, thousands of protestors thronged to the rally, venting their anger against Bush as well as General Musharraf. 'Down with Bush' and 'Down with Musharraf' were the most common slogans. The unprecedented public response to the MMA's protest call had visibly boosted their confidence and brought a new stridency to their supporters.[13]

The Islamists successfully manipulated the popular revulsion against the American attack and increased their credentials as the country's major political force. They were not yet in a position to force the ousting of Musharraf, but they had certainly forced the government into a tight corner and dictated their own political agenda. Musharraf tiptoed on a tightrope. While trying to maintain its cooperation with the USA in the war on terror, his administration scrambled to desperately identify itself with the feeling on the streets and prevent public anger from boiling over into an anti-government uprising. Massive anti-war protests and across-the-board anti-American sentiment forced the government to carry out a delicate balancing act by distancing itself from the US operation, while at the same time not alienating the USA or allowing the Islamist alliance to stoke anti-American fires to an explosive point.[14]

Pakistan's stance of not supporting the US attack on Iraq helped the government to some extent in defusing public anger, but Musharraf's long-term political problems continued to simmer on the back-burner. Islamabad's support for Washington was balanced against two powerful forces at home: the religious conservative forces that had gained tremendous political support and the military that did not seem to be happy with the war in Iraq.

Riding on the wave of popular anti-war sentiments and emboldened by their new-found public support, Islamic groups intensified their attack on Musharraf, calling him an 'American stooge'. MMA leaders tried to use anti-American sentiment to vent their anger against the government's pro-West policies and to gain maximum political mileage from a potentially volatile situation. The Islamists grabbed the opportunity to expand their support base in Punjab and Sindh.

There was a visible rise in the activities of the outlawed Islamist extremist groups which were back in the field exploiting anti-Americanism. The militant leaders, recently freed from house arrest, returned to the mosques to rally the Muslims against the United States and recruit volunteers for a new 'holy war'. Hundreds of Pakistani volunteers enrolled themselves to fight in Iraq after an Islamic cleric issued a fatwa that it was obligatory for all Muslims to join 'the jihad' against the invasion of a Muslim country by American forces.

Rising anti-American sentiments, coupled with a surge in support for conservative Islamist groups, had a significant fall-out in neighbouring Afghanistan where the US-led coalition forces were locked in battle with the remnants of al-Qaeda and the Taliban. There was an alarming rise in the number of attacks by insurgents in southern Afghanistan. The increasing number of rocket attacks targeting coalition bases was a testimony to the support for the Afghan resistance from the pro-Taliban administration in the North West Frontier Province and Balochistan. For the first time since their ousting, some key former Taliban leaders resurfaced and openly operated from inside Pakistan.[15]

Musharraf managed the balancing act quite well. Tightly wedged between the mullahs and a hard place, he emerged unscathed from the crisis. After narrowly escaping a series of assassination attempts, Musharraf got some much-needed respite when, in December 2003, he won a protracted constitutional battle legitimizing his rule. A vote of confidence by Parliament allowed him to stay on as President for the next four years. It was the second boost for the military ruler in a week. On the last day of the year, lawmakers approved a series of amendments in the constitution making him an all-powerful leader, vested with the authority to dismiss an elected government as well as Parliament.

Musharraf owed his triumph solely to the hardline religious groups that had hitherto been at odds with him over his pro-US policies as well as his domestic crackdown on Islamic militants. In return for their support for his presidency, Musharraf had agreed to shed his military uniform by the end of the year. 'There comes a time in the lives of nations when important decisions must be taken,' he said. 'That time has come.' The President hoped the move would end the political deadlock, which had paralysed Parliament since the elections 14 months earlier.

The deal between Musharraf and the MMA had revived the traditional alliance between the mullahs and the military.[16] It also strengthened the Islamists' hold over the bordering provinces where the Taliban had regrouped. This 'marriage of convenience', however, had not deterred the more extremist elements from plotting to kill him. Ironically, the suicide attack on the President's convoy came just a day after the signing of the deal between the MMA and the government. He was a marked man and they were after his life. Musharraf did not realize that he could not ride on both boats.

The Islamists tried to make the best of their new-found political clout. Besides pushing for the adoption of Islamic sharia laws, the administration pledged to end co-education and close down movie theatres, which it considered to be a western violation of traditional norms and values. The administration ordered schools to replace shirt and trouser uniforms with the traditional *shalwar kameez*, describing the wearing of western dress as 'un-Islamic'. In order to Islamize the education system, more Islamic texts were used in school and college curricula. The MMA's agenda to end co-education was the first step towards the total segregation of women in public life.[17]

These retrogressive measures were part of an attempt to impose a Taliban-like orthodox Islamic system. The MMA government increased the role of religion in political and social life. The Chief Minister, Akram Khan Durrani, had to grow a beard after some Islamic leaders said he lacked this criterion of a 'good Muslim'; under the strict sharia law, Muslim men were expected to wear beards. The MMA demanded abolition of the 25 per cent of seats reserved for women in the national and provincial assemblies, saying they had no business to be in Parliament.[18] These measures fuelled intolerance and gave a free hand to the mullahs, who opposed female education. In Peshawar, thousands of Islamic zealots smashed billboards carrying pictures of female models, declaring them un-Islamic.

Non-governmental organizations working in the field of female education were particularly targeted by the mullahs, who often accused them of spreading 'obscenity'. 'We feel very vulnerable,' said Marium Bibi, a tribal woman who had provoked the wrath of the Islamic zealots by opening schools for girls in remote villages. Her organization, Khewndo Khor (Sisters' House), ran more than forty schools in the most conservative parts of the province. One of its offices was bombed after Bibi refused to close down the schools.

In July 2005, the North West Frontier Province provincial assembly passed a controversial *hisba* (accountability) law, which envisaged setting up a watchdog body to ensure people respected calls to prayer, did not engage in commerce at the time of Friday prayers and that unrelated men and women did not appear in public places together. The law also prohibited singing and dancing. Reminiscent of the infamous Department of Vice and Virtue, the law proposed the appointment of a *mohatasib* (one who holds others accountable) to monitor the conduct of the populace so that it was in accordance with Islamic tenets. The actions taken by the mohatasib, chosen from among the top clerics, could not be challenged in any court of law. He had the powers of the judges of the High Court to punish anyone obstructing his authority. He was also to monitor the media to ensure that they were 'useful for the promotion of Islamic values'. Spying and anonymous denunciation were encouraged. Any citizen could complain to the Mohatasib against any other person for not observing 'Islamic values'. It was clearly a step towards Talibanization and the establishment of religious fascism.[19] The enactment of the law was stopped after a ruling by the Supreme Court of Pakistan declared that it violated the constitution. But the Islamic government appeared determined to enforce it with some changes.[20]

The mullahs were encouraged by Musharraf's policy of accommodation of the religious right and his backtracking on his pledge to regulate madrasas, most of which were run by MMA component parties. His move to marginalize liberal political forces gave the Islamists tremendous space to carry out their agenda. A weak civilian set-up was unable to fight Musharraf's battle, in Parliament as well as in public. Most of the ruling party members were ideologically much closer to the MMA and considered it their natural ally. They were reluctant to fight for Musharraf's reform agenda and his so-called 'enlightened moderation'.

It was not a great surprise when President Musharraf, on 30 December 2004, formally declared that he was not doffing his military uniform, breaking a public pledge that he had made exactly a year earlier. 'My stepping down from the post of army chief at this critical juncture would be dangerous for the country,' he asserted in a televised address to the nation. Musharraf defended his decision, saying that he was a marked man and that the situation had changed since he made his promise. He claimed that the 'renaissance' he led would be in serious jeopardy if he retired from the army.[21]

The renaissance, however, in terms of tackling extremism, did not amount to much. The military's reluctance to make a clean break with its traditional allies among radical Islamist groups, coupled with the suppression of liberal political parties, left the country hostage to extremist elements. Blinded by the demands of regime survival, the military continued to patronize the religious right to counter its secular and democratic opposition. Half-hearted measures, largely taken under international pressure, totally lacked conviction. Musharraf's so-called vision of 'enlightened moderation' might have brought a marked improvement in the country's cultural atmosphere and won him applause from the West, but that was where it ended. On most key issues, he had backtracked under pressure from his own right-wing allies and the mullahs. The much-touted education reforms had long been stalled after top ruling party leaders and the MMA strongly opposed changes in the school curriculum which inculcated retrogressive ideology.

In December 2004, Parliament passed a bill mandating a stiffer penalty in all cases where men killed female relatives on suspicion of having illicit relations. But the legislation was so diluted as to be ineffectual. The new rules did not outlaw the practice of the killer being able to buy his freedom by paying compensation to the victim's relatives. They also allowed the victim's family to pardon the perpetrators. Since the killer was often a close family member himself, he would invariably get amnesty. Human rights groups contended that, because of loopholes in the laws, crime against women had risen.

In 2005, the government acquiesced to the demand of Islamic radicals to include people's religious affiliations in their passports. The new passport not only identified the religion of every Pakistani, but also his or her sect. Religious minorities feared the passport would widen the sectarian divides that had plagued the country. Senior government officials rejected the argument that Musharraf coddled extremists, maintaining that the pace of reform was determined by the capacity of society. They argued that because of the odds facing him, Musharraf had adopted an incremental and gradual approach towards implementation of his reform agenda. 'He does not want to act hastily and in the process evoke an extremist backlash,' argued a military spokesman. 'Breaking away from deeply held customs will take some time. We believe in bringing change not through revolutionary, but evolutionary means.' Musharraf also had to contend with the armed forces who were deeply steeped in General Zia's culture.

Because of his government's failure to deliver, to any substantial degree, on pledges to contain the growth of jihadist networks, religious extremism in Pakistan continued to pose a threat to domestic, regional and international security. Many Pakistani madrasas continued providing recruits to extremist groups. In July 2005, following the terrorist attacks in London, Musharraf had admitted his government's failure in implementing madrasa reforms. He argued that he was not politically strong enough to push through measures to curb militant madrasas. He vowed to clamp down on them, but there has not been much progress made. The leaders of extremist religious organizations continued to enjoy virtual immunity from the laws and carried on preaching their jihadist sectarian ideology, using mosques and madrasas to recruit new cadres for their cause.

Giving in to pressure from the religious right, the Musharraf government also backtracked on its pledge to reform discriminatory Islamic laws that were open to abuse by religious fanatics. Existing legislation against the incitement of sectarian hatred and violence was rarely enforced. The jihadist media continued to flourish; audio and videotapes, books and pamphlets that propagated the most virulent sectarian views were easily available. The government even failed to disarm the jihadist private armies which Musharraf had publicly denounced. The horizontal and vertical fragmentation of society along political, religious and ethnic lines, which has intensified over the past few years, posed the most serious problem for both Musharraf's and Pakistan's survival.

11

FAULT
LINES

Musharraf appeared visibly uncomfortable as he stood by Bush at their joint press conference on 4 March 2006, and heard the US President say that he had come to Islamabad to determine whether or not the Pakistani leader was as committed as he had been in the past to the war on terror. The comments reflected the growing frustration of the American administration over Musharraf's failure to stop Taliban insurgents using Pakistani territory as a base for attacks on the coalition forces in Afghanistan. The issue had become a sour point in the relations between Washington and Islamabad as the escalating violence in Afghanistan resulted in heavy casualties among US troops. More American soldiers were killed in the fighting in early 2006 than in the last four years following the ousting of the Taliban regime in December 2001.

On the day of Bush's visit, Islamabad looked like a fortified city with some ten thousand troops and police deployed on security duty and anti-aircraft guns installed in the surrounding hills. Marksmen had taken up positions on the rooftops. The extraordinary security measures were necessary as the shadow of al-Qaeda continued to hang heavy over Pakistan.[1] The administration was visibly nervous. A day earlier, a suicide bomber had rammed his vehicle into a car outside the American consulate in Karachi, killing an American diplomat. During his 24-hour stay in the Pakistani capital, Bush came closer than he had ever been before to Osama bin Laden, who was believed to be hiding in the tribal region bordering Afghanistan.

While praising Musharraf for his 'courage', Bush called upon his 'buddy' to do more to curb Islamic militancy and stop cross-border infiltration of Taliban insurgents into Afghanistan.[2] The public admonition caused serious embarrassment to the Pakistani military leader, who had risked his life by supporting the USA in the war on terror. Pakistani military authorities were deeply disappointed with Bush's visit. While a day earlier, in New Delhi, the US President had hailed India as an emerging world power and awarded it an unprecedented, civilian nuclear technology deal, all Musharraf got was a lecture on getting tougher with the Taliban and vague promises of future economic, military and technological assistance.[3] Although Pakistan remained central to US security interests in the region, this raw deal raised scepticism among Pakistan's army officers, who had little trust anyway in any long-term US commitment to Pakistan. The Bush administration continued to back Musharraf as a valuable ally, but he stood on weaker ground than ever.

Musharraf appeared to be in an impossible position. His politics of expediency had given huge latitude to the radical Islamists. Despite his promise to reform them, thousands of madrasas across the country remained breeding grounds for Islamic extremism, fomenting sectarian violence. The military had been completely bogged down in Waziristan where three years of military campaign against al-Qaeda-backed militants had produced few results. Hundreds of soldiers were killed in the war which seemed to have no end. Islamist militant groups continued to operate freely, despite their proscription, as Musharraf battled to perpetuate his rule.

To make matters worse, the devasating earthquake of October 2005 highlighted how much more power and effectiveness the jihadist groups had on the ground compared to the government. The 2002 ban had caused many of the main militant groups, such as Lashkar-e-Taiba, Jaish-e-Mohammed and Harkat-ul-Mujahideen, to reinvent themselves as welfare organizations. With their grassroots networks, their well disciplined cadres were the first to reach the quake-stricken areas and, within hours of the tragedy, had begun to rescue those trapped under the debris of collapsed houses, as well as providing emergency treatment to the injured. Laying down their arms, hundreds of militants carried relief goods, sometimes on their backs, to those remote areas which could only be reached by helicopters.[4]

Jihadist groups could react quickly and remain active in the quake-hit areas for a number of reasons. Their training camps and bases had operated freely in the North West Frontier Province and Azad Kashmir despite the government's claim of proscribing them. The militants had well-equipped facilities close to the areas worst hit by the quake. Hardly anyone was as familiar with the mountainous region of Azad Kashmir as the militants. They knew only too well the terrain through which they had been sneaking into Indian-controlled Kashmir.[5]

Ironically, American troops were brought over from Afghanistan to work side by side with the jihadists in bringing relief to remote parts of Pakistan. The Bush administration was visibly unhappy with such coexistence; it wanted the Pakistani military to take over control of the entire relief work and squeeze out those charities and aid groups that promoted a radical brand of Islam. The US Ambassador, Ryan Crocker, alleged that the relief work gave the jihadist groups a chance to promote militant ideas. He called on the Pakistani government to stop their activities. 'If the militant organizations are seen to be delivering the goods, and the government is not, it is going to be in trouble,' he said at a press briefing. The White House repeated the message during Vice President Dick Cheney's 20 December meeting with Musharraf.

Though the growing influence of the Islamists might have been cause for concern, there was little the military government did to stop them. Musharraf admitted that he was battling to assert the administration's competence in the face of stiff competition from the militant Islamist groups. He said that he could not stop them from relief work, but warned that they would not be allowed to exploit the situation and solicit new recruits.[6] In his 20 October interview with CNN, General Musharraf said, 'I know that some extremist outfits placed on the government's watch list are participating in relief activities in the quake-affected areas. Their activities are being watched closely and anyone found involved in extremist acts will be punished. However, everyone is motivated right now to help the quake victims. And I am not going to prevent anyone from helping the people.'

With the credibility of the government and the army at its lowest ebb, it was difficult to contain the Islamists. The success of jihadist groups in providing earthquake relief had, indeed, strengthened their claims to legitimacy in Pakistan. While the popularity of the jihadists soared, the government seemed directionless, leading Pakistan onto dangerous ground. The jihadist efforts were greeted with heartfelt gratitude by survivors and local officials alike. In an unprecedented gesture, Azad Kashmir's Prime Minister, Sardar Sikandar Hayat, received the Jamaat-ud Da'awa chief, Hafiz Mohammed Saeed, at his official residence in Muzaffarabad and thanked him on behalf of his government. The same day, the Azad Kashmir President, Lt.-General (retd) Sardar Mohammad Anwer Khan, visited the group's camp in the city.[7]

Their new-found prestige had indeed bolstered the influence of the radical Islamists and that was quite evident during the nationwide protests in the second week of February 2006 against the publication of cartoons of the Prophet Mohammed by a Danish newspaper. One of the 12 drawings, which were reprinted in several other European countries, showed the Prophet wearing a bomb-shaped turban with a lit fuse. Islamic tradition bars any depiction of the Prophet Mohammed, favourable or otherwise, to prevent idolatry. As in other Muslim countries, the Danish cartoons fuelled anti-western sentiments in Pakistan too. The Islamists took full advantage and turned the protests into a violent anti-government agitation.

Among those in the forefront were the jihadist outfits. Hundreds and thousands of people took to the streets across Pakistan on the call of an alliance of Sunni Muslim organizations formed in the wake of the caricatures. Chanting 'Death to America' and 'Death to Musharraf', the protests turned violent, burning down western financial institutions and food chains like KFC and McDonalds.[8] The furore over the Danish cartoons had exposed the fissures that had widened over the preceding years. For the first time since Musharraf had seized power in October 1999, there were frequent and violent protests in the country, drawing out thousands of people.

Musharraf and his army's unwillingness to cede power, and the lack of democratic progress, were the main reasons why no headway was made in countering Islamic extremism. The Musharraf government had failed to build independent state and political institutions, or establish free and fair elections, thereby providing a conducive environment for extremism to flourish. Any steps Musharraf took to introduce a modicum of democracy were countered by measures to increase his or the military's power. He also beefed up the military's already substantial powers by creating a National Security Council that he and the military dominated.

Musharraf's military-led government has been widely credited with turning the economy around from the verge of bankruptcy. From near insolvency, it managed to steer the economy to a more than eight per cent growth in 2005, with aid from the USA and other western nations contributing in this upturn. Pakistan also benefited post-9/11 from massive foreign exchange remittances from Pakistani expatriates, which boosted both the stock market and real estate. Pakistan witnessed the emergence of a new middle class, fuelled by remittances and rising domestic incomes. This drastically changed spending patterns, spurring demands for motorcycles, cars, and other consumer goods.

But there is a downside. Despite an improvement on the financial front, Pakistan remains plagued with problems of rising poverty and unemployment. Around one third of the population still lives below the poverty line. The highest incidence of poverty is in the rural areas which comprises 60 per cent of the population. According to a World Bank report, one third of Pakistan's population lives in poverty with two thirds in the rural areas. 'Their poverty is both deeper and more severe than urban poverty,' says the report. The high economic growth achieved by Pakistan has not produced a corresponding social improvement. This has created an explosive social situation that could easily be exploited by religious extremists.

In the US war on terror, few world leaders have produced results like President Musharraf. His security forces have captured and delivered to the USA several of the most wanted al-Qaeda terrorists, including Khalid Sheikh Mohammed and Ramzi bin al-Shibh, the masterminds of the 11 September attacks. There is, however, little evidence of him showing the same kind of resolve when it comes to dealing with Islamic militancy at home. In fact, within Pakistan his performance in the fight against Islamic extremism is abysmal. The alleged Pakistani link to the suicide bombings in London on 7 July 2005 and the foiled plot to blow up flights from London to the USA in August 2006 indicate that the international terrorist network continues to operate from Pakistan.

A major reason for Musharraf's failure to root out extremism and jihadist forces is a lack of consistency in his policies. Most of his actions lack commitment, having been taken under pressure from the USA and the international community.

Because of its strategic position, external factors play a huge role in shaping Pakistan's destiny. Although forces of radicalization have roots inside the country, events in the region have a direct bearing on Pakistan. The instability in Afghanistan has had a strong spill-over effect in the border areas inhabited by the Pashtuns. With the Taliban operating from both sides of the Durand Line, the war in Afghanistan has already spread to Pakistan. Although Musharraf has renounced the use of militancy as an instrument to fight Pakistan's battle in Kashmir, the lack of any headway in the conflict resolution may force the military to go back to its old ways. While Musharraf has taken some positive steps in easing tensions with India, the peace process remains tenuous and prone to accidents. Any reversal could be disastrous for regional security and infuse fresh life into militancy.

The war against militancy and Islamic extremism can be best fought – and won – in a liberal democracy. Musharraf's authoritarian rule has blocked any hopes of a democratic process taking root. It is very clear that the restoration of democracy in Pakistan is not a priority for Washington, because a leader in military uniform can deliver far more than a democratically elected one. An army general ruling Pakistan does not trouble the West, so long as he happens to be an effective ally in the war against terror. Washington's backing may have given Musharraf a huge boost, but that cannot change realities at home. Anger at Musharraf's close relationship with the US has long generated support for Islamic radicals among many Pakistanis.

Despite the backing of the army and America, Musharraf is living on borrowed time. He has spawned a system that is a hybrid of military and civilian rule. It is certainly not a democracy. So far, the military's backing has given the system a semblance of stability, but it is crumbling under the weight of its own contradiction. There is no succession principle in his system, which will inevitably lead to a takeover by another army general in the event that something happens to him. There is always a danger of the vacuum being filled by radical Islamists, both inside and outside the military.

Pakistan may not be facing any imminent threat of an Islamic fundamentalist takeover, but there is a real danger of fragmentation with radical Islamists controlling part of the country. The growing influence of militant Islam, particularly in the strategically located North West Frontier Province and the western province of Balochistan, is ominous. The militants, who fashion themselves on the legacy of Afghanistan's ousted Taliban regime, have already established rigid Islamic rule in the Waziristan tribal region. The situation is more worrying as their influence spills over to other areas of the North

West Frontier Province. In many parts of the province, the militants have forcibly closed down video and music shops, as well as Internet cafés, declaring them un-Islamic. The barbers are warned not to shave beards, people are prohibited from playing music, even at weddings, and from watching television. Women are barred from coming out of their homes on their own. The Talibanization of Waziristan and the rising power of the radical mullahs in parts of the North West Frontier Province present a disturbing scenario. It will be difficult to contain the spread of this trend to other parts of the country.

Musharraf's support for the US-led war on terror, his tactical cooperation with certain militant groups, and his refusal to embed a culture of democracy and accountability have intensified social, ethnic and religious differences in Pakistani society. These are the faultlines from which a geo-political earthquake could at some point erupt – an earthquake which would make the current regional security situation look positively calm by comparison. Pakistan's battle with itself is far from over.

TIMELINE

14 August 1947	The Muslim state of Pakistan is created by the partition of India at the end of British rule. Hundreds of thousands die in widespread communal violence and millions are made homeless. Mohammed Ali Jinnah becomes the first Governor General of the new state.
October 1947	Armed tribesmen from Pakistan's North West Frontier Province invade Kashmir. The Maharaja requests armed assistance from India.
September 1948	Jinnah dies. The first India-Pakistan war over the disputed territory of Kashmir breaks out. Fighting continues throughout the year.
January 1949	The war ends and a ceasefire is arranged by the United Nations. Both India and Pakistan agree to hold a referendum in the state, which to this date has never been held.
March 1956	The Constitution proclaims Pakistan an Islamic republic.
October 1958	Army Commander in Chief, General Mohammed Ayub Khan seizes power. A pro-western and secular leader, he rules the country for more than a decade.
September 1965	The second India-Pakistan war breaks out after Pakistan launches a covert offensive across the ceasefire line into Indian-administered Kashmir.

	India retaliates by crossing the international border at Lahore. After three weeks, both India and Pakistan agreed to a UN-sponsored ceasefire.
January 1966	Leaders of India and Pakistan meet at Tashkent and sign a declaration agreeing to solve their disputes through peaceful means. They also agree to withdraw to pre-war positions.
March 1969	Field Marshall Ayub Khan steps down and hands over power to the military after violent anti-government protests paralyse the country. General Yahya Khan becomes President and imposes martial law.
December 1970	General Yahya's military government holds Pakistan's first general elections. The Bengali nationalist party, Awami League, led by Mujibur Rehman, sweeps the polls in East Pakistan and secures an absolute majority in the National Assembly. The military regime declines to convene the assembly.
March 1971	Pakistan launches a military operation to crush East Pakistan's attempt to secede, leading to a civil war.
December 1971	India intervenes on behalf of Bengali separatists, triggering the third India-Pakistan war. The Pakistani military surrenders to Indian armed forces. East Pakistan becomes the independent state of Bangladesh. General Yahya Khan steps down after a revolt by young army officers. Zulfikar Ali Bhutto becomes President.
January 1972	Bhutto and India's Prime Minister, Indira Gandhi, sign the Simla peace agreement, which creates a new Line of Control in Kashmir.
August 1973	Zulfikar Ali Bhutto becomes Prime Minister after the National Assembly approves a new constitution.
July 1977	Chief of Army Staff General Zia ul-Haq seizes power in a bloodless coup. Martial Law is imposed and Bhutto is sent to prison.
April 1979	Bhutto is hanged after a dubious trial on a charge of murder.
December 1979	Soviet forces enter Afghanistan.

1980	The USA removes sanctions on Pakistan. With the help of Pakistan's Inter-Services Intelligence (ISI), the CIA launches its biggest ever covert operation against the Soviet forces in Afghanistan.
April 1986	Zulfikar Ali Bhutto's daughter Benazir returns from exile to lead a campaign for restoration of democracy.
August 1988	General Zia, the US ambassador and top Pakistan army officials die in a mysterious air crash.
November 1988	Benazir Bhutto's Pakistan's People's Party wins election. Benazir becomes the first woman in the Muslim world to be elected as Prime Minister.
August 1990	Benazir is dismissed as Prime Minister on charges of corruption. The USA imposes sanctions on Pakistan for its nuclear weapons programme.
November 1990	Nawaz Sharif becomes Prime Minister after his Islamic Democratic Alliance (IDA) wins the elections.
July 1993	President Ghulam Ishaq Khan and Prime Minister Nawaz Sharif both resign under pressure from military.
October 1993	Benazir returns to power for the second time.
October 1996	President Farooq Leghari dismisses the Bhutto government amid corruption allegations.
February 1997	Nawaz Sharif returns as Prime Minister after his Pakistan Muslim League party sweeps elections.
May 1998	Pakistan conducts its own nuclear tests after India explodes several devices.
May 1999	Incursion by Pakistani-backed forces into the Kargil region in Indian-controlled Kashmir triggers a new conflict between the two countries. Their troops clash in the mountains, raising fears of a nuclear escalation. More than 1,000 people are killed on both sides. Under US pressure, Pakistan pulls back.
October 1999	General Pervez Musharraf seizes power, overthrowing Prime Minister Nawaz Sharif. Sharif is sentenced to life imprisonment on hijacking and terrorism charges. He is later sent into exile to Saudi Arabia.

December 1999	Islamic militants hijack an Indian airlines jet with 155 passengers on board after it takes off from Kathmandu, Nepal, and force it to land in Kandahar. Three militant leaders are freed by Indian authorities and flown to Kandahar to end the hijacking. Among them are Masood Azhar, the later head of Jaish-e-Mohammed, and British-born militant Ahmed Omar Saeed Sheikh.
June 2001	General Pervez Musharraf names himself President while remaining head of the army.
July 2001	Musharraf meets Indian Prime Minister Atal Bihari Vajpayee in the Indian city of Agra, in the first summit between the two neighbours in more than two years. The meeting ends without a breakthrough or even a joint statement because of differences over Kashmir.
September 2001	After the 9/11 attacks in New York and Washington, Musharraf pledges support for the USA in its fight against terrorism, facilitating US attacks on Afghanistan. The USA lifts some of the sanctions imposed on Pakistan after the nuclear tests.
December 2001	India threatens to attack Pakistan after a suicide attack on the Indian parliament allegedly by Pakistani based militant groups. Both countries amass more than one million troops on their borders.
January 2002	Daniel Pearl, a *Wall Street Journal* reporter is kidnapped in Karachi while researching a story on terrorism. Under pressure from the USA and India, Musharraf outlaws five Islamic extremist groups including Lashakar-e-Taiba (LeT) and Jaish-e-Mohammed (JEM), the two groups blamed for the attack on the Indian parliament.
April 2002	Musharraf wins another five years in office in a controversial referendum.
May 2002	14 people, including 11 French technicians, are killed in a suicide attack on a bus in Karachi.
June 2002	12 people are killed in a suicide attack outside the US consulate in the city. Britain and the USA urge their citizens to leave India and Pakistan as the

	two South Asian nuclear neighbours come close to war.
September 2002	Pakistani security forces capture Ramzi bin al-Shibh, one of the masterminds of the 9/11 attacks.
October 2002	First general election since the 1999 military coup, results in a hung parliament. Religious parties fare better than expected. Mir Zafarullah Jamali elected as Prime Minister by the National Assembly. He is the first civilian premier since the 1999 military coup and a member of a pro-Musharraf faction of the Pakistan Muslim League.
April 2003	Khalid Sheikh Mohammed, mastermind of the 9/11 attacks, is captured in a raid on a house in Ralawalpindi cantonment area.
December 2003	Pakistan and India agree to resume direct air links and allow overflights by each other's planes after a two-year ban. President Musharraf narrowly survives an attempt on his life when Islamic militants ram their explosive packed vehicles into president's cavalcade in Rawalpindi.
January 2004	President Musharraf and Indian Prime Minister Atal Bihari Vajpayee meet on the sidelines of the South Asian regional conference in Islamabad. Musharraf pledges not to permit use of Pakistani soil for terrorist activities, clearing the way for a historic peace process between the two South Asian rivals.
February 2004	Dr Abdul Qadeer Khan, father of Pakistan's nuclear bomb, admits selling nuclear technology to Libya, North Korea and Iran. He is put under house arrest.
March 2004	Pakistan launches a major military operation to capture al-Qaeda fugitives in the Waziristan tribal region. Some 700 soldiers are killed during a 30-month operation.
August 2004	Shaukat Aziz, a former Citibank executive, is elected as Pakistan's new Prime Minister.
December 2004	President Musharraf declares he will stay on as head of the army, having previously promised to relinquish the role.

April 2005	Bus services commence running the first service in 60 years between Muzaffarabad in Pakistani-administered Kashmir and Srinagar in Indian-controlled Kashmir.
October 2005	An earthquake, with its epicentre in Pakistani-administered Kashmir, kills tens of thousands of people.
September 2006	Musharraf launches his controversial autobiography, *In the Line of Fire*, which ignites an international debate on Pakistan's role in the war on terror.

NOTES

PROLOGUE

1. The detail was gathered through a series of interviews with close aides of Musharraf and senior government officials. Part of the information was taken from Musharraf's interview with the BBC programme *Frontline Pakistan*, broadcast in August 2005.
2. Musharraf interviewed on Pakistan Television, 25 December 2003.
3. Zaffar Abbas, 'What happened?' *Herald* magazine, June 2005.
4. Interview with General Musharraf, October 1999.
5. In *Business Recorder*, Karachi, 16 October 1999; see <www.presidentofPakistan.gov.pk/biography.aspx>.
6. See <www.presidentofPakistan.gov.pk/biography.aspx>.
7. Mangla is the headquarters of the Pakistani army's main strike corps.
8. Interview with a retired senior army officer in 2004.
9. Ibid.
10. Interview with a former member of Nawaz Sharif's government in 2002.
11. From the transcript of evidence presented in court during the trial of Nawaz Sharif.
12. Zahid Hussain, 'From prison to palace', *Newsline*, January 2001.
13. Ibid.
14. Field Marshall Ayub Khan (1907–1974) was commissioned in the Royal British Indian army in 1928. At the time of Independence, he was the most senior Muslim officer in Pakistan's army and became the first native commander-in-chief in 1951. The army was directly involved in politics for the first time when Ayub Khan, serving as army chief, was inducted into the Cabinet as Defence Minister. He played a key role in Pakistan's entry into US-sponsored cold war military alliances, the Central Treaty Organisation (CENTO) and the South East Asian Treaty Organisation (CEATO). On 7 October 1958, Ayub Khan imposed martial law for the first time in Pakistan. After nearly 11 years of rule, his generals forced him to resign in 1969 in the wake of public protests.
15. Adnan Adil, 'Murder in God's name', *Newsline*, June 2002.

16. See Chapter Three, 'Inside Jihad'.

17. Zahid Hussain, 'In the shadow of terrorism', *Newsline*, February 2000.

18. Ibid.

19. Hussain, 'General on a mission', *Newsline*, July 2001.

20. Ibid.

CHAPTER ONE

1. Zulfikar Ali Bhutto (1928–1977). A protege of Pakistan's first military ruler, Field Marshall Ayub Khan, Bhutto served as his foreign minister before launching his political party, the Pakistan People's Party, in 1969. The PPP won a landslide victory in West Pakistan (today's Pakistan) in the 1970 general election. He became President and chief martial law administrator after the secession of East Pakistan (now Bangladesh) in December 1971. He gave the country a new constitution in 1973 and became its first elected Prime Minister. Bhutto's government was overthrown by General Zia ul-Haq in July 1977 and he was executed two years later after a dubious trial.

2. Mohammed Ali Jinnah (1876–1948). A lawyer, statesman and founding father of Pakistan, Jinnah became the country's first Governor General after its creation on 14 August 1947.

3. General Yahaya Khan seized power in March 1969. He was forced to step down in December 1971 after a revolt in the army.

4. Ahmedis or Qadianis is a sect that followed the teachings of a nineteenth-century Punjabi cleric, Mirza Ghulam Ahmed, who claimed he had direct revelations from Allah. His claim clashed with the basic Islamic tenet that Mohammed was the last and final prophet.

5. In *Jang* newspaper, August 1988.

6. 'The man behind Tablighi movement', *The News*, 5 September 1997.

7. Hassan Abbas, Pakistan's Drift into Extremism, p. 90.

8. Maleeha Lodhi and Zahid Hussain, 'The invisible government', *Newsline*, October 1992.

9. Steve Coll, *Ghost Wars* (Harmondsworth: Penguin), p. 63.

10. Ahmed Rashid, 'The Taliban exporting extremism', *Foreign Affairs*, November–December 1999.

11. Jason Burke, *Al-Qaeda* (London: I.B.Tauris).

12. Lodhi and Hussain, 'The invisible government'.

13. Ibid.

14. Hasan Askari Rizvi, *Military, State and Society in Pakistan* (Lahore: Sang-E-Meel Publications), p. 181.

15. Ibid.

16. Stephen Cohen, *The Pakistan Army* (Oxford University Press, Pakistan, 1968 edition), p. 95.

17. Ibid.
18. Brigadier S.K. Malik, *The Quranic Concept of War* (Lahore: Wajid Ali Ltd, 1986).
19. Mushahid Hussain, 'Changing profile of Pakistan army', *Frontier Post*, 13 February 1993.
20. Ibid.
21. Khalid Ahmed, *Pakistan: State in Crisis* (Lahore: Vanguard Press).
22. Interview with General Hamid Gul, 1990.
23. General Zia was killed when his C130 military aircraft crashed soon after take-off near Pakistan's southern Punjab city of Bahawalpur on 18 August 1988. The US ambassador, Arnold Raphael, and several senior Pakistani army generals were also among dead. The cause of the accident remains a mystery.
24. Lodhi and Hussain, 'The invisible government'.
25. 'Tough days ahead for Asad Durrani', *Frontier Post*, 9 May 1997.
26. Maleeha Lodhi, 'The ISI's new face', *Newsline*, May 1993.
27. Hussain Haqqani, Pakistan: *Between Mosque and Military* (Lahore: Vanguard Books).
28. Lodhi, 'The ISI's new face'.
29. Rahimullah Yousufzai, 'Here comes the Taliban', *Newsline*, February 1995.
30. Ahmed Rashid, *Taliban* (London: I.B.Tauris), pp. 186–7.
31. Michael Griffin, *Reaping the Whirlwind* (London: Pluto Press), p. 8.
32. Rashid, *Taliban*, pp. 186–7.
33. Ibid.
34. Ibid.
35. Zahid Hussain, 'To the rescue', *Newsline*, 1998.

CHAPTER TWO

1. Interview with Pakistan's ambassador to Washington, Maleeaha Lodhi.
2. Steve Coll, *Ghost Wars* (Harmondsworth: Penguin), p. 508.
3. Ibid.
4. Interview with Ambassador Lodhi.
5. Interview with Musharraf in January 2002.
6. Ibid.
7. Bob Woodward, *Bush at War* (London: Simon & Schuster), p. 59.
8. Interview with Ambassador Lodhi.
9. Woodward, *Bush at War*, p. 59.
10. Interview with Ambassador Lodhi in 2006.
11. In the *New York Times*, 21 October 2001.
12. The 9/11 Commission Report, p. 183.
13. Ibid.

14. Ibid. p. 123.

15. Ibid. p. 207.

16. Ibid.

17. Interview with a minister in Musharraf's government in June 2005.

18. The text of President Musharraf's speech, *The News*, 20 September 2001.

19. Interview with Musharraf.

20. Interview with a senior Pakistani foreign ministry official in 2005.

21. Former interior minister Moinuddin Haider narrated the incident to me.

22. 'Rubble without a cause: Despite international outrage and dissent within their own ranks, hard line Taliban extremists have systematically destroyed Afghanistan's pre Islamic heritage', *Newsline*, April 2001.

23. 'A general turn around', *Newsline*, February 2003.

24. Ibid.

25. The 9/11 Commission Report, p. 117.

26. See Chapter Ten.

27. Interview with a senior retired Pakistani army officer.

28. Interview with Musharraf, January 2002.

29. In his remarks at a joint press conference with Colin Powell in Islamabad on October 2001, President Musharraf said: 'We agreed that a durable peace in Afghanistan would only be possible through the establishment of a broad based, multi-ethnic government representing the demographic contours of Afghanistan freely choosen by the Afghans without outside interference. Former King Zahir Shah, political leaders, moderate Taliban.' Press release US State Department.

30. 'After arm twisting, Afghan factions pick interim government and leader', *New York Times*, 6 December 2001.

31. Interview with Musharraf, January 2002.

32. Akbar Zaidi, *Pakistan's Economic and Social Development* (Delhi: Rupa & co), p. 81.

33. Ibid.

34. Interview with a senior ISI officer.

CHAPTER THREE
1. In *The News*, 13 January 2002.

2. Interview with Musharraf in January 2002.

3. Hassan Abbas, Pakistan's Drift into Extremism, p. 201.

4. International Crisis Group (ICG) report, *Pakistan: Madrasas, Extremism and the Military*, July 2002.

5. Ibid.

6. Interview with Hafiz Saeed in January 2001.

7. Amir Mir, *The True Face of Jehadists* (Lahore: Mashal Press), pp. 107–8.

8. Ibid.

9. Ibid.
10. Amir Rana, *Jihad and Jihadists* (Lahore: Mashal Press), p. 21.
11. Marium Abou Zahab and Olivier Roy, *Islamist Networks: The Pakistan-Afghan Connection* (London: Hurst & Co), p.32.
12. Ibid, pp. 33–4.
13. Ibid p. 35.
14. Amir Zia, 'The soldiers of Islam', *Newsline*, February 2001.
15. Ibid.
16. Ibid.
17. Zahid Hussain, 'Inside jihad', *Newsline*, February 2001.
18. Zahab and Roy, *Islamist Networks*, p.36.
19. 'Inside jihad', *Newsline*, February 2001.
20. ICG report, *The State of Sectarianism in Pakistan*, April 2005.
21. Hussain, 'Inside jihad'.
22. Mir, The True Face of Jehadists.
23. Zahab and Roy, *Islamist Networks*, p. 40.
24. ICG report, *The State of Sectarianism in Pakistan*.
25. Ibid.
26. Zahab and Roy, *Islamist Networks*.
27. CNN.
28. 'Jihad until world is rid of injustice: Saeed', *The News*, Rawalpindi, 21 November 2002.
29. Ibid.
30. Interview with Yahya Mujahid in 2005.
31. Mir, The True Face of Jehadists.
32. Ibid. p. 87.
33. Ibid. p. 91.
34. I was present at the rally.
35. Amir Rana, *Jihad and Jihadists*, pp. 31–2.
36. Zahab and Roy, *Islamist Networks*, p. 27.
37. Ibid.
38. In the *Daily Dawn*, Karachi, 1998.
39. In the *Daily Telegraph*, 27 February 2002.
40. ICG Report, *Pakistan: Madrasas, Extremism and the Military*, July 2002.
41. '12 die in raid on Indian parliament', *Daily Telegraph*, 12 December 2001.
42. According to a senior Pakistani senior security official.
43. For details, see Chapter Seven, 'War Comes Home'.
44. 'Plotter's death perks up Musharraf', *Daily Times*, Lahore, 25 July 2005.
45. 'Secret agencies had cleared the bomber', *Daily Dawn*, Karachi, 29 December 2003.
46. Rana, Jihad and Jihadists, pp. 43–4.

47. Ibid.
48. Zahab, 'The regional dimension of sectarian conflict', in Christophe Jaffrelot (ed.), *Pakistan: Nationalism without a Nation* (London: Zed Books), p. 120.
49. 'Cracking open Pakistan's jihadi core', *Asia Times*, 12 August 2004.
50. Zahid Hussain, 'Islamic warriors', *Newsline*, 1995.

CHAPTER FOUR

1. Jamal Malik, *Colonialization of Islam* (Lahore: Vanguard Press), p. 208.
2. ICG report, *The State of Sectarianism in Pakistan*, April 2005.
3. Malik, Colonialization of Islam, p. 142.
4. The rate of Zakat, the Islamic tithe, is 2.5 percent deducted from all bank accounts over a variable limit, according to the price of gold on the eve of the first day of Ramadhan.
5. ICG report, *Pakistan: Madrasas, military and Extremism*, July 2002.
6. Ibid.
7. Ibid.
8. Malik, *Colonialization of Islam*.
9. ICG report, *The State of Sectarianism in Pakistan*.
10. Ibid.
11. Joe Stephens and David B. Ottaway, 'The ABC's of jihad in Afghanistan', *Washington Post*, 23 March 2002.
12. In *Newsweek*.
13. Ibid.
14. Ibid.
15. Sara Jess and Gabriel Beek, *American Taliban* (University Press, California), p. 138.
16. Ibid.
17. 'Awakening a sleeping giant', *Newsline*, October 2003.
18. Ibid.
19. Ibid.
20. See Chapter Seven.
21. Ibid.
22. Ibid.
23. 'New wave of British terrorists are taught at schools, not in the mountains', *The Times*, 14 July 2005.
24. Ibid.
25. ICG report, *Pakistan: Madrasas, extremism and the military*, July 2002.
26. Ibid.
27. Interview with Maulana Noor Mohammed in Quetta in 2003.

CHAPTER FIVE

1. 'Much ado about nothing', *Newsline*, March 2003.
2. 'Valley of death', *Newsline*, August 2003.
3. ICG report, The State of Sectarianism in Pakistan, April 2005.
4. In *Newsline*, March 2003.
5. ICG report, The State of Sectarianism in Pakistan.
6. Abbas Rashid, The Politics and Dynamics of Violent Sectarianism.
7. S.V. R. Nasr, The State and Rise of Sectarian Militancy, p. 89.
8. Ibid.
9. ICG report, The State of Sectarianism in Pakistan.
10. Ibid.
11. Nasr, The State and Rise of Sectarian Militancy, p. 97.
12. Ibid.
13. Deoband is a town in Uttar Pradesh, India. In 1867, a Darul Uloom ('House of Knowledge') was set up there with the objective of countering the 'polluting' influence of western ideas and Hindu culture through madrasa education. Ahle Hadith originated in the nineteenth century and were inspired by Wahabi movement, though they do not subscribe to the title.
14. ICG report, The State of Sectarianism in Pakistan.
15. Ibid.
16. Marium Abou Zahab, 'The regional dimension of sectarian conflict', in Christophe Jaffrelot (ed.), *Pakistan: Nationalism without a Nation* (London: Zed Books), p. 118.
17. Ibid.
18. Ibid. p. 119.
19. In Newsline.
20. Rashid, The Politics and Dynamics of Violent Sectarianism.
21. 'Bomb on Pakistan's PM's route kills three', Reuters, 3 January 1999.
22. 'Sipah-e-Mohammed and Lashkar-e-Jahngvi banned', *The News*, August 2001.
23. LeJ's cadres overlapped with JeM and the two organisations coordinated several terrorist attacks in Pakistan including the assassination attempt on Musharraf.
24. In *Newsline*, April 1995.
25. Ibid.
26. 'Riaz Basra, 3 others die in encounter', *Daily Dawn*, 15 May 2002.
27. 'Key Pakistani militant dead', *BBC News*, 12 December 2002.
28. 'Suicide city', *Newsline*, June 2004.
29. 'An eye for an eye', *Newsline*, October 2003.
30. Ibid.
31. The blast ripped through a crowd of mourners at the overnight rally attended by several thousand in the city of Multan, a city 425 km (250

miles) south-west of the capital, Islamabad, to mark the first anniversary of the shooting of Azam Tariq. Most at the rally were members of Sipah-e-Sahaba Pakistan ('Soldiers of Mohammad's Companions'), an outlawed Sunni group that Tariq headed and which has been blamed for many attacks on minority Shia Muslims who make up about 15 per cent of Pakistan's mainly Sunni population of 150 million.

32. A suicide bomber blew himself up in a mosque packed with more than 1,000 Shia worshippers during Friday prayers in the eastern Pakistani city of Sialkot.

33. ICG report, The State of Sectarianism in Pakistan.

34. 'The New face of al Qaeda', *Newsline*, August 2004.

CHAPTER SIX

1. 'President Musharraf reassured Prime Minister Vajpayee that he will not permit any territory under Pakistan's control to be used to support terrorism in any manner. President Musharraf emphasized that a sustained and productive dialogue addressing all issues would lead to positive results,' *Daily Dawn*, 7 January 2004.

2. The Kashmir dispute dates back to 1947 after the creation of Pakistan on the basis of separate Muslim nationhood. Pakistan based its claim on Kashmir, a princely state, on the basis of Kashmir's Muslim majority population and its geography. But the Hindu ruler signed the Instrument of accession with India. The move led to a war between India and Pakistan in 1948 that left the state divided, with Pakistan controlling one third of it. UN Security Council resolutions in 1948 and 1950 called for a plebiscite in the disputed state to determine the wishes of its people for accession to either Pakistan or India, but they were never implemented. The dispute remained the main cause of conflict between the two South Asian nations.

3. 'Pakistan to pull out part of its troops from LOC', *Daily Dawn*, 21 December 2000.

4. 'General on a mission', *Newsline*, July, 2001.

5. Subhash Kapila, 'The United States and the Agra summit', South Asia Analysis Group, paper no 291, 10 August 2001.

6. 'A bridge too far', *Newsline*, August 2001.

7. Celia Dugger, 'India and Pakistan End Talks over Kashmir in Bitterness', *New York Times*, 17 July 2001.

8. 'A bridge too far', *Newsline*.

9. 'Not All Lost In the Talks Between India And Pakistan', *New York Times*, 18 July 2001.

10. ICG report, Pakistan: Madrasas, Extremism and the Military.

11. 'Pakistan blamed for Kashmiri atrocity', *Daily Telegraph*, 3 October 2001.

12. Brahama Chellaney, 'India is ready to defend itself', *New York Times*, 28 December 2002.
13. See Chapter Three.
14. Text of President Musharraf's speech, *The News*, 13 January 2002.
15. Hussain Haqqani, 'Musharraf echoes dictators of the past', *Gulf News*, 9 May 2002.
16. 'Pakistan's dubious referendum', *New York Times*, 1 May 2002.
17. Interview with a senior Pakistan Army General in June 2002.
18. Barbara Crossette, in her report published in the *New York Times* on 30 May 2002, quoted Pakistan's ambassador to the UN, Munir Akram, as stating: 'We have not said we will use nuclear weapons. We have not said we will not use nuclear weapons.'
19. In *Daily Dawn*, 29 May 2002.
20. Ibid.
21. 'Powell wants proof of Pakistan's militant clampdown', Reuters, 31 May 2002.
22. 'State Dept issues India advisory', Associated Press (AP), 31 May 2002.
23. Glenn Kessler, 'A defining moment in Islamabad: A US brokered "yes" pulled India, Pakistan from brink of war', *Washington Post*, 22 June 2002.
24. Ibid.
25. Ibid.
26. 'Pakistan reviews support for Kashmir', *Daily Telegraph*, 23 May 2002.
27. Interview with General Hamid Gul in May 2002.
28. Interview with a senior foreign ministry official.
29. Interview with a senior foreign ministry official.
30. In *Newsline*, November 2004.
31. Interview with Mirwaiz Umar Farooq in Sirinagar in April 2005.
32. 'We will continue our struggle to liberate Kashmir', interview with Syed Slahuddin, supreme commander Hezbul Mujahideen, *Newsline*, June 2003.
33. Interview with Geelani in April 2005.

CHAPTER SEVEN

1. 'Four al-Qaeda men among six killed', *Daily Dawn*, 4 July 2002.
2. A Tora Bora mountain in eastern Afghanistan runs along the border with Pakistan. Bin Laden with up to 1,000 al Qaeda fighters was rumoured to have retreated with up to 1,000 al Qaeda fighters to the deep bunkers in that mountainous range built during the Soviet occupation. US forces launched a massive land and air operation in December 2001 aimed at killing Bin Laden. But Bin laden got away.
3. 'How al Qaeda slipped away', *Newsweek*, 19 August 2002.

4. Ibid.
5. Ibid.
6. In the Washington Post.
7. 'Deadly cargo', *Time*, 21 October 2002.
8. 'Pakistan says a suspect in reporter's killing has links to a regional web of militants,' *New York Times*, 25 February 2002.
9. 'Missing in action', *Newsline*, February 2002.
10. See also Prologue.
11. Ibid.
12. Ibid.
13. Interview with Mariane Pearl in Karachi in January 2002.
14. 'Missing in action', *Newsline*, February 2002.
15. 'Police knew of Pearl's death for several days', *Gulf News*, 23 February 2002.
16. According to a senior Pakistani security official.
17. 'The missing week', *Newsweek*, 11 March 2002.
18. Ibid.
19. In The Times.
20. James Risen, *State of War* (Free Press), pp. 21, 22.
21. According to a senior Pakistani security official.
22. 'Raid netted top operative of al Qaeda', *Washington Post*, 2 April 2002.
23. Ibid.
24. 'Key Bin Laden deputy captured', *BBC News*, 1 April 2002.
25. 'Key al Qaeda recruiter captured', *BBC News*, 3 April 2002.
26. 'How the perfect terrorist plotted the ultimate crime', *The Observer*, 7 April 2002.
27. 'Capture of Bin Laden's aide boosts US anti terror fight', *Financial Times*, 3 April 2002.
28. 'Car bombing jolts Pakistan government', *Washington Post*, 9 May 2002.
29. 'Pistols at noon', *Newsline*, October 2002.
30. Ibid.
31. Ibid.
32. The 9/11 Commission Report, p. 161.
33. Ibid. pp. 165–6.
34. 'Pistols at noon', *Newsline*, October 2002.
35. According to a senior police officer involved the capture of KSM in Quetta.
36. 'Closing in?' *Newsline*, March 2003.
37. Ibid.
38. 'Al Qaeda arm in Pakistan is tied to 12 years of plots and attacks', *Wall Street Journal*, 6 August 2004.
39. Ibid.
40. Ibid.

41. 'Closing in?' *Newsline*, March 2003.
42. Ibid.
43. Ibid.
44. 'Noose tightens', *Newsline*, March 2004.
45. According to top Pakistani intelligence sources.
46. 'Bin Laden's back channel', *Newsweek*, 5 August 2004.
47. 'Al Qaeda planned attack on airports', *Daily Dawn*, 6 August 2004.
48. 'Al Qaeda whiz was top terror planner', *The News*, 5 August 2004.
49. 'Al Qaeda's new face', *Newsline*, August 2004.
50. Ibid.
51. 'Bin Laden's back channel', *Newsweek*, 5 August 2004.
52. 'British raids net a leader of al Qaeda', *Washington Post*, 5 August 2004.
53. 'Pakistan holds top al Qaeda suspect', *Washington Post*, 30 July 2004.
54. According to intelligence sources.
55. 'Khalfan says he plotted attack on Pakistan leaders', *Daily Nation*, 4 August 2004.
56. 'Al Qaeda number three Faraj al Libbi arrested', *Daily Dawn*, 5 May 2005.
57. 'Bin Laden aide had ten strong British network', *The Times*, 6 May 2005.
58. 'Senior al Qaeda commander killed', *Daily Dawn*, 3 December 2005.
59. 'Everyone's mastermind: Al Qaeda operative killed in Pakistan', *Newsweek*, 26 December 2005.
60. 'Al Qaeda's new face', *Newsline*, August 2004.
61. Ibid.
62. Ibid.

CHAPTER EIGHT

1. 'Massive hunt launched for Mehsud', *Daily Dawn*, 10 October 2004.
2. For Tora Bora, see Chapter Seven, 'War Comes Home'.
3. 'Guantanamo detainees say Arabs, Muslims sold for US bounties', Associated Press (AP), 31 May 2005.
4. According to a Pakistan army spokesman.
5. See Chapter Seven.
6. In the Wall Street Journal.
7. 'Tribal tribulation: A campaign to flush out Islamic militants hiding in Pakistan's wild west tests the will of Islamabad and the US', *Time*, 17 May 2004.
8. 'US pledges long term strategic partnership: Pakistan designated major non NATO ally', *Daily Dawn*, 19 March 2004.
9. 'The warrior tribes', *Newsline*, April 2004.
10. Olaf Caroe, *The Pathans* (Oxford: Oxford University Press), p. 393.
11. Akbar S. Ahmed, *Resistance and Control in Pakistan* (London:

Routledge), p. 17.

12. The Durand line is a controversial 2,640-kilometre (1,610 miles) border between Afghanistan and Pakistan. Named after Sir Mortimer Durand, Foreign Secretary in the British Indian government, the border was demarcated after an agreement between the representatives of Afghan government and the British Empire in 1893. The border was intentionally drawn to cut through those tribes that the British feared. In 1947, Afghanistan's *Loya jirga* (grand assembly) declared the agreement invalid, and since then the issue has remained a major cause of tension between the two countries. Today the line is often referred as one 'drawn on water', symbolizing the porous nature of the border.

13. Rizwan Hussain, Pakistan and the Emergence of Islamic Militancy in Afghanistan (London: Ashgate Publishing), p. 53.

14. The Pashtun nationalists led by Khan Abdul Ghaffar Khan demanded political autonomy for Pakistan's North West Frontier Province and its renaming as 'Pashtunistan'. The movement, backed by Afghanistan, was very strong in the 1950s and 1960s, but petered out after the Soviet invasion of neighbouring Afghanistan.

15. See Chapter Ten.

16. 'The new frontier', *Newsline*, April 2004.

17. Ibid.

18. Ibid.

19. Ibid.

20. Ibid.

21. In The Times.

22. Musharraf's interview with CNN.

23. Lawrence Wright, 'The man behind bin Laden', *New Yorker*, 16 September 2002.

24. Ibid.

25. Ibid,

26. Ibid.

27. 'All quiet on the north western front', *Newsline*, May 2004.

28. Ibid.

29. 'Night raid kills Nek and four other militants', *Daily Dawn*, 19 June 2004.

30. 'Troubled frontier', *Newsline*, July 2004.

31. 'Militants were paid to repay al Qaeda debt', *Daily Dawn*, 9 February 2005.

CHAPTER NINE

1. 'Nuclear experts may have links with al Qaeda', *New York Times*, 9 December 2001.

2. 'Pakistani atom experts held amid fears of leaked secrets', *New York*

Times, 1 November 2001.

3.   'Pakistanis linked to papers on anthrax weapons', *New York Times*, 28 November 2001.

4.   'Nuclear experts briefed bin Laden, Pakistanis say', *Washington Post*, 12 December 2001.

5.   Amir Latif, *Islam Online*, at <www.islam-online.net/English/news/2001>, 24 October 2001.

6.   Zahid Malik, *Dr. A.Q. Khan and the Islamic Bomb* (Islamabad: Hurmat Publications), p. 38.

7.   Ibid, p. 52.

8.   Leonard S. Spector, *The Spread of Nuclear Weapons: The Undeclared Bomb*, Carnegie Endowment for International Peace (Cambridge, Mass: Ballinger Publishing Company), p. 120–1.

9.   Zahid Hussain, 'Deliberate nuclear ambiguity', in Samina Ahmed and David Cortright (eds.), *Pakistan and the Bomb: Public Opinion and Nuclear Options* (Indiana: University of Notre Dame), p. 32.

10. Zulfikar Ali Bhutto, *If I Am Assassinated* (New Delhi: Vikas, 1979).

11. Malik, *Dr. A.Q. Khan and the Islamic Bomb*, p. 70.

12. Spector, *The Spread of Nuclear Weapons*, p. 103.

13. Zahid Hussain, 'The bomb controversy', *Newsline*, November 1991.

14. In *Nawa-i-Waqt*, 10 February 1984.

15. Spector, The Spread of Nuclear Weapons, p. 127.

16. David Albright, 'India and Pakistan's nuclear arms race: Out of the closet but not in the street', *Arms Control Today*, June 1993, p. 15.

17. Zahid Hussain, 'Whodunit', *Newsline*, April 1994.

18. George Perkovich, 'A nuclear third way in South Asia', *Foreign Policy*, Summer 1993.

19. Interview with Dr Khan, 30 May 1988.

20. Albright and Corey, 'Documents indicate A.Q. Khan offered nuclear weapon design to Iraq in 1990: Did he approach the other countries?' Institute for Science and International Security (ISIS), 4 February 2004.

21. 'In North Korea and Pakistan, deep roots of nuclear barter', *New York Times*, 24 November 2003.

22. 'The evil behind the axis?' *Los Angles Times*, 5 January 2005.

23. 'Pakistan's nuclear hero throws open Pandora's box', *The Guardian*, 31 January 2004.

24. 2004.

25. Pervez Hoodbhoy, 'For God and profit', *Newsline*, February 2004.

26. 'Confession or cover up', *Newsline*, February 2004.

27. Pervez Hoodbhoy, 'Pakistan: Inside the nuclear closet', *Chowk*, March 2004, available at <www.chowk.com/show_article.cgi?aid=00003200&channel=civic%20center&threshold=1&layout=0&order=0&start=50&end=59&page=1>.

28. 'As nuclear secrets emerge in Khan inquiry, more are suspected', *New York Times*, 26 December 2004.

29. According to a senior Pakistani foreign ministry official.

30. 'At least 7 nations tied to Pakistan nuclear ring', *Washington Post*, 8 February 2004.

31. Seymour M. Hersh, *Chain of Command* (New York: HarperCollins), pp. 315–16.

32. 'As nuclear secrets emerge in Khan inquiry, more are suspected', *New York Times*.

33. In *The Guardian*, 31 January 2004.

34. 'Beg asked Nawaz to give nuclear technology to a "friend" says Ishaq Dar', *Daily Times*, Lahore, 25 December 2003.

35. Interview with General Aslam Beg in February 2004.

36. 'Dr Khan linked to nuclear black-market', *The News*, 28 January 2004.

37. 'Confession or cover up', *Newsline*, February 2004.

38. According to a senior Pakistani official.

39. 'Pakistan aided Libya in N-plan', *New York Times*, 5 January 2005.

40. 'Confession or cover up', *Newsline*, February 2004.

41. 'Pakistan aided Libya in N-plan', *New York Times*, 5 January 2005.

42. According to a top Pakistani official.

43. 'Confession or cover up', *Newsline*, February 2004.

44. Seymour M. Hersh, *Chain of Command*, p. 312.

45. In *Newsline*, February 2004.

46. 'Dr. Khan admits to nuclear proliferation', *The News*, 5 February 2004.

CHAPTER TEN

1. Aimal Kansi was a native of Quetta, a Pakistani city on Afghanistan border. He spent four years on the FBI's ten most wanted fugitive list after he shot dead two CIA operatives at the entrance of CIA headquarters in Langley, Virginia on 25 January 1993. He fled to Pakistan, where he remained in hiding for four years. He was captured on 15 June 1997 and, following a trial, was executed by lethal injection in the US state of Virginia in 2002.

2. MMA comprised six mainstream parties that included Jamaat-i-Islami (JI), Jamiat Ulema Islam – Fazalur Rehaman faction (JUI-F), Jamiat Ulema Islam-Samiul Haq faction (JUI-S), Jamiat Ulema Pakistan (JUP), Tehrik Nifaz Fikha Jaffaria (TNFJ) and Jamiat Ahle Hadith.

3. 'The Mullah's fight back', *Newsline*, October 2002.

4. 'President Musharraf goes all out to establish a shadowy military state in the garb of democracy', *Newsline*, July 2002.

5. 'How to steal an election: The ISI working behind the scenes to engineer a victory for the King's Party', *Newsline*, September 2002.

6. 'The General's selection', *Newsline*, October 2002.

7. Benazir Bhutto, who faced a litany of corruption, lived in exile between London and Dubai since 1998. Nawaz Sharif, who faced life imprisonment on sedition charges, was exiled to Saudi Arabia in 2001.

8. Interview with several MMA leaders.

9. JI has links with Hezbul Mujahideen, a Kashmiri militant organisation fighting the Indian forces. Many of the JI cadres have participated in the anti Soviet war and fought in Kashmir. Thousands of JUI cadres joined the Taliban forces in Afghanistan. The organisation had close links with Harkat ul Mujahideed (HuM).

10. 'Observers term polls seriously flawed', *Daily Dawn*, 13 October 2002. Also see ICG report, *Pakistan: the Mullahs and the Military*, March 2003, p. 15.

11. 'We will not allow our soil to be used by any foreign power – Qazi Hussain Ahmed', an interview with Qazi Hussain Ahmed, the chief of Jamaat-i-Islami, *Newsline*, November 2002.

12. Siddiq Baluch, 'What the formation of Balochistan government foretells', *Daily Dawn*, 19 December 2002.

13. 'The war within', *Newsline*, April 2003.

14. Ibid.

15. Ibid.

16. 'Dangerous liaison', *Newsline*, January 2004.

17. ICG report, Pakistan: the Mullahs and the Military, p. 21.

18. 'Backward march: The MMM government attempts to turn the clock back through a series of extreme measures', *Newsline*, July 2003.

19. 'Pakistan "moral laws" spark row', BBC News, 11 July 2005 at <http://news.bbc.co.uk/2/hi/south_asia/4672067.stm>.

20. 'The great election farce', *Newsline*, September 2005.

21. 'Backward march', *Newsline*, January 2005.

CHAPTER ELEVEN

1. 'Beating around the Bush', *Newsline* March 2006.

2. 'Pakistan is tense as Bush arrives on 24-hour visit', *New York Times*, 4 March 2006.

3. 'US give India applause, Pakistan a pat on the back: President Bush's dealings with the two nuclear rivals illustrated the shifting balance of power in the region and the world', *New York Times*, March 2006.

4. Steve Coll, 'Fault lines: After the earth quake, some strange new alliances', *New Yorker*, 21 November 2005.

5. 'Militant philanthrophy', *Newsline*, November 2005.

6. 'Too little too late', *Newsline*, November 2005.

7. 'Militant philanthropy', *Newsline*.

8. 'The invisible hand', *Newsline*, March 2006.

INDEX